NEIL KINNOCK

NEIL KINNOCK

Eileen Jones

ROBERT HALE · LONDON

© *Eileen Jones 1994*
First published in Great Britain 1994

ISBN 0 7090 5239 1

Robert Hale Limited
Clerkenwell House
Clerkenwell Green
London EC1R 0HT

2 4 6 8 10 9 7 5 3

Photoset in North Wales by
Derek Doyle & Associates, Mold, Clwyd.
Printed in Great Britain by
St Edmundsbury Press Ltd, Bury St Edmunds, Suffolk.
Bound by WBC Ltd, Bridgend, Mid-Glamorgan.

Contents

List of Illustrations		7
Acknowledgements		9
Prologue		11
1	A Rather Loud Ginger Person	19
2	Waiting in the Wings	32
3	Leader	48
4	Of Miners and Militants	61
5	Roses and Thorns	76
6	On the Defensive	88
7	Back to the Drawing-board	103
8	Meet the Challenge, Make the Change	117
9	Fit to be Prime Minister?	133
10	Of Leaders and Leadership	145
11	Almost There	158
12	The Last Rally	172
13	Never Mind, Miss, At Least You Came Second	187
14	Whatever Next?	201
Postscript		208
Bibliography		211
Index		213

Illustrations

Between pages 96 and 97

1 Freckle-faced Neil Kinnock, age 7
2 As a cub scout, age 9, in 1951
3 Neil, age 11, with his father, Gordon, on holiday at Southsea, 1953
4 Kinnock, age 17, in his final year at Lewis School, Pengam
5 Summer rehearsal camp for the Glamorgan Youth Choir and Orchestra at Ogmore by Sea, 1959
6 Kinnock, age 18, with the Lewis School Choir
7 Kinnock and the wreckage of his car which crashed on the M4 in July 1983
8 Kinnock prior to his first confrontation with the Prime Minister as Opposition Leader on 24 October 1983
9 The new Labour leader and his deputy at Brighton in October 1983
10 Neil and Glenys Kinnock at a Euro-election campaign rally in Leeds in 1984
11 Neil and Glenys with their children leaving for Athens on an official visit to Greece in January 1984
12 Kinnock putting across the message of the new policy review following the 1987 election defeat
13 Kinnock at the controversial pre-election rally in Sheffield, April 1992
14 Appealing to the voters at Leeds Town Hall in June 1987
15 Kinnock on a visit to a Midland Bank staff nursery at the Arlington Business Centre in Yorkshire in June 1990

Between pages 152 and 153

16 Here Kinnock visits a school in Clitheroe, Lancashire, prior to the county council elections in 1993
17 The Kinnock family's Victorian house in Ealing

18 Addressing supporters on the steps of Labour's Walworth Road headquarters after the election defeat
19 Listening to a speech with Tony Benn at the 1984 party conference in Blackpool
20 Relaxing with Glenys at the end of the conference week
21 Kinnock at Labour Party Conference in Blackpool in 1988
22 Breakfast at a scout camp in October 1991
23 Neil and Glenys with Rachel and Stephen in the spring of 1992

PICTURE CREDITS

Kinnock family: 1–6. White and Reed, Reading: 7. Press Association: 8, 9, 11, 17. *Yorkshire Post*: 10, 13–15. *Manchester Evening News*: 12. Jack Barry/*Clitheroe Advertiser*: 16. *Guardian*: 18. *Blackpool Evening Gazette*: 19–21. Labour Party: 22. Brenda Prince/ Format: 23.

Acknowledgements

The life of any leading politician in Britain will always be well documented, and this is certainly true in the case of Neil Kinnock. However, this is the first time that the story of his life, from his childhood to the aftermath of Labour's election defeat in 1992, has been told within the covers of one book. There is an emphasis on more recent times, bearing in mind that two earlier biographies – by Robert Harris and George Drower – appeared some ten years ago, and that Michael Leapman wrote a detailed account of the first few years of Kinnock's leadership of the Labour Party. I thank these writers, and others whose works are credited in each chapter, for permission to quote from their books. (See *Bibliography* for full list of sources.)

I have also referred to accounts of contemporary political history from the national and regional press. I have talked to Neil Kinnock's friends, colleagues and critics. But, most importantly, I have had Neil Kinnock's full co-operation. I am immensely grateful for the time he devoted to talking to me and answering a barrage of queries over a period of months, for providing copies of his speeches and lending family photographs. I am also very grateful to his personal assistant, Jan Royall, for her support, encouragement and generous help at every stage.

There are many others to whom I am indebted, among them Kath Lapsley and Wendy Broadbent at Manchester Central Library; Irene Hughes and staff at Hebden Bridge Library; Kathleen Rainford and Michael Rhodes at the *Yorkshire Post* library; Eileen Brooks; Barbara Castle; Charles Clarke; Matthew Cox; Julie Crowley and Jackie Stacey at Walworth Road; Peter Devine; John Humphrys; Beryl Marshall; Suzanne Miles; and Tom Sawyer. And thanks to my family – Steve, Michael and David – for their patience and support; to my sister and my mother; and to my father, Fred Jones, who died at Christmas 1992. For a lifetime of inspiration and encouragement I dedicate this book to him.

The excerpt from *That Hideous Strength* is reproduced with the permission of the Bodley Head and the estate of C.S. Lewis.

And sons of the mountains and sons of the valleys
O lift up your hearts, and then
Lift up your feet.

'Land of My Mothers'
The Collected Poems of Idris Davies
Gomer Press

Prologue

Resilience is vital if you want to survive in politics.

The man who very nearly became Prime Minister early in 1992 ended the year as a popular television personality and radio presenter instead. He had been hailed for his overhaul of the opposition Labour Party. He was described as the toughest leader the Labour Party ever had, as one of the tragic heroes in history and as the 'nearly man'.

For Neil Kinnock, the man who once refused to contemplate the possibility that he might not move into No. 10 Downing Street, the general election defeat of 9 April was a personal and political tragedy. He was fifty, with no inclination for early retirement, and all the dreams and hopes of a lifetime's work at an abrupt end. The years of his leadership, he maintained, were entirely wasted. Yet within moments of the defeat ... and his subsequent resignation as leader of the Labour Party ... he could claim with apparent sincerity that his concern was for the people of Britain who would suffer as a result; that personal despondency would be destructive.

Instead of taking to the despatch box for Prime Minister's question time, Neil Kinnock took to the airwaves, and his performances on TV and radio won a level of popular acclaim, which, ironically, had failed to win him a mandate to govern. The media, which had dogged his leadership years with criticism, now feted him. There were still issues of political note on which he was called to give his assessment; there were few television chat shows or panel games whose proceedings were not enlivened by his wit.

Kinnock's personality was said to be one of the reasons for Labour's failure. It was widely held that he was sufficiently disliked by a proportion of the electorate to allow the re-election of a none-too-popular government during a recession. He was, said his detractors variously, ruthless, arrogant, autocratic, devious, untrustworthy – even being Welsh was considered by some to be a character defect. One commentator maintained that he had endured more public insults over a longer period than any other figure in British public life.

Yet by the end of his own *'annus horribilis'* Kinnock appeared confident, relaxed and entertaining, one of the heroes of popular culture. He played disc jockey on BBC Radio Two when Jimmy Young went on holiday. He played stand-up comic to Clive Anderson's straight man when he appeared on the late night chat show (Channel 4). He stood his ground in the arena of vicious satire on the panel of the quiz show *Have I Got News For You* (BBC 2). And he made a guest appearance to announce one of the winners of the British Comedy Awards (ITV). His arrival on stage that night was greeted by a level of thunderous applause which most professional entertainers would envy. 'Just listen to that,' said the show's host, Jonathan Ross. 'It makes you wonder where all this lot was on a certain night a few months ago.'

On that 'certain night', the Labour Party suffered its fourth successive election defeat. Kinnock, who had led the party since 1983 – the longest-serving opposition leader in the history of British politics – had appeared to be tauntingly close to victory according to the opinion polls. But in spite of wiping eighty seats off the Conservative majority, the Labour defeat was conclusive. Days later Kinnock announced that he would be stepping down.

His character had been savaged by the tabloid papers during his leadership, during the campaign, and especially so during the final few days, and Kinnock maintained that the 'Conservative-supporting press has enabled the Tory party to win yet again'. He said afterwards that the relationship between those papers (notably the *Daily Mail, The Sun* and the *Daily Express*) and the Conservative party was a fact of British political life. 'I did think that it would be possible this time to succeed in achieving change in spite of that. Clearly it wasn't.' (The one exception among the tabloids, the *Daily Mirror*, by nature of its political and historical tradition, had been generally supportive, although not always uncritical, throughout the Kinnock years.)

The tabloids had not finished, and even some traditional areas of Labour support had little sympathy for Kinnock in their search for a scapegoat: at best he was accused of being a bad loser. The election inquest became a personal post-mortem, while even kindnesses were doubled-edged. 'Kinnock is resolutely of his place – principled, passionate, sentimental,' wrote Stuart Hall in the *New Statesman* '– and by that token, he is not for these times.'

Hindsight eventually gave a broader view of failure, and one where the blame could not fairly be placed on one personality. Hugo Young in *The Guardian* argued that the election result made clear that Kinnock was not the sole impediment to a Labour victory. 'Something far deeper than the frailties of one man accounts for the tenacious inability of the Labour Party to secure more than 35 per cent of the popular vote.'

Nevertheless, the inquest appeared to run indefinitely, with witnesses offering contributions both wise and fanciful. Denis Healey, a former deputy leader of the Labour Party, maintained during a television discussion in December (TV-am, *Even on Sunday*) that one of the reasons for defeat was Kinnock's physical appearance on television which repelled some women voters. (Though it was Lord Healey who later described Kinnock as one of the great tragic heroes, akin to Gorbachev.)

According to Hugo Young, Kinnock had been patronized by some of his friends, despised by most of his enemies. 'He needed the thickest skin of any man alive and in eight years he developed this impregnable carapace. But it did not secure him against insidious attack, year after year, for not being a winner.'

Yet Kinnock had held on to the Labour leadership with a tenacity admired even by his enemies; they had to acknowledge that – at the time – no one else could do the job. His victory in winning the tenure in 1983 had been overwhelming. Since then his personal rating in the opinion polls had fluctuated, rarely matching that of Margaret Thatcher at any period during her premiership. At the beginning of the 1992 election campaign John Major's personal rating was 18 per cent ahead of Kinnock's, with 20 per cent of Labour supporters – and 54 per cent of trade union members – claiming to be dissatisfied with Kinnock's personal performance.

He retained a few critics in the Parliamentary Labour Party, especially among his old allies on the left. Kinnock had been a persistent left-wing critic of the Labour governments between 1974 and 1979, and was closely associated with the Tribune group in the PLP, and with the *Tribune* newspaper. In the early 1980s when the Labour left fragmented and he refused to vote for Tony Benn in the 1981 deputy leadership contest, he became distanced from the hard left. They were, he believed, too concerned with their own status and dogmatic posturing to challenge the Conservatives.

Kinnock aimed for party unity above all else, as the only way to make Labour electable. He achieved that unity, largely, because most MPs would much rather be in government than in opposition, of course. And at certain points in his career, it looked as though he had made Labour electable. Such a high point occurred towards the end of 1989 and early in 1990; unfortunately it did not coincide with the calling of a general election. And after that the Conservatives played what Kinnock sees as their trump card, replacing their unpopular leader with a 'new man'.

With Labour again defeated and Kinnock's role under scrutiny, there was nevertheless a sizable – and vociferous – body of support for the 'lost leader'. (Kinnock was interviewed by David Dimbleby in a BBC

TV programme, which went out under the title *The Lost Leader*. The quotation comes from a poem by Robert Browning in which an unnamed poet, presumed to be Wordsworth, is condemned for abandoning principles.) And Kinnock's allies proved to be passionate in his defence. After the election he received an astonishing 30,000 messages and letters of support and sympathy. There was the single daffodil and a note saying 'Sorry' delivered by a small boy to his home in Ealing; and there were declarations of loyalty from his political allies, whose reactions were equally intense.

Among these was Baroness Castle of Blackburn, the grand dame of British socialism whose 'back to socialist basics' speech was one of the highlights of the Sheffield pre-election rally. In *The Guardian* guest's diary, the week after the election, she hit back at the critics. 'I mourn the loss of one of the bravest leaders I have known,' she wrote.

> The Tories had in fact paid Neil a compliment they did not intend when they directed so much of the Tory machine fire and venom on him personally. I was interested to detect some racist undertones emerging during the campaign. Neil's 'unfitness to govern', it appeared, had something to do with his being Welsh. Tories don't respect the Welsh whom they regard as a nation of mere plebs and poets.

Barbara Castle, now in full flight, condemned the tabloids for their accusations of 'whingeing by a bad loser'.

> The truth is that the Tories are the biggest whingers of the lot. They have never believed in a level playing field but only one that is perpetually biased their way. So they whinge when the BBC gives a brilliantly impartial coverage of the election because such impartiality puts Labour policies in a better light than the Tory press intends to do. I hope the BBC mandarins have put on their bullet-proof vests and are ready to fight back. I am. Blandness has got us nowhere. Our enemy is too dangerous. It is passion we need now.

With less passion but no less poignancy was the expression of regret from poet John Hegley, also in *The Guardian*, in 'Happy Easter, Mr Kinnock':

> You were a pilot
> different from Pontius
> championing justice
> unenvious of the selfishly conscious.
> Amid the movement to release the thief
> you gave me belief
> and it was you they wanted to nail

for the sin
of wanting to take the tin
from those who could afford it.
Lord it was a rum do.
The vinegar of too few blue losses
unsweetened by your own constituency win
and you bore the ballot box crosses
big with dignity.
Neil
you made me feel
hope
even though the electorate
said nope.

Few political leaders have had their demise mourned in verse.

It is evident that few people were indifferent to Kinnock as a personality: either they revered or reviled him, and perhaps it had been so throughout his career. But when post-election diagnosis ran out of momentum, after the summer recess, Neil Kinnock, back-bench MP and TV personality, appeared to be enjoying his highest ever public rating. It was not a season noted for any high degree of integrity among politicians, of course. By late autumn, with John Major's new government spectacularly sinking in the public esteem due to a combination of economic and political factors and internal scandals, and with the opposition voice of John Smith yet to prove its strength, Neil Kinnock was viewed in a different light. The political diarist Alan Watkins wrote in *The Observer* in December that Kinnock's principal comfort at the moment 'must be that his period of opposition is being cast in a retrospective glow. Unlike Lord Wilson's, his reputation is being rehabilitated even before it has had time to go into a decline.'

Not that Kinnock had bounced back into the public arena as if nothing had happened. His first television performances, both from the back benches, and noticeably on BBC 1's *Question Time* in November, were marked by a lack of ease and self-confidence. In debate Kinnock seemed less colourful and less abrasive, in appearance he looked thinner, even gaunt. Hugo Young in *The Guardian* in December presented a rather melodramatic description: 'Looking now at his emaciated form, surely the product of something more than dietary restraint, you see the shattered ghost of a man who gave up a serious part of his life to make Labour the party of the aspiring majority.' In fact, it was precisely that – dietary restraint. Kinnock had decided to lose some weight.

When the bruised ego began to recover, the public appearances became more frequent and more positive in tone. The level of exposure was surprising because Kinnock, after all, had only nearly become Prime Minister and had behind him no credentials in government service. When ITV made a four-part documentary about his leadership years, one commentator noted that even former President de Gaulle had merited only two programmes. Some believed that having lived in the limelight for nearly nine years, Kinnock still enjoyed the public arena and was using the obvious medium – and his undoubted talents – to reach an audience. Perhaps astute programme makers were taking advantage of the availability of an undisputed crowd-puller who might have an enhancing effect on their viewing figures? Certainly there now appeared to be a sense of genuine liking for a man who was no longer required to prove his trustworthiness with every appearance. Perhaps the demands of office had been such that his true nature became sublimated to duty; released from that burden was he now more relaxed and more approachable?

Among the reasons why he had been chosen as party leader in 1983 were Kinnock's positive image, his skills as a communicator, and his ability to perform well on television. Now, freed from the constraints of office, that ability was again allowed freedom of expression. The result was far more than a talent for entertaining: a candid interview with David Dimbleby on BBC television in December gave the impression of an able statesman, a humanitarian socialist, a man willing to acknowledge publicly his faults and failings. Just the sort of man to win the trust of the electorate, perhaps, had that side of the man been seen earlier. By the time that the series *Kinnock: The Inside Story* was shown on ITV, viewers appeared to have forgotten what – if anything – it was about him that they did not trust. But the frankness and candour were more than would have been allowed a man still in office.

'He's a very interesting man and a deceptive man, in the sense that the more you see, the more you talk to him, the more there is to see, the more depth there is,' says broadcaster and journalist John Humphrys, who conducted several post-election interviews with Kinnock for TV and radio. 'It's true that he doesn't do himself justice when he appears on TV. He is an immensely warm man, and TV often doesn't help get this across.'

'People cannot articulate now what it was that they didn't trust about him,' says admirer and NEC ally Tom Sawyer, the deputy leader of NUPE. 'But they are not being asked to evaluate him as a prospective prime minister now.' The problem, says Sawyer, probably dates from the early period of Kinnock's leadership. 'He did not establish the statesman credentials early enough. There was always the touch of the "boyo" about him. I grew up the same way that he did. I'm a typical working class lad and we don't make prime ministers.'

But why should it be a bad thing for a politician to be one of the boys, asks John Humphrys. 'I don't see why a politician should be remote. We are prepared to accept the elite and arrogant in a politician, yet not so much the down to earth. I suspect that aspect of him, being one of the boys, is what people associate with being lightweight, although I don't see why you have to be aloof to be taken seriously.' Humphrys says that in meeting many politicians over thirty years, he became increasingly confused as to how they saw themselves. 'Humility isn't something that readily springs to mind, but in an odd sort of way there's a humility about Kinnock, yet without the pretension that other politicians have.' Yet ultimately, Humphrys believes, Kinnock was unsuccessful more for personality reasons than any other. 'There is a kind of latent anti-Welshness among the English and that is his bad luck, that and his hair colour. It is often the case that the things that don't matter at all that have the greatest influence over your destiny.'

That 'Welshness' arises regularly in conversations about Kinnock. It is a shallow and meaningless description: Kinnock was born in Wales and represented a Welsh constituency; he speaks with no more than a gentle hint of accent; he has a passable knowledge of the Welsh language but does not claim to be a speaker of Welsh; and he was a fierce opponent of plans for Welsh devolution. And he insists that he has never used the word 'boyo' in his life. But the label persists, even when it is seen as a virtue. MP Ken Livingstone, talking to *The Guardian* about politicians and their television appearances, described Kinnock on *Have I Got News For You?*

He went back to being the Welsh boyo as if there hadn't been an intervening nine years. Of all the non-professional comedian guests they've had on, I thought he was the best, with all these snappy one-liners he'd forced himself to drop. And one of the reasons people didn't want Kinnock was because they recognised the person they were seeing was false, he had shed half his personality.

Kinnock was further accused in some quarters that in his efforts to unite the Labour Party, and in his single-mindedness to see Labour elected, he became increasingly inaccessible, remote and isolated from his colleagues. Some have criticized the level of his determination to see a Labour government elected – and himself as Prime Minister – overlooking the fact that all the socialist principles in the world are meaningless without the power to implement them. Neil Kinnock nearly made it: he made the Labour Party electable and then failed to see it elected. In the words of Roy Hattersley, he removed the reasons for not voting Labour. It was not quite enough, but Kinnock's life and career have taught him how to survive defeat. 'There has been no self pity from him, no looking back with gloom, or ahead with doom,' says Glenys Kinnock, sharing that resilience. 'I suppose politicians can cope with these things. That's what makes them politicians, but I wasn't surprised by his bravery.'

1   A Rather Loud Ginger Person

In the heart of the mining country of South Wales, into a family of miners, Neil Gordon Kinnock was born in Tredegar on 28 March 1942. His father, Gordon, was a coal miner, as were both his grandfathers and several uncles. His mother, Mary, was a district nurse who also came from a mining family. They had two rooms in a small, terraced council house at 1 Vale View, although within a few years of Neil's birth the family moved to Awelfa, to a prefabricated bungalow on a new council estate.

The new house gave the Kinnocks comforts undreamed of by the previous generation: a fridge, a bathroom, and central heating. And as Neil was an only child, resources were not stretched as they had been for his parents' families: Gordon was one of seven children and Mary came from a family of four surviving children. But comfort was relative. Gordon Kinnock's work in the pit caused industrial dermatitis on his hands which became so severe that he was forced to leave mining. He was unemployed for a year, and then took a job as a bricklayer's labourer at the Ebbw Vale steelworks where his duties included ripping out the linings from the blast furnaces. His already damaged hands had to be bandaged every morning.

Mary Kinnock went back to work as a district nurse once young Neil was at school. But they were considered to be relatively well-off. 'We weren't poor,' Kinnock recalls. 'My father worked till he dropped. He always worked long hours. My mother worked as well. Most years we had a holiday. I was never conscious of any real shortage of money, although we never had a car. It couldn't have been thought of in any way as a poor household.'

Neil Kinnock was born and brought up in the constituency of Aneurin Bevan, Labour's architect of the National Health Service, who was to become his political hero. Kinnock's father was a good trade unionist, but his parents were not politically active until they retired, although they both supported the Labour Party. Robert Harris, author of *The Making of Neil Kinnock*, relates a story about Mary Kinnock's habit on polling day of 'using a Tory car to take her to the polling booth, kindly inviting the driver in for a cup of tea and keeping him talking for anything up to an hour on the tactical grounds that "while he's taking my tea, he's not taking anyone else's votes".'

But Mary Kinnock did not join the Labour Party until she retired. Employed as a nurse by Monmouthshire County Council, she did not want anybody to think that she would gain preferment as a consequence of political contact. 'The very idea that anyone would think that of her was laughable,' Kinnock says. The day she finished work she and her husband joined the local Labour Party.

Mary Kinnock wanted the best for her only son, recognizing that education was the one means of escaping the traditional poverty of the area, and sent him to a good junior school at Georgetown at the far side of Tredegar. Neil proved to be a minor rebel, resentful of authority but always a lively and happy boy. 'I had a good time as a kid,' he recalls. There were occasional bouts of bad temper during his childhood, it is said, but they were short-lived. In spite of a tendency to spend more time than he should playing football, rugby and cricket, he passed the eleven plus, gaining marks which enabled him to go to the super-selective, boys only Lewis School at Pengam, which was a fourteen-mile journey from home. 'My mother thought that Tredegar Grammar School was fine – I just happened to do well enough at eleven plus to get one of the reserved places in Pengam. I think there were eight allocated to Tredegar boys every year for the top scorers.'

As in many single-sex grammar schools at the time there was a certain amount of bullying, and as a new boy Kinnock was picked on for a few weeks. The particular initiation rite was being beaten with a leather strap in a railway carriage. 'They used to do it to all the new boys. Most sensibly put up with it, but I couldn't – I hit back. And my life became much happier. Up to then I had been a very happy kid. But it means that I know what fear feels like.' (Kinnock says that he has never felt fear as an adult. 'I have never been intimidated by individuals or threats from organisations. I'm lucky, I suppose.')

For the first couple of years at Pengam he was a little overweight: 'I look at photographs of myself now and I wasn't tremendously fat, it was just a slight complication, but I felt like Billy Bunter.' He admits to being 'a bit of a flop' as a schoolboy, and developed an intense dislike for the 'super dooper' grammar school with its smart uniform, did as little work as he could get away with, and had plans to leave at fifteen to be a coalminer or a soldier or a policeman. He took the initial steps in applying for each job, but when his parents found out 'there was hell' and Neil remained at school to take – and resit – his O-levels. (The first time round he passed only his three favourite subjects, English, history and geography.) In the sixth form he began to enjoy school life, and took part in end-of-term plays as well as starring in the debating society. He played rugby, in his own view 'with more enthusiasm than talent', and he was a member of the Ebbw Vale youth team. Academically he was not regarded as a high flyer, but he passed A-levels in economics, history and English, and won a place at University College, Cardiff.

But Neil's political education was under way before he left school. He joined the Labour Party just before his fifteenth birthday, and at sixteen he had his first encounter with Bevan. Kinnock and some similarly under-age friends went out of town to a pub where they hoped they would not be recognized. They went in to buy a drink, and fled in awe when they saw Nye Bevan standing at the bar. He had already heard his hero speak, of course, at public meetings which he attended with his father. According to Robert Harris, the myths surrounding Neil Kinnock's political awakening rose like mists from the South Wales valleys. 'Go to Billy the Barber's in the centre of Tredegar, in the square by the town clock, and you will hear stories of how the Infant Kinnock, son of Mary, would dazzle local miners with his oratory at the age of eight.'

His socialism was certainly born from experience rather than ideology but, says Harris, 'his great good fortune was to have been born at a time, in a family, in a community, where it was still possible naturally to drink in a radical, pragmatic form of socialism without having to suffer the poverty and hardship which originally produced it.'

Kinnock had read Bevan's *In Place of Fear* when he was fourteen, adding inspiration to experience. Years later he wrote a foreword to a new edition of the book. Soon after joining the Labour Party he joined local discussion groups where he displayed a talent for arguing with people much older, and learned from 'those who had been through the mill of the twenties, thirties and forties, with all of the political, philosophical and industrial tumult of those times'. His mentor was a miner and county councillor called Bill Harry, a friend of his family, who introduced Neil to the people, the ideas and the writings of the Labour movement.

(Years later, during the leadership campaign, Kinnock wrote to thank Harry for his guidance: 'I so much share your regret that Mam and Dad aren't around to see all of this. One way and another I didn't give them very much success until the last couple of years of their lives and they always stuck with me. I only hope I can show the same understanding of my kids. Anyway, the only success that really matters is to help people like my mother and father – and there are millions of them. That's what I go on trying to do, just like you – yes, you more than anyone other than my folks – started teaching me to do all those years ago.')

His political education continued at Cardiff where he enrolled in

October 1961 to study history and industrial relations. This was the beginning of the decade when to be a student was an end in itself, when young people with jobs emulated the student lifestyle and philosophy. If teenagers had dominated the fifties, then the sixties belonged to college and university students. They were seen and heard far beyond their campus boundaries. They demonstrated noisily about causes mainly dear to the heart of the left. They made life uncomfortable for visiting politicians while warmly welcoming the pop musicians around whom the culture of the time was built. They learned to play hard and work almost as hard, while freed from the burdens which preoccupied their successors: graduate unemployment was a fear virtually unknown during the sixties.

It was into this invigorating environment, both stimulating and diverting, that Neil Kinnock threw himself energetically. He played a lot of cricket and rugby, he sang with folk musicians and skipped lectures to go to the cinema in the afternoon, he joined protests and debates, and spent a bare minimum of time working. It was hardly surprising that after three years he failed one of his papers in his history finals, and had to resit the exam the following year before he was awarded a degree.

He also took an active part in student politics; increasingly so when a neck injury during a rugby match curtailed his sporting activity. (As a rugby player his ability was much the same as it had been at school, enthusiastic more than gifted. At 5′ 9″ he is only slightly built, but, as Kinnock points out, the build is not crucial. 'You don't have to be big to be good – look at Cliff Morgan and Gareth Edwards! I had the strength, but not the ability.') His performances switched indoors, to the University Union refectory where Friday night debates would attract a boisterous audience of hundreds of students. Invited speakers were often treated mercilessly; students taking part in the debates knew that they had a fierce crowd to control.

Kinnock did not speak during his first year. But his début came as a result of a challenge presented by a 'stunningly attractive' brunette whom he met in the lunch queue. Glenys Elizabeth Parry, a former Miss National Savings queen from Anglesey, had arrived at Cardiff to study history and education in 1962. She remembers a 'rather loud ginger person' who offered her a leaflet about the Socialist Society.

He was instantly captivated. But he realized that it would take more than his image as a good-time member of the rugby club with a tendency to fool around to win her heart. Kinnock learned that she admired people who could speak fluently in public, and so his first speech in a debate was made directly to impress Miss Parry. The subject of the debate, he thinks, was something to do with the greatness of Britain. Its relevance was lost, possibly the debate too, but the heart was won. 'I made an effort to impress her and it worked,' he says.

Glenys was born in Roade in Northamptonshire where her father was a railway signalman: the family lived at 2 Railway Cottages. Her father's job took them all back to Anglesey, where the family had come from, when Glenys was three. Cyril Parry, her father, was an active trade unionist and secretary of the local Labour Party, and Glenys and her older brother were always included in political discussions: it was a more actively socialist background than Neil's. Cyril Parry had pushed one-year-old Glenys around in her pram when he was delivering leaflets during the 1945 election campaign. At sixteen she joined the Labour Party herself, and also became a member of CND.

At school she was head prefect, keen on drama and singing – she always dodged sport, but has a good voice and has always been very literary. She was a hard worker, gregarious and popular with both staff and pupils. But she was not a keen or active public speaker herself at that time.

At home, a rented house, the family was not well-off. 'My dad worked very, very hard, mostly 12-hour shifts with one Sunday off in three.' Glenys's father, who had run off to sea at the age of fourteen, was a strong, articulate, romantic and humorous man, she says, and being affectionate with each other 'was part of the way we were. Which was quite unusual, I think, in a working class home.' He had travelled widely with the merchant navy, and his stories of those days gave his children what Glenys calls a global sense of life. 'I never look in to the borders of this country, I am always looking out.'

Her mother was a great home-maker, very organized, a wonderful manager of money and a perfectionist. She was brought up fairly strictly: make-up was forbidden, so Glenys would take a compact with her and use the mirror in a public telephone kiosk on her way out. Religion, and the chapel, were important to the Parry family, but Glenys herself stopped being a believer when she was about sixteen.

At Cardiff Neil and Glenys were a well-matched team, and not only romantically. They always regarded each other as best friends too, and they shared political convictions. They were active members of CND, organizing protests against apartheid and the imprisonment of Nelson Mandela. They went on marches together, and campaigned together for the Labour Party during elections. Neil became chairman of the Socialist Society and Glenys its Secretary. Their courtship was less balanced: Neil was quite crazy about Glenys, she more cautious by nature. One summer vacation she stormed back home to Anglesey after a row but Neil followed her in his old Standard Ten car to make amends.

During the university vacations, Kinnock managed to get labouring jobs in the Ebbw Vale steelworks. He would often work double shifts, and on some occasions he managed treble shifts – 24 hours without a break. 'That was because I went to three different foremen and got each to give me a shift, without telling each of the others. They used to call me "The Hobbler", because if you hobbled a shift, it meant you worked straight from one to the other – and I would do anything.' He has always managed to function with very little sleep, and has never doubted the strength of his energy level.

During his third year at Cardiff, Neil failed in an attempt to win the presidency of the Students' Union. But he continued to work for the Socialist Society and the Debating Society, where his popularity grew, and by 1965, having gained his degree and about to start on a post-graduate teaching course, he was elected president of the union, having campaigned on the slogan 'Kinnock for efficiency, initiative, approachability, experience'. In that role, he says, he introduced a much more democratic constitution, and took the union finances into substantial profit. He also organized a well-received 'freshers' week' for the new intake of students, which included performances by top groups of the period like Brian Poole and the Tremeloes at the Freshers' Ball.

Glenys became secretary of the Cardiff branch of the National Union of Students at the same time, and later became chairwoman. She would join Neil in organizing student demonstrations, such as the march through Cardiff protesting against the regime of Ian Smith in Rhodesia. But the students' union irritated Kinnock. All too often its members were more interested in the social events and bar opening times, while the president battled against their apathy in attempting to hold serious meetings, discuss pertinent issues and make policy. At one stage Kinnock ordered the bar to be closed for the evening when meetings were being held.

It was said that his 'dictatorial' rule brought him a certain amount of unpopularity, and as a result of the style of his administration a minority anti-Kinnock faction emerged, attacking him in the Cardiff student newspaper. (It was this paper which first labelled Neil and Glenys 'the power and the glory'. 'Originally I was the power, she was the glory,' says Kinnock. In later years the national press inverted the label when trying to suggest that Glenys was in fact the more powerful influence in their relationship, a claim which she has always treated with contempt.) In the event, Kinnock resigned as president two months before the end of his term of office, not bowing to the pressure of his critics but as a gesture of solidarity when Glenys was attacked for her policy of selecting delegates to the NUS conference on the basis of their work through the year. It was a matter of principle, but he was also frustrated by the apathy among his fellow students. From then on, he and Glenys devoted their time instead to the Labour Party.

Kinnock was to say later that in his political career he never made a calculation about the levels of doing things. 'The idea of becoming an MP was simply beyond the realms of thought.' But that was in his early days. Glenys has said that from the time she met him at university he always wanted to get into Parliament. Certainly his choice of career helped him meet the people who were to influence his future in that direction.

After taking his teaching certificate Kinnock found a job with the Workers' Educational Association as an organizer and tutor. The WEA, funded mainly by the trade unions and the Department of Education, was founded with the aim of increasing the opportunities and broadening the horizons of working people. Its former president, R.H. Tawney, was one of Kinnock's favourite writers of philosophy and politics, and the organization itself gave him the opportunity to meet the leading lights of the local trade union movement as well as Labour Party activists. He also proved to be an excellent teacher, well-respected by his students who were often much older than him. Many of the classes were actually held in the factories, and teaching there gave Kinnock new insights into the conditions and the concerns of trade union members.

Glenys began her teaching career at Abersychan Grammar School; and in 1967, on 25 March, she and Neil were married in the chapel near her family's home at Holyhead, Anglesey. (Glenys wears a wedding ring made of Danish silver: she didn't want South African gold because of their strong opposition to apartheid, and they had been unable to find Welsh gold.) Neil had never had any other long-term girlfriend, and Glenys was the only one to meet his mother's eventual approval. The two women were said to be extremely wary of each other at first, and it is possible that Mary Kinnock was slightly jealous of her daughter-in-law for quite a few years. Glenys believes that Mary relied on Neil for intellectual stimulation, although she was very religious and mother and son would have arguments about Christianity.

The newly weds bought a three-bedroomed terraced house in the village of Pontllanfraith, near Tredegar (borrowing the deposit from Neil's father), and transferred to the local Labour Party there, which was in the Bedwellty constituency. Bedwellty – later to become Islwyn – was made up of fifteen towns and villages which Kinnock describes as 'the Bible belt of rugby football'. Neil formed a branch of the WEA in one of the towns, Blackwood, and through that he met the man who was to become one of his closest friends (and election agent), Barry Moore. He also consolidated his friendship with Michael Foot who had moved to Tredegar when he became MP for Ebbw Vale. Kinnock had first met Foot in 1960 during the Ebbw Vale by-election which followed the death of Nye Bevan. In February 1963 they teamed up again when Neil and Glenys went out walking with Foot and his wife, Jill Craigie. The two couples became very close.

Kinnock stood at the time firmly on the left of the Labour Party. Robert Harris quotes a colleague from those days, Terry Burns, who was later to become a supporter of Militant: 'If there was a left wing within the constituency in those days, I was it. So I was a natural ally of any other left-winger – which Neil certainly was. I'd say his political position at that time was like mine: midway between Militant and Tribune.' Supported by Burns and Barry Moore, Kinnock became youth officer for the Bedwellty party, and he was soon respected for his enthusiasm and hard work, which he combined with a natural wit and good humour.

But there were times when the Labour leadership pushed Kinnock to the brink of leaving the party altogether. He had little time or charity for Harold Wilson, whom he thought pompous, and he was appalled by the Labour government's support for the US 'adventure' in Vietnam, the 1968 wage freeze and the looming trade union legislation contained in the Labour Party publication *In Place of Strife*. According to Robert Harris: 'No taunt angers Kinnock so much as the accusation of some on the left that he is a 'new Wilson', Labour shorthand for a man who masquerades as a socialist as long as it suits him and then abandons his former beliefs when he acquires power.' In fact it was a sign of Kinnock's emergent realism and pragmatism that he saw the value of working for reform from within the Labour Party, and he was soon gaining prominence as an effective – and popular – speaker. In particular he made a name for himself during a by-election in 1968 at Caerphilly when he campaigned for the Labour candidate against a strong challenge from Plaid Cymru, and it was less than a year later that the chance came for the 26-year-old Kinnock to make his own bid for Westminster.

The sitting member for Bedwellty, Harold Finch, who was seventy years old, announced abruptly at a meeting of the constituency party that he intended to retire before the next election. His was one of the safest Labour seats in Britain and his majority at the 1966 election had been more than 25,000. Kinnock, who was then assistant secretary of the local party, took the minutes of the meeting at which Finch casually announced his intention to retire. After the meeting he went for a drink with some friends and asked them: 'Who shall we get to stand in his place?' They replied: 'You will, you bloody idiot!'

His rival was the official NUM candidate, Lance Rogers, who was an obvious favourite at the start of the campaign. Barry Moore took on the job of Kinnock's agent, rounding up support from Labour Party and trade union branches. An early sign of luck was the nomination of the Transport and General Workers' Union (to which Kinnock himself belonged); to luck, Kinnock added the support of the younger members of the constituency, and a formidable degree of intensive canvassing. On the other hand, he was considered by many to be too young and inexperienced, and in a mining area it was understandable that NUM nominations would go to the mining candidate.

Four candidates stood in the first ballot at the selection meeting in Blackwood parish hall on 6 June 1969. Kinnock received the highest number of votes, but not enough to win outright. Two of the candidates were eliminated and Kinnock and Rogers were left to fight it out in a second round. The result of this ballot was a draw – seventy-five votes each – and the two candidates were required to speak yet again to the meeting. Kinnock rose to the occasion, making one of the most sparkling – and crucial – speeches of his career.

When the final ballot was cast, the votes were Rogers seventy-four, Kinnock seventy-six. Bedwellty was such a safe seat that this was, in effect, Kinnock's ticket to Westminster. 'I rang my mother after the selection meeting to tell her the news,' he remembers. 'Glenys was six months pregnant at the time, and my mother said, "That's excellent, now you go home and have a nice cup of tea and get Glenys to put her feet up." ' Kinnock's father, too, would not put aside his natural caution. 'I said to him, "Westminster next stop, dad," and he said, "Oh, you don't know. People can be funny." '

Denis Healey, who was Defence Secretary at the time, recalls in his memoirs, *The Time of My Life*, that he went to Bedwellty in November 1969 to speak at the farewell dinner of the retiring MP, Harold Finch. 'I was met at Newport station by the new candidate, a red-haired young WEA lecturer with a pretty wife who was pregnant. He made a rousing speech over the cold ham and salad in the Miners' Institute, with excellent and unfamiliar jokes which I wrote down in my diary along with his name.'

Neil Kinnock's election to Parliament now depended only on the date chosen by the Wilson administration to go to the polls. In the meantime he worked more ferociously for the Labour Party than many a candidate in a marginal seat. He was still considered to be politically naive and aware of this he sought to prove himself, making speeches at meetings throughout the constituency and beyond, where he was happy to campaign for other MPs. When the general election was held on 18 June 1970, Kinnock won the seat with a huge majority, in spite of a national swing against Labour. The Conservatives now had an overall lead of thirty-five seats, but in Bedwellty the crucial figures were:

Neil Kinnock	28,078
Paul Marland (Conservative)	5,799
Charles Davey (Plaid Cymru)	3,780

His majority was higher than that of party leader Harold Wilson's tally in Huyton. Locally, his majority was around 2,000 votes down on that of his predecessor Harold Finch in 1966. But that had been at the time of Labour's landslide victory. Now, with a huge swing against Labour nationally, Kinnock's result was seen as a triumph.

From his familiar corner of Wales where he was already a prominent figure on the political scene, Neil Kinnock arrived at Westminster in the summer of 1970 to find himself a very small fish in a large pond. At twenty-eight, he was one of the Labour Party's youngest MPs, and he had never before stepped inside the House of Commons even as a visitor. But he was not so much awestruck as aware of the pride felt by his family – his parents in particular – at his achievement. His first letter sent to him as an MP at the Westminster address came from his mother, and he sat down in the library, records Robert Harris, to reply to her. 'While I was there, Winston Churchill walked across in front of me, and Jeremy Thorpe went in the other direction. And so I wrote saying ... a Churchill and a Thorpe have just walked past and it's the first time a Kinnock's sat here.'

He was soon to make the whole House aware of the name of Kinnock with his maiden speech on 13 July. This parliamentary tradition is normally used as a formal way in which a new member can introduce himself or herself, usually with a tribute to their predecessor and a description of their constituency, perhaps with a little humour, but certainly not with any controversy. That at least is the custom. But as the new member for Bedwellty announced that day to jeers from the Tory benches: 'There is no order of the House that demands that I make a non-controversial speech.' He would have found such a demand virtually impossible, speaking as he did during a debate on the National Health Service, which had been created by his hero, Bevan. 'There has been a lot of talk about compassion, and this from a party whose very existence is an illustration of rapacity and selfishness. To me and to the people of South Wales that is what Conservatism means.'

The Government, he said, was prepared 'in the name of the god "choice" to encourage the development of private alternatives in education, welfare and health.' He accused the Conservatives of planning 'extensive mining operations' on the NHS, and then came the part of his speech which, like no other from his parliamentary career, was to be used time and again to illustrate Kinnock's cry for justice:

> Compassion is not a sloppy, sentimental feeling for people who are under-privileged or sick, to be used as a tear-jerker or as an expedient at the time of an election. It is an absolutely practical belief that, regardless of a person's background, ability or ability to pay, he should be provided

with the best that society has to offer. That is compassion in practice and anything less than that is sheer sentimentality.

His fluency and confidence were admired by more experienced MPs, and during his first two years Kinnock was to practise his oratory frequently and on a wide spectrum of subjects, among them nursery schools, the mining industry and coal pensions, handicapped children, the brewing industry and school milk. But he found sitting on the back benches an experience confusing and bewildering initially, and he often wondered if his decision to stand for Parliament had been the correct one. His concerns were with the people in his constituency but he was surprised how little he seemed able to achieve on their behalf, however hard he worked. He was also homesick, living at first in a small hotel near Paddington and later in lodgings in north London with two other Labour MPs, Kevin McNamara and Don Concannon. He had left Glenys at home with their young son Stephen, who was born in January 1970, and missed them desperately. He travelled back to Pontllanfraith every weekend, as it was difficult for Glenys and the baby to visit him in London. She was both miserable and lonely, and by 1971 when she was expecting their second child, the strain of separation was beginning to affect them both.

Tragedy hit the family at the end of 1971 when Neil's parents died within a few days of one another. Gordon Kinnock, then aged sixty-four, collapsed with a heart attack and died in hospital shortly after his son arrived to see him; Mary Kinnock died soon after her husband's funeral. 'It was not a coincidence,' Neil Kinnock says. 'I think my mother died of a broken heart. She suffered from bronchial asthma, and I think that the strain and sense of grief was too much for her. It was a searing experience.' Glenys has described it as 'the worst time of our lives. It was a terrible tragedy. I felt so deeply for Neil. I loved them very much and I wanted my children to know them. I still wish that they had known them.' A few days after the second funeral, Glenys gave birth to a daughter Rachel, two weeks overdue.

Left alone during the week with two young children – and with mice in the house, of which she was terrified – Glenys began to suffer from depression, and Neil began to wonder if his political career was worth the sacrifice of family life. Eventually he decided that the whole family should move to London, even though he had previously vowed that he would always live in his constituency. The local party members were not at all pleased with the decision; it was a choice similar to that made by Bevan when he left Tredegar for a country house in Buckinghamshire, and he too had been criticized. But the Kinnocks bought a small terraced house in Pontllanfraith to use at weekends, and over the years his constituents came to realize that Neil Kinnock served them conscientiously in spite of his weekday absence. He held regular surgeries every other weekend in different towns and villages, and followed through all the correspondence from the voters of Bedwellty who took their problems to him.

He also made drastic changes to the working practice of the local party. The general management committee had met, under his predecessor Finch, just once a year. Kinnock made those meetings at first twice-yearly, and then quarterly, eventually monthly. Kinnock believed that an MP should be accountable but not subservient to the wishes of his local constituency party, and he would give regular parliamentary reports of what he had been doing at the Commons. This local accountability did not just apply to the local Labour Party. In April and September each year he arranged public meetings at three or four venues in the constituency, where he would speak on his work as an MP. So the move to London was eventually accepted by Kinnock's critics. The family bought a semi-detached house in Dysart Avenue, Kingston upon Thames, which was on the right side of London for setting off on the journey back to Wales. (Later they moved to a slightly bigger house near Lammas Park in Ealing.)

During his first few years as an MP, Kinnock was regarded as on the left of the Labour Party. One of his early friendships was with Dennis Skinner, and they both joined the left-wing Tribune Group: Kinnock was to become a regular contributor to the *Tribune* newspaper. Chris Mullin, who edited *Tribune* in the seventies and is now MP for Sunderland South, was an early friend of Kinnock's in London and was always impressed by him, his charisma and his humour. Robert Harris recalls him saying: 'I remember thinking very early on that he was bound to be leader unless he was hit by a bus.'

Kinnock was a strong opponent of entry into the Common Market, which he saw as bringing no benefits whatsoever to his native Wales, and he was to maintain this opposition throughout the seventies. And yet he did not believe that those Labour MPs who were pro-Marketeers – in defiance of the official party policy of the time – should be rebuked. According to George Drower, author of *Neil Kinnock: The Path to Leadership*, he believed that an MP's right to act according to his conscience was paramount. 'He believed that while MPs should consult their local parties as much as possible, this did not mean that an MP should merely be a delegate of his constituency party. This was a belief that he maintained from the start of his parliamentary career.'

In the House of Commons he rose to speak with increasing regularity, and during his first four years in Parliament he asked no less than 239 written questions. But Kinnock says that it was not until the miners' strike of 1971–2 that he really felt he was doing a worthwhile job at Westminster. The mining industry belonged to his personal background, and the cause was one on which he could focus his antipathy to the Conservative Government. He was in demand as a speaker at public meetings throughout the country, and when he spoke on the subject in the Commons it was with a passion based on experience and first-hand knowledge.

In one notable speech he drew a picture of life on the miners' picket lines.

> If they [the Conservatives] had been on strike for five weeks, if their families' total income was seven pounds a week social security benefit ... if they were worried about paying the rent, and they saw some cowboy coming along driving a bald-tyred wagon without a road-fund licence, what would their reaction be? What would be the instinct of any red-blooded man in this House, having put his family to all that inconvenience and near-misery, if he saw someone riding roughshod over his picket line? I know what my attitude would be.

In those days the language of his oratory, which sometimes spilled over into anger, and the physical power of his delivery while speaking, were the features which brought him to prominence, almost as much as the substance of what he was saying. There was said to be a recklessness about his manner if he was defending a matter of principle, and it was soon apparent that few who heard him were indifferent to Neil Kinnock: either they strongly admired him or they hated him. That was the manner, the force of presence, which brought Kinnock to the attention of the political world; it came to be tempered with time and the burden of authority. Like other mortals he was to mature with age.

2   Waiting in the Wings

The miners continued to play a dominant role in British politics, and when a further dispute with the Conservative Government over a pay claim came to a head in the winter of 1973, the Prime Minister, Edward Heath, sought to settle the issue by calling a general election. The date chosen was 28 February 1974, and Labour came back to power, with five seats more than the Conservatives but no overall majority. But there was nothing close about the result in Bedwellty where Neil Kinnock's majority was 21,637.

He had played a prominent role in the campaign, proving to be an effective and popular television personality; this, and the fact that his speechmaking at Westminster had drawn the attention of the Labour leadership led to a request from Harold Wilson that Kinnock should second the new Government's response to the Queen's Speech – a role which is usually a harbinger of later ministerial office for a young backbencher. (Wilson, returning for his second term of office as Prime Minister, strengthened Labour's presence later that year after calling another election in the autumn.)

Kinnock was naturally enthusiastic about his party's return to power, but still critical of Wilson as leader. His need for the freedom to voice that criticism meant that he did not want to be constrained by government office. But he had come to the attention of several members of the new Cabinet who asked in turn if he would serve them as a Parliamentary Private Secretary. This junior role, acting as a messenger and assistant to a senior minister, can be useful grounding for a young MP, but Kinnock believed that his talents could be more usefully exploited in other directions. Somewhat reluctantly, he made an agreement to work for Michael Foot, the new Employment Secretary, for a twelve-month period.

He was relieved when that year was over. Kinnock felt he had too many disagreements with the Government and was concerned that he could be an embarrassment to Foot, whose views he would traditionally be expected to reflect. Freed from any obligation to defer to a member of the Labour Government, he was able to speak out if the leadership appeared to be veering away from the route to socialism as he saw it. He had been one of the first signatories of the Campaign for Labour Party Democracy (CLPD), a pressure group whose objectives were to secure mandatory reselection, popular election for the leader, and greater democracy in policy making.

The CLPD proved in time to be a major force in restructuring Labour's constitution, attracting those activists on the left of the party keen enough to make the fine detail of procedural rules work to their advantage. Kinnock was not one of these active members. He did not support the idea of mandatory reselection of all candidates between elections, as a method of making individual MPs accountable to their local party, for example. But he was in favour of one of their tactics: the attempt to change the constitution to widen the franchise for the election of party leader, a move which would in due course be to his enormous advantage. In the mean time, his attacks on Wilson's government came from the floor of the House, over such matters as increased allowances for the Royal Family; the policy towards South Africa (including a call for the cancellation of the British Lions rugby tour); and the sale of arms to Chile.

Kinnock had also been a member of the Campaign for Nuclear Disarmament since his student days. He took a keen interest in anti-fascist and anti-racist organizations, becoming a founder member of the Anti-Nazi League, and joined protests against the activities of right-wing regimes worldwide. In Parliament he gradually dropped the occasional jokey style of speechmaking, but saved his humour for television where he was increasingly in demand for discussion programmes. And while few outside the Labour Party had heard of the Campaign for Labour Party Democracy, Kinnock was summoned by programme makers when the subject of parliamentary reform was on the agenda. He was a relaxed and confident TV performer, ready to accept almost any invitation to take part (as indeed he would accept invitations from all and sundry to speak at events throughout the country, to the exasperation of his family).

Kinnock used the newspapers too, writing a series of articles for *The Guardian*, for *Labour Weekly* and – most intensively – for the socialist paper *Tribune*, where he added his voice to criticism of the Wilson government's economic policies. *Tribune* at that time was read widely among the rank and file of Labour's active membership, and the regular exposure in print was yet another way that Kinnock's name and views became widely known.

Along with most of the Labour left at the time, Kinnock was an active anti-Marketeer, but Britain had voted in a referendum in June 1975 to stay in the Common Market, by a two-to-one majority. 'I thought that the referendum result was inevitable and I was very disturbed by the nationalistic arguments of some in the "No" campaign.' Kinnock has since said publicly that he wished he had made it clear immediately after the result that 'we should then commit ourselves to Europe and make the best of it.'

This was a minor setback. It was only a few months before Kinnock enjoyed one of his biggest political triumphs to date, at the Labour Party Conference in Blackpool. The *Tribune* newspaper midweek rally had long been regarded as one of the great rituals of Labour politics. Robert Harris describes how more than 2,000 left-wing delegates would gather 'in a revivalist atmosphere to listen to the left's leading speakers of the day ... To the radical wing of the party, an invitation to address it is an important mark of distinction.' Kinnock shared the platform that night with Michael Foot and Ian Mikardo. He was there, ostensibly, to make the traditional appeal for funds, rather than as a key speaker – he was well aware by then of his reputation for being the 'life and soul of the party'. He was on particularly good form that night: his speech won a standing ovation, as well as a record collection and a host of admirers from the constituency parties whose support would later be crucial. Among fellow MPs he was seen as the star of the show, and Barbara Castle recalled that it was one of the funniest speeches she had ever heard.

At the party conference the following year, 1976, Kinnock stood for the first time as a candidate for Labour's ruling body, the National Executive Committee (NEC). Thanks to the friends he had won the previous year he polled 155,000 votes – not enough to win election but an impressive tally for a newcomer. (Most local Labour parties cast a block of 1,000 votes in the constituency section.) But the 1976 party conference also saw Kinnock in action in his personal crusade against plans for devolution for Wales and Scotland. In a speech which won another ovation he maintained that such a move would guarantee 'disharmony, disunity, conflict and competition throughout the whole of Britain'. But in spite of Kinnock's personal appeal, conference voted heavily in support of devolution.

The question had first been raised when a promise to the regions was made in Labour's election manifesto in October 1974. Kinnock was wholeheartedly opposed to the idea and believed that his views were shared by the majority of his constituents. He would point to Ulster where 'we have learned that legislative autonomy without economic solvency and the support of the whole community is a bloody tragedy'. In 1976 his views were polarized against those of his old friend and colleague, Michael Foot, who became deputy party leader with special responsibility for devolution. (Foot, for example, thought that a failure to grant independence to Ireland in the nineteenth century had brought disunity.)

Harold Wilson had announced his resignation in March 1976 and in the subsequent leadership contest Kinnock was one of the leaders of Foot's campaign team. James Callaghan won that election and he became Prime Minister on 5 April. (It was during this period that Kinnock first raised the idea of an electoral college to choose the party leader when he wrote in *Tribune* that the whole of the Labour movement should be involved in the decision, not just MPs.) The new administration was determined to go ahead with proposals for devolution, and throughout the debate Foot and Kinnock maintained opposing stances, without their friendship being damaged in the long run. Kinnock's opposition was fundamental and determined: it was he, together with fellow Gwent MP, Leo Abse, who eventually tabled a Commons resolution calling for a referendum on the subject.

The issue is regarded somewhat differently today, in the broader perspective of the European Community; at the time devolution raised passions on a par with the European debates of the early nineties. The Labour Government, with a very small majority in the Commons, was concerned about the rise in popularity of Plaid Cymru and the Scottish Nationalist Party. These two parties were thought to be taking votes which would traditionally have gone to Labour, and the leadership believed that there was a clear and popular demand for Welsh and Scottish assemblies, a belief which Kinnock insisted was mistaken. His view was that 'the emancipation of the class which I came to this House to represent … can best be achieved in a single nation and in a single economic unit'.

Kinnock led the campaign against devolution, almost single-handedly, until the referendum in March 1979. In Wales he lost both supporters and personal friends because of his determination. Nationalists were thought to have been behind threats to his life and rumour-mongering designed to damage his political career. According to George Drower in *The Path to Leadership*, Kinnock's fight against devolution was 'an act of immense personal and political courage … While he had the support of his own constituency, his anti-devolutionist stance put his career at great risk. He flew in the face of the party hierarchy and upset many Labour supporters and voters in South Wales.' At the Welsh Labour Party Conference in the spring of 1978 he was accused of being a traitor. But, says Drower, his attitude was to meet the devolutionists head on, to fight and then defeat them. 'Unlike Foot, but like Margaret Thatcher whom he despised, he was a conviction politician. Kinnock's conviction was not to do with socialism or Labour Party policy, it was gut British thinking and common sense.'

In an article in *The Times* a year later, Caroline Moorehead described how people had been surprised by the degree of passion Kinnock brought to the cause.

> Neither the emotion he showed, nor the stand he took, were entirely in keeping with the package of views he shares with fellow members of the Tribune group. But devolution revealed just how far he is prepared to speak out when he feels committed, just how impatient he is with prevarication, and it dispelled for a few local sceptics the image of Neil Kinnock as a man obsessed by personal ambition.

The referendum result was a clear vindication of Kinnock's long campaign: in neither Wales nor Scotland was there anywhere near the 40 per cent of the total electorate required to win. In Wales the majority was four to one against the establishment of an Assembly. The victory belonged to Kinnock: ultimately even among those who disagreed with his views he mostly won respect.

The years of the Callaghan administration proved to be a period of gradual advancement for Kinnock. His highly individual and often rebellious approach won him more friends than enemies within the Labour movement. At the same time he was accused of occasional disloyalty to the hierarchy. In March 1976 he abstained in the voting on the Government's economic policy after a Budget declaration that there would be no increases in government spending for three years, and a promise of tax cuts if the unions would limit pay demands to 3 per cent. Kinnock was among left-wingers who wanted to see an increase in public spending. And he opposed what he saw as an attempt to blackmail the trade unions who had accepted the terms of the social contract and earlier wage limits.

An image as a rebel did no harm at all: at the Labour Party Conference at Brighton in 1977, Kinnock moved a step closer to the NEC when he increased his votes to 244,000. He also received star billing in the conference comedy review, 'End of the Peers Show'. Glenys Kinnock attributed his impressive voting tally to her husband's intensive public speaking throughout the country, and his frequent television appearances. A talent for making people laugh was also useful. Figures on the right of the Labour Party, including Shirley Williams, David Owen and Bill Rogers, had recommended constituencies to vote for Kinnock whom they saw as on the 'respectable' left. One reason for Kinnock's respectability with the right was the humour in his speeches – for wit was a rare feature amongst left-wingers. George Drower says that much of Kinnock's popularity among the constituency parties at the time was his working-class image 'which gave him an aura of trustworthiness and stability; an additional strength was that he did not have a working class accent. He has the self assurance and articulation of the middle classes and his pleasant sense of humour means that they do not feel threatened by his ideas.'

TV appearances certainly helped to boost Kinnock's popularity, as well as ensuring that his name became a household one. In 1976, for example, he appeared on BBC television seventeen times, and the following year spoke on twenty-four BBC radio programmes (from *Any Questions* to the *Jimmy Young Programme* – of which he was to be a host years later). In 1980 he clocked up fifty-five TV appearances in one year, and it was ı ımoured that he had been offered a job as a television presenter, a role scorned then by Kinnock but accepted by his Labour MP colleague Brian Walden.

Nevertheless Kinnock accepted just about every invitation to appear on screen, whatever the topic under discussion. The exposure paid off, and in 1978 he won critical approval within the Labour Party with election to the NEC. That year the annual conference was held in Blackpool, and when the votes were counted, Kinnock's total of 274,000 gave him not just a place among the Executive, but fourth place from thirty-four candidates. There was a champagne celebration with Glenys – his campaign manager – and a party of close friends. In the conference hall his name was greeted with applause.

But beyond the walls of the conference centre there was little cause for celebration in the autumn of 1978. Against all expectation, James Callaghan ruled out a general election in October. Kinnock thought the decision misguided; he foresaw trouble escalating as a result of the imposition of a 5 per cent limit on pay rises. He was to be proved right as Britain headed into a winter for which the description 'discontent' is perhaps too mild. Strikes by NHS staff, by lorry drivers, water-board workers, local council staff and others brought areas of the country virtually to a standstill. Kinnock accused the Labour Government of 'totally operating Tory policies' and warned that 'if we have an election now, we face slaughter'.

The result of the devolution referendum pushed Callaghan to a decision which he would have been wise to make the previous autumn. Having lost the support of the Scottish Nationalists, Labour's small majority failed to survive a confidence motion in the House on 28 March 1979 – by just one vote. Callaghan had little option but to put his case to the electorate.

Kinnock has since expressed his regret about his approach to the Labour government of 1974–9. 'I did not give enough credit to fellow members of the Labour Party who were trying to deal with major problems,' he says. (He also, incidentally, cast aside misgivings about home rule ten years later when he made a pledge to make political devolution – for Scotland, at any rate – a priority for an incoming Labour government.) But in the general election on 3 May 1979, Labour lost office with a 5.2 per cent swing to the Conservatives and their leader, Margaret Thatcher. Significantly in Bedwellty, where Kinnock's majority was more than 20,000, the Plaid Cymru candidate lost his deposit.

Through his stand against devolution Neil Kinnock had helped to bring about the downfall of the Labour Government. It was an administration which he believed had been heading further and further to the right and losing sight of all socialist principles, hence his defiance of the leadership and his refusal of ministerial posts. Now, in opposition, the individualistic stance of the rebel was less appropriate and he decided it was time to join the team and work from within to create a Labour Government for the future. Kinnock stood for election to the Shadow Cabinet, and took fourteenth place. The first twelve MPs in the poll go forward automatically to the front bench, but minor roles are at the discretion of the party leader.

With some persuasion from Michael Foot, Callaghan offered Kinnock a more senior post than he might have expected: education spokesman. Kinnock accepted, on 18 June 1979: it was, he says, 'put up or shut up time'. The decision put him firmly on the promotional ladder within the Labour Party, to the surprise of some observers. At thirty-seven he was among the youngest 'senior' MPs, and not only had he played no part in the Callaghan government, he was one of its strongest critics. But Callaghan apparently bore no political grudges. He liked Kinnock personally, having known him closely since Kinnock campaigned for him in Cardiff in the 1960s, and evidently considered him able enough.

Although his own experience in education, as a WEA tutor, had been short-lived, Kinnock had been kept up to date from the teacher's point of view by Glenys, who had by then worked in grammar, secondary modern, comprehensive and special schools. He had also followed the education debate closely throughout his parliamentary career: he had early clashes as a young MP with the then Education Secretary Margaret Thatcher on issues concerning polytechnics and student loans. And he had taken up causes such as adult literacy and youth unemployment during the seventies.

Colleagues on the left of the party were not impressed. To some it seemed that Kinnock had betrayed his principles by joining a team led by a right-winger. But the move was well judged. Robert Harris says that Kinnock's decision to take the education post proved to be the hinge upon which his career turned.

It demonstrated that for Kinnock politics is not about striking heroic stances: it is about power. Between 1974 and 1979 he wielded more power by staying outside the Government than he would have had if he had taken up the offer to take a place inside. The election defeat altered that. A place in the Shadow Cabinet offers its occupant more scope to display his talent than a junior ministry.

At a time when the Conservatives were encouraging the growth of private education, Kinnock found that his new job gave him ample opportunity to unleash the passion of his socialist convictions on the Government. He enjoyed speaking at conferences, joining demonstrations against cuts in education spending and generally displaying his enthusiasm for the subject. What he found less acceptable was the amount of reading matter presented for his perusal, and on educational theory he might not have been entirely thorough. But he had regular contact with the NUT and with classroom teachers in schools and colleges of all kinds. And he made a lasting impression in his attacks on private education, with repeated promises that a future Labour Government would repeal Tory legislation and work towards a fully comprehensive system.

He published a discussion document, which proposed the elimination of all public support for private schools over a ten-year period: they were, he believed, 'the very cement in the wall that divides British society'. It was a cause he championed wholeheartedly, with the worst aspects of his own grammar-school education always at the back of his mind. But his critics saw too great an influence of the politics of class warfare in Kinnock's own plans for the education system. They were, according to some observers, essentially impractical, both remote and obsolete as Labour itself was to be under the leadership of Michael Foot, reflecting its increasingly isolated beliefs.

Caroline Moorehead in *The Times* said that for all his standing ovations, Kinnock did not have an easy ride as shadow education spokesman. 'His baptism was sharp and not particularly happy ... he was given a subject which, though dear to his heart as inseparable from the furthering of socialism, has nonetheless enmeshed predecessors in the labyrinths of its acts and policies and revealed itself a notable graveyard for good schemes.'

Nevertheless, the attacks which Kinnock made on such institutions as grammar schools and private education won him support among traditional Labour voters. And at the party conference in Brighton that autumn of 1979 he won a standing ovation after a speech in which he attacked spending cuts. The Tories, he said, 'cripple our children and then taunt them for being lame'. It was a fiery speech and hailed for its oratory and passion. Only afterwards did Kinnock admit that he had taken the rare precaution of jotting down some notes beforehand, only to lose them before he stood at the rostrum.

That same week he moved up into second place in the NEC elections, winning 484,000 votes – just 3,000 fewer than Tony Benn. Few people in the Labour movement were so popular. In the public memory Kinnock was not associated with the failed Callaghan regime; in the press he was beginning to be considered as a possible future leader of the party.

It was a relatively carefree period for Kinnock. His career was established and in the ascendant, yet he had few of the cares and responsibilities of the 1980s. He had his family nearby, well settled in London, the chilren were growing up but not yet growing away. (Stephen and Rachel gave the appearance of standing back from their father's career, Kinnock recalled later. 'But in retrospect they have shown an almost uncanny memory for detail – times, dates, impressions. What transpires is that they talked to each other a lot about the things that were going on, but never wanted to provoke discussion, or make Glenys and me worry.' They each joined the Labour Party when they reached the age of fifteen – 'They just went off and did it. I think partly as an act of solidarity, but also because they have got the right convictions. We're very proud of that.')

But if times were good for Kinnock, they were proving to be more than a little uncomfortable for Callaghan and the leadership team. At the conference where Kinnock scored such a personal success, they came under fierce attack for alleged mismanagement of power and control of the election manifesto. The left, who saw the Wilson and Callaghan regimes as tragically lost opportunities, claimed that proposals representing majority interest – such as the abolition of the House of Lords – had been dropped by the unelected political advisers who drew up the manifesto. (Similar charges by the left followed subsequent election defeats, of course, but in 1979 the NEC was righteously angry that its own policy – not just the recommendations of conference – was not put to the voters.)

This was one of the issues being pursued by the Campaign for Labour Party Democracy, that the NEC alone should have control of the manifesto, and they were disappointed that Kinnock's vote had swung the NEC in favour of deferring a decision. The proposed change which would in time have the most significant effect on Kinnock's career – the electoral college to choose the party leader – was also deferred. Those in the Labour Party who were battling for greater democracy and accountability had to be content with one significant conference decision – the mandatory reselection of MPs.

Although Kinnock had won his ovation, he had also started to alienate the left wing. There were further signs of movement away from their ideology when the shadow education spokesman, the following year, refused to make a definite promise that a future Labour administration would restore Tory cuts in school milk provision, meals and travel. Here was evidence of the pragmatism which would mark Kinnock's future career. He would no longer commit himself to courses of action which he saw as impossible to fulfil, lacking in common sense, or ignorant of economic realities. He said to a meeting of the Parliamentary Labour Party where MPs had called for unequivocal undertakings to restore arts funding: 'If you want an Education Spokesman to promote that the moon is made of green cheese, get another Education Spokesman.'

'We have too often in the past made promises we could not keep and we must not do so again and destroy our credibility,' he told a meeting of the Bedwellty Labour Party. For the first time he was faced with some criticism from his local management committee; not for the first time he was unpopular among his colleagues at Westminster. Some of them were pleased to see him publicly embarrassed, as when he claimed that Tory policies had led to the need for drawing lots for books and equipment in some schools. His Conservative opposite number, Mark Carlisle, produced figures which showed that his party was actually spending more on school books than had the last Labour administration.

But by the autumn of 1980 Kinnock was beginning to be seen as a serious contender for the Labour leadership. Caroline Moorehead wrote in *The Times*:

> Today there are few members of Parliament on either side of the House who do not at least speculate about his role as a possible future leader of the Labour Party, even if they ask themselves, somewhat perplexed, just why it is that a 37-year-old Welshman with great charm, but almost nothing in the way of a past, has suddenly come to look so promising.

She said that on both sides of the House there were those who saw his 'disregard for homework a failure of ability, who mistrust his flights of Welsh rhetoric and the fact that he does not operate with an Oxford trained English mind'.

But there were others, she wrote,

> more prepared to admire a man who is not ashamed to admit that the principles of politics are more interesting to him than the details, people delighted to find such an orator in such a dim age of oratory, such a golden boy when there are so few about, such a genuinely international socialist whose inspiration is derived from the heart of the labour movement and the classics of socialism.

By the time that the 1980 party conference opened in Blackpool on 29 September Kinnock had begun to consider the possibilities seriously himself. He knew that the prospect was slight under the current rules for electing a leader, with only members of the Parliamentary Labour Party eligible to vote, for Kinnock was not an all-round favourite at Westminster. The right wing of the old school regarded with suspicion his rebellious past, while the left wing were concerned that he had never been wholeheartedly committed to their ideology, and now appeared to be moving steadily away from it. But Kinnock's popularity in the Labour movement generally continued to grow.

Further reassurance came that week when he took second place, once again behind Tony Benn, in the NEC election, with 432,000 votes. And so the motion put to the conference in the middle of the week had particular significance for him. A small majority voted to approve in principle the idea of an electoral college to choose the party leader. The finer details, concerning the percentages of votes to be given to MPs, the unions and the constituencies, were deferred, after much agonizing, to a further special one-day conference, but the implications were quite clear to Kinnock and his undisguised pleasure was noted by all at Blackpool that day. Years later Roy Hattersley reflected that in their obsession with proposed changes over the election of leader, the reselection of MPs, and the manifesto, 'Nobody was thinking about what the Labour Party stood for, even less how its principles should be applied in the modern world.'

But before the special conference had convened, James Callaghan resigned as leader of the Labour Party in November 1980, and the election for his successor was held in the traditional way, with votes being cast only by MPs. The popular candidate was Denis Healey, Callaghan's own choice, but not a favourite among those on the left. Kinnock considered Healey a 'cert', although not his preference. 'I'd told Michael Foot in October 1980 that it was impossible for him to get enough PLP votes to win. And I didn't want him to have to endure what I thought would be defeat. He was talked into standing by Moss Evans [TGWU] and Clive Jenkins [ASTMS, the Association of Scientific, Technical and Managerial Staffs]. When Michael said he would stand, I told him: "You know what I think, but I'll work like hell for you." '

Foot, though seen as a left-wing rebel himself, was well respected at Westminster as a man of principle and honour, and was admired for his keen intellect and his occasionally brilliant speeches. However, he was initially a reluctant candidate, believing that at sixty-seven he was too old for the post; only the thought that he might be able to bring about party unity convinced him to go ahead. Foot was duly elected, more as the 'stop Healey' choice than through any faith in his qualities of leadership among MPs, and certainly as a result of some vigorous campaigning by his young friend Kinnock. Kinnock was elected to the Shadow Cabinet and resumed his role as education spokesman. (Roy Hattersley was to declare, a decade later, that 'by electing Michael we decided, at least subconsciously, that the next election was as good as lost'.)

In January 1981, the Labour Party met for a one-day conference at Wembley to consider how future leaders would be chosen. Change was already inevitable, the form of that change was now at issue. On the right, David Owen and Roy Hattersley advocated 'one member, one vote', but the massive weight of the trade union block votes was against them: the unions wanted to retain the power that they held. An electoral college was agreed, and after a day of bitter argument, tactical trading and vote switching, the proportion of votes was set at 30 per cent from the constituencies, 40 per cent from the trade unions and 30 per cent from the PLP – the formula advocated by the hard left.

Foot, who had preferred a 50-25-25 proportion but had not spoken in the debate, attempted to ignore the now apparent divisions of opinion in the party and made a fierce speech attacking the Conservative Government. According to Robert Harris, this first conference speech set the pattern for all the rest.

> Right and left would brutally attack one another all week, pausing to listen to Foot orating about unemployment, disarmament and the need for unity, give him an ovation, and then immediately resume fighting. His leadership speeches were not the keynote of a conference: they were occasional commercial breaks for socialism.

There were two momentous reactions to the Wembley conference. The first was the announcement, already planned and judiciously timed, by four senior right-wingers – David Owen, Roy Jenkins, Shirley Williams and Bill Rogers – of a new Council for Social Democracy. Their statement, the 'Limehouse Declaration', stopped short of resignation from the Labour Party at that stage, but their call for 'a realignment of British politics' was the first move towards the creation of the Social Democratic Party, officially launched two months later. They regarded the outcome of the Wembley conference as 'calamitous' in that 'a handful of trade union leaders can now dictate the choice of a future Prime Minister'. From the start, Kinnock denounced the SDP as traitors, and he attacked their decision at every opportunity. He was equally critical of the second Wembley spin-off, the announcement by Tony Benn that he would challenge Denis Healey for deputy leadership of the party.

Kinnock saw Benn's move as public evidence of civil war in the Labour Party and believed that the challenge could do nothing but harm to prospects for unity or election victory. 'I thought we needed a contest like we needed bubonic plague,' he said at the time. Benn, on the other hand, saw elections as being 'quite unifying' rather than divisive, but he believed that as Healey had been allowed in unopposed (coming second behind Foot in the leadership contest) there was now a genuine vacancy. According to his diary: 'I am sure I will be clobbered if I stand, but I don't think that is really the issue,' he told Foot.

Kinnock was always suspicious of Benn, of his aristocratic background and original position on the right of the party: Kinnock's own socialism was inherited and instinctive rather than intellectual. But his opposition to Benn's challenge was based on more than personality differences. Kinnock was a realist, and Benn's proposals for what a future Labour Government would do – and in how short a time (such as immediately abolish the House of Lords and pull out of the EEC) he saw as visions of fantasy. Such an attitude damaged Labour because people could not take it seriously; it was both arrogant and insulting, he maintained. And Benn's decision to make a challenge only undermined an already weakened Labour Party, he believed.

During a family holiday in Italy, Kinnock wrote a long and bitter article for *Tribune*, 'Personality, Policies and Democratic Socialism', justifying his belief. 'Those who scorn appeals for unity ... desert the millions of people for whom a Labour government would be the only means of deliverance from insecurity, poverty, unemployment and despair.' Benn, he wrote, had

> fostered antagonism within the party ... undermined the credibility of credible policies by oversimplification, he has not disowned those who insist upon support for his candidature as the test of loyalty to Labour policy. I believe that through an inaccurate analysis of the position and power of the Labour movement and by a tactically mistaken decision to contest the deputy leadership, Tony has significantly harmed the current standing and electoral opportunities of the Labour Party. By doing so he has inadvertently harmed those who I am sure he most wants to help.

Peter Kellner, who introduced a collection of Kinnock's speeches in the book *Thorns and Roses*, wrote that this article was significant for three reasons.

> First, it demonstrated a degree of political courage. He put into words what many on the left thought but nobody of his stature had said; and he said it in the Left's own weekly newspaper. Second, the article worked. That is, thirty-seven Labour MPs abstained in the second round of the contest. Such was the closeness of the result that had just thirteen of those abstainers backed Benn, he would have won. Third, Kinnock's article, and the abstentions, marked the beginning of a chain of events

that was to lead eventually to the isolation, and finally impotence, of the radicals.

Unwilling to stand himself, and unable to back Healey because of fundamental policy differences – among them unilateral nuclear disarmament – Kinnock had decided to vote for John Silkin in the first ballot. The deputy leadership contest reached its conclusion in Brighton in autumn 1981 at the annual conference. Far from being 'clobbered', Benn had mustered considerable support and came a very close second to Healey in a second ballot, in which Kinnock abstained, after Silkin had been eliminated in the first. It is generally held that abstention by Kinnock and other Tribunite MPs prevented Benn from winning by a margin of less than 1 per cent of the vote. It was a decision Kinnock later regretted. He said years later: 'I wish I had voted for Denis instead of abstaining.'

Barbara Castle wrote in her memoirs, *Fighting All the Way*, that Kinnock had agonized over his choice.

> It was at this conference that he first made his impact on me as a political figure to be taken seriously. Feeling for Benn was running high in the constituencies. Neil's own local party of Bedwellty was Bennite to a man and woman, but Neil made it clear that he was going to vote for John Silkin and then, if necessary, abstain. It was a courageous move which put him at odds with the majority of local parties and with his own constituency, and he could only have taken that step as a man of principle.

Lady Castle recalled that she and her husband found themselves behind Neil in the procession waiting to file on to the platform for the opening ceremony. ' "There goes a future leader of the party," I said to Ted audibly. Neil smiled at us over his shoulder and said modestly, "Thank you, but I do not want the job. It would mean too much disruption of my family life." '

The campaign had raised fiercely partisan feelings among Labour's rank and file, and Brighton that week saw hostility spill over into warfare, with rival groups scuffling. Kinnock himself was involved in an incident when he was attacked by a stranger at the Grand Hotel. And he had a vicious confrontation with Arthur Scargill during a discussion on BBC's *Panorama* when Scargill accused him of dishonesty. Kinnock retorted that when Benn was a member of the pre-1979 Labour Cabinet 'which he now claims to despise, I was voting against it and campaigning to try and divert that Government back to what I believe is the socialist path and I won't take claims of dishonesty from you or anybody else'. To make a bad week worse, Kinnock saw his share of the vote in the NEC elections drop to 371,000 and only fifth place, a protest vote after his opposition to Benn.

According to Barbara Castle, Kinnock shrugged off a vitriolic attack by one of the Bennites, Margaret Beckett, claiming that she would not have dared speak her mind if he had been present. Lady Castle wrote: 'I realised that this light-hearted, witty, idealistic left winger had a mind of his own and a will to follow his own course.' Years later she had questioned him about the incident and asked him: 'So you never set out to become leader of the party?' He had replied, 'Not at that time', and had explained to her what had actually happened.

> The majority of the Tribune group had lost patience with Tony Benn and wanted to put up their own candidate. They asked Neil to stand but he refused, arguing that it would be divisive and they should abstain. The group therefore nominated John Silkin, who was wiped out on the first ballot. This time Neil persuaded them to abstain. By now he had become the standard bearer of the sane left and their obvious candidate when the leadership issue came up again.

But while the left saw his action as tantamount to treason, the moderates in the Labour Party were grateful to Kinnock and his fellow members of the Tribune group of MPs who had abstained in the second ballot, thus allowing Healey his narrow margin of victory. His constituency party in Bedwellty was less pleased: they had backed Benn and were outraged by their representative's act of defiance. Kinnock had to suffer considerable hostility on home territory before he was reselected, under the new rules, by a majority of 65 to 12 at the Bedwellty General Committee meeting in March 1982.

There was no appeasing the far left of the party nationally, however. Kinnock had further lost their favour in opposing them when the NEC voted to open a new inquiry into the activities of the Militant tendency, a faction within the Labour Party said to have Trotskyite leanings who were gaining considerable control of constituency parties in some areas. They had some support in Wales, and in Kinnock's own constituency, not enough to be a threat to him but certainly enough to make him aware of their activities – and to be alarmed by them.

This was not the first indication of trouble on the Militant front. During the 1970s, Reg Underhill, the Labour Party's national agent, had drawn up a report which catalogued evidence claiming that Militant were a party within a party. Underhill had seen the growing drift to the left in the constituencies and at grass-roots level, but he and his colleagues were bitterly disappointed when the NEC chose to take no action. After his retirement in 1979, Underhill – at his own expense – circulated the findings of his report to every constituency party, so that none in the Labour movement could claim to be ignorant of what was involved. (Many believe that if the Underhill report had been acted upon in the seventies, then much of the later damage done to the party could have been avoided.)

The NEC decided to make another examination of Militant's stand at the same time as their refusal to endorse Peter Tatchell, a left-winger, as prospective parliamentary candidate for Bermondsey in South London. Although Tatchell was not a Militant supporter, his views on extra-parliamentary action to fight the Government had set danger signals in front of the traditionalists. (Tatchell had advocated a siege of the House of Commons, among other forms of action, to protest about unemployment.) Kinnock spoke and voted against Tatchell's endorsement out of loyalty to Michael Foot and because of his own instincts: ironically when the issue was raised again months later, Foot backed down, but Tatchell was subsequently defeated at the by-election, losing one of Labour's safest seats to the Liberals. Labour has so far never regained the seat.

The episode was not forgotten by Kinnock's opponents who saw it as an example of his further drift away from his roots on the left. Attempts were made to discredit him and some members of the Tribune group of MPs called for his removal from their 'slate' of candidates for the NEC elections because he could no longer be considered a left-winger. 'I pointed out at the time that my removal from the "slate" would be difficult – I'd never been on it!' Kinnock says.

But Kinnock survived, and his popularity among the moderates began to rise. He had to work hard to win that popularity, however, and he did it at the expense of parliamentary engagements. From being a persistent speaker and questioner in the House of Commons, Kinnock now put in very few appearances, using his time instead to tour the country and address meetings of trades unions and local constituency parties. Their support was crucial to his re-election to the NEC and, obviously, to any ambitions he might have for climbing the ladder within the party. His speaking tours paid off: at the 1982 autumn conference he held on to his NEC place – although with a lower percentage of the vote – and his education speech won him another standing ovation. He described an education system 'subject to unremitting attack from a government which is supposed to have not only moral but legal responsibility for safeguarding the educational interests of the nation'. A few weeks later Kinnock climbed from seventh place to second in the elections to the Shadow Cabinet.

3   Leader

The Labour Party was suffering badly in the opinion polls at the end of 1981. Internal wrangling did little to impress an already mistrustful electorate; as it happened, the Conservatives were also performing poorly and Margaret Thatcher was said to be the most unpopular Prime Minister in living memory. But her fortunes and those of her party were to change dramatically due to external forces which in turn led to a backlash against Labour and its leadership. The Falklands War with Argentina erupted in April 1982 after a British guard ship had been withdrawn from the South Atlantic. The Falkland Islands, a British colonial outpost, were then invaded by Argentina. George Drower, in *The Path to Leadership*, described how Margaret Thatcher and her defence secretary John Nott ignored advice from James Callaghan – acknowledged as an expert on colonial matters – over the withdrawal of the guard ship HMS Endurance. Although Thatcher and Nott were competent in the administration of the Falklands War, says Drower, 'no one in Britain was more responsible for the war taking place. That they were able to enhance their reputations in spite of this is among the most disgraceful injustices of modern British politics.'

There is no question that the Falklands factor played an immense part in the Conservatives' revival, although the beginning of the economic recovery that was to become the credit-led Tory boom probably had more effect on the subsequent Tory election victory. Labour were seen as half-hearted in their support for the Government's use of military force; Kinnock agreed that dispatching the task force was necessary, and then spent much of his time defending his party leader.

Michael Foot was considered by the right to be un-patriotic because he was a member of CND, and by the left as disloyal to his party because he supported the Government's action. But when Argentina surrendered and the Conservative Government was riding on the crest of a nationalistic wave, Kinnock told a by-election meeting that the Tories were 'stooping into the very sewer of public emotion' if they decided to hold a general election on the basis of a crisis 'for which they are very largely responsible'. Mrs Thatcher was to wait another year, until June 1983, to test the popularity of her leadership during the Falklands War, but even before Labour's spectacular election defeat it seemed inevitable that Michael Foot's days as leader were numbered.

Neil Kinnock's own ambitions appear to have crystallized around 1981 when he told a friend in Wales, Gwyn Evans, that he would probably have to stand for the leadership when Michael Foot resigned. It was something which he and Glenys joked about. But the prospect began to look a distinctly serious one early in 1983 with a general election looming. Foot's ability to lead Labour to victory was doubted by many within the party and beyond it: Kinnock was one of the few still to show any faith and loyalty. Whereas a huge majority of Labour MPs when questioned thought that Foot should go before an election, Kinnock refused to persuade him to stand down. 'I am proud to stand by such a man,' he said at a rally in March that year. 'I want him to be the leader of our country for I trust him with my children's lives. I trust him with the future of our people.' Had Foot resigned that spring, then his deputy Healey would have become a caretaker of the party until the autumn conference.

Kinnock was seen as a possible challenger for the post of deputy in that event. He had been education spokesman for four years, but more importantly he had achieved a position of acceptability by both the right and the left – with the exception of the extreme left of the party. Had Labour lost a crucial by-election in Darlington at the end of March, then Foot might well have made his move. But Labour held on to the seat, and Foot stayed, scarcely with a great deal of confidence, to lead his party when Margaret Thatcher named 9 June as the day for the general election.

Under more normal circumstances, the Conservatives would have struggled to defend their poor record. More than three million people were unemployed, British manufacturing output was at an all time low, and an unprecedented number of companies had collapsed. And yet the Tories began the election campaign with a huge lead over Labour in the opinion polls: 47 per cent to Labour's 34 per cent, with the SDP at 19 per cent. The Falklands factor was crucial. In spite of the growing number of critics who pointed out that Mrs Thatcher could have avoided the dispute in the first place, and in spite of the high cost in servicemen's lives as well as the £2,000 million said to have been spent, public opinion still hailed a military victory and gave credit to the Conservatives who had been at the helm.

The Labour Party had to share some of the blame, too, for their own low standing in the polls. For four years they had been viewed as an opposition at war with itself, too distracted by internal disputes to present feasible alternative policies. (Kinnock was to say later that the

Tories won because of a 'false boom' and because of two wars – a real one in the Falklands and a political civil war in the Labour Party.) The Walworth Road headquarters was said to be riddled with incompetence, which did no positive good to the image of a major party. It was little wonder that the 1983 election campaign suffered from a severe lack of organization or coherence.

The election manifesto, for example, proved difficult reading for even the most staunch Labour supporter. It was 15,000 words long, a poorly presented assortment of ideas from apparently unconnected departments. It has been labelled variously 'a triumph of policy over presentation', 'a compilation of numerous half-digested ideas', and, most pertinently by Gerald Kaufman, 'the longest suicide note in history'. But if Labour presented itself as the party almost destined to lose, Kinnock looked like a man determined to win. It was the first election he had fought from within the senior ranks of the party and, finding little in the way of organizational support or backing – much to his disgust – he set about campaigning with a vigour which put colleagues to shame.

He toured the country, visiting more than a hundred constituencies and making speeches everywhere along the way, in village halls, in factories, in front of audiences of several hundred or just a handful. His enthusiasm appeared never to waver, although the schedule he had set for himself was unrealistic and he developed a reputation for being late – a reputation which he found hard to shake off over the years, as he always tried to do more than was humanly possible within rigid timetables. It was also a mammoth task for what seemed like a one-man campaign, and he was frustrated by the level of incompetence which he met. He also spoke so often that he was not only exhausted but also in danger of losing his voice. And yet his speeches were hailed as among the best made by anyone during the campaign. 'By concentrating on the caring side of Labour's programme, unemployment, the welfare state, and education, he avoided getting caught in arguments on defence and the Common Market,' wrote George Drower. 'If others had followed his lead, Labour's gap might have been lessened.'

Defence was the key issue on which Labour's public approval lay balanced. Their policy reflected the views of Foot and Kinnock, both arch-unilateralists who were determined that a future Labour Government would scrap all nuclear weapons irrespective of the actions of other powers. Kinnock's view remained resolute throughout that campaign, even though he could see that voters were being discouraged by the issue of unilateralism, and in spite of an intervention by former Prime Minister Callaghan who stated that the weapons should not be dismantled 'for nothing in return'. This step out of line led to further argument within the party, from which Kinnock tried to distance himself. However much he was angered by Callaghan's views, he saw that another disagreement among the Labour hierarchy would only fuel public mistrust. Callaghan, he said, had a personal opinion and was entitled to voice it. 'The Labour Party has a non-nuclear defence policy and the Labour government will implement the policy.'

But it was a controversy concerning conventional warfare which marred Kinnock's own campaign. During the final week before polling day he took part in a live televised debate with a studio audience and the subject of the Falklands War was raised, as it had been regularly. Kinnock was furious that the Tories were still living off the credit for a military victory, and when a voice shouted out, 'At least Mrs Thatcher's got guts,' he replied: 'And it's a pity that other people had to leave theirs on the ground at Goose Green in order to prove it.' This brought an inevitable outcry from the Conservatives, but rather than retract his remarks, Kinnock later announced that he was sending a letter to the families of all servicemen killed during the conflict. In this he apologized for any offence caused, while reiterating his belief that their loss had led to Mrs Thatcher's 'reputation for fortitude'. His remarks, he said, were unpremeditated and he would never consciously or unconsciously add to the anguish felt by those bereaved. He added: 'I honestly felt then and continue to honestly feel now that it was and is a pity – a tragic pity – that with or without her intention, the Prime Minister's reputation was advanced through such sacrifice.'

The incident illustrates Kinnock's ability to retrieve the initiative, but whether the episode won him friends or lost votes was irrelevant at the time, for Labour were already beyond redemption. As Robert Harris relates, the *Daily Mirror* had already wistfully put away the front page it had been planning to print in the event of a sensational Labour victory: the banner headline 'GOTCHA!' over a picture of Mrs Thatcher leaving 10 Downing Street.

Kinnock, the physical weariness of the campaign showing in his face, and his voice painfully hoarse, was to make one last fierce attack on the Conservatives, at a meeting in Glamorgan two days before the election:

> If Margaret Thatcher is re-elected as Prime Minister on Thursday, I warn you.
>
> I warn you that you will have pain when healing and relief depend on payment.
>
> I warn you that you will have ignorance, when talents are untended and wits are wasted, when learning is a privilege and not a right.
>
> I warn you that you will have poverty, when pensions slip and benefits are whittled away by a Government that won't pay in an economy that can't pay.

I warn you that you will be cold when fuel charges are used as a tax system that the rich don't notice and the poor can't afford.

I warn you that you must not expect work; when many cannot spend, many more will not be able to earn. When they don't earn, they don't spend. When they don't spend, work dies.

I warn you not to go into the streets alone after dark or into the streets in large crowds of protest in the light.

I warn you that you will be quiet, when the curfew of fear and the gibbet of unemployment make you obedient.

I warn you that you will have a defence of a sort with risk and at a price that surpasses all understanding.

I warn you that you will be home bound when fares and transport bills kill leisure and lock you up.

I warn you that you will borrow less, when credit, loans, mortgages and easy payments are refused to people on your melting income.

If Margaret Thatcher wins on Thursday, she will be more a leader than a Prime Minister. That power produces arrogance and when it is toughened by Tebbitry and flattered and fawned upon by spineless sycophants, the boot-licking tabloid knights of Fleet Street and placemen in the quangos, the arrogance corrupts absolutely.

If Margaret Thatcher wins on Thursday, I warn you not to be ordinary. I warn you not to be young. I warn you not to fall ill. I warn you not to get old.

On election night, with the results coming in, Kinnock was asked on television if he expected to be the next leader of the Labour Party. Such speculation, he said, was foolhardy: Michael Foot was leader and had not made a declaration otherwise. But events that night were fuelling the speculation. Tony Benn was defeated and lost his seat in a Bristol constituency which had been altered by boundary changes, and the candidates for the leadership of the Labour Party had to be MPs. But if one of his rivals was now displaced, Kinnock had little else to celebrate at the time. Labour's defeat was the most humiliating since the early part of the century. The Conservatives won 397 seats, Labour 209. (The Liberals won 17 and the SDP 6.) The party had taken only 27 per cent of the vote, and no fewer than 119 Labour candidates lost their deposits. The working class had deserted in their millions, with fewer than 40 per cent of trade unionists and less than half the unemployed voting Labour.

Boundary changes had affected Kinnock's constituency, now renamed Islwyn. That accounted in part for an apparent drop in his support. Kinnock believes, however, that some 8,000 votes which went to the SDP candidate were gained from 'rooted Labour supporters who wanted to teach the party a lesson' and quotes several conversations with constituents to support the argument. Nevertheless, he still retained a majority of more than 14,000 over his SDP rival.

Kinnock was now a favourite in the leadership race, for it was certain that Foot would resign after such a devastating defeat. Roy Hattersley was another likely contender, while Denis Healey was to make it clear that he would not be standing. An election for a new leader would not be held until the party conference in October, yet within a few days of the election, and pre-empting Foot's formal resignation, the race was under way.

Starter's orders were called by two leading trade union officials, Clive Jenkins of the ASTMS and Moss Evans of the TGWU, Kinnock's own union. They agreed to formally nominate Michael Foot for reselection, should he wish to stand again, but they also agreed that in the likely event of Foot's resignation, their votes would go instead to Kinnock. It was Jenkins who contacted Foot on the Saturday after the election, offering support; it was Jenkins who was first told that Foot was standing down. And it was he who broke the news to Kinnock that, with the blessing of Michael Foot, the two powerful unions had made their nomination for leader of the party. The word came with a flourish of publicity when both Kinnock and Jenkins were being interviewed separately for *The World This Weekend* programme on Radio Four. Kinnock, said Jenkins, was a young and sophisticated politician with 'dash, sparkle, imagination and a persuasive quality'. Michael Foot, it appeared, had resigned by default, and had allowed his favoured successor to take an effective early lead before any other candidates were aware that the race had started.

The new electoral college system of choosing the party leader was going to work in Kinnock's favour, it was clear from the start. His nationwide campaigning and public speaking tours of the past decade meant that he was a known – and approved – quantity in constituencies all over Britain. Equally his tours had taken in many trade union venues, and considerable support was forthcoming immediately from the unions with their block votes: the TGWU, for example, as the largest union, could offer a potential 1.25 million votes. By the end of the first week of campaigning, Kinnock was assured of nominations from other major unions including USDAW (the shopworkers' union) and the railwaymen's union, ASLEF. There were complaints from the hard left that the unions were not consulting their membership before making nominations; this was evidently the case to some extent when so many block votes were guaranteed so early in the campaign.

But an opinion poll a month later confirmed that Kinnock really did have immense popularity among union members as well as their leaders, and this was reinforced when the unions did consult branch and shop-floor members. Even among the Parliamentary Labour Party, where Kinnock might have expected to fare less well, there was wide agreement on the need for change and for a younger, more dynamic figurehead. And ironically the tabloid press, who would play a role in Kinnock's downfall a decade later, were at the time enthusiastic in their backing for the 'tough, angry young leader', as the *Daily Star* proclaimed him. But Kinnock was not content to let his reputation work for him, and in the months leading to the leadership election he staged a very determined campaign, managed by Robin Cook, a fellow Tribunite and MP for Livingston.

It is easy to overlook the fact that Kinnock actually had three rivals in the race: Roy Hattersley, Eric Heffer and Peter Shore. Hattersley would possibly have fared better under the old rules for election, when only MPs voted, and he did tend to concentrate his appeal for support among their ranks. But there had been a shift away from the right among the PLP; also the average age of Labour MPs was now considerably younger, and Kinnock seemed to be a more natural choice of the new intake. He was still only forty-one, and was heard to say at one stage that he could lead the party for ten years, retire at fifty-one and still be younger than Hattersley was then: an ominous prophesy, with hindsight.

Robert Harris points out, though, that Kinnock had occasional periods of self-doubt, and that like many extroverts he had darker moods. 'At times during the campaign he expressed reservations about the suddenness with which he was being pitched into the leadership. It had all come too soon: the children were at an age when they needed more attention; he would miss seeing them grow up; he and Glenys were still young enough to travel and enjoy themselves; why should he burden himself with the additional work?' He was also acutely aware of his lack of experience: four years as Shadow Education Minister was perhaps not sufficient training for bouts at the dispatch box with Margaret Thatcher.

The Shadow Cabinet members almost all backed Hattersley, who had seemed the natural successor when Denis Healey decided not to stand. Hattersley did have experience as a government minister, as a former consumer affairs secretary in the Cabinet, but even this could not always be judged as an advantage over Kinnock whose popularity with some members of the Labour movement was precisely because he had not been a member of an unpopular administration. Both Kinnock and Hattersley, as gestures towards party unity, were also standing for the deputy leadership, along with Michael Meacher, Gwyneth Dunwoody and Denzil Davies, and each had stated publicly that they would happily work with the other.

But throughout the summer of 1983 it became increasingly clear in which capacity each would succeed. George Drower wrote that Hattersley's campaign appeared desperate. 'While Kinnock's success had appeared to be effortless, Hattersley lost much prestige by appearing to try.' And he noted that Hattersley's 'uncharacteristically aggressive campaigning' gave him the air of a loser. 'Traditionally the Labour moderates had been the best organised in the party but now Kinnock's presidential style of campaigning impressed many by its efficiency.' At one stage Hattersley looked like losing even the deputy's post to left-winger Michael Meacher, which worried those who feared further defections to the SDP. The combination of Kinnock and Hattersley began to be referred to as the 'dream ticket' which would hold the party together.

But the dream was not yet a reality, and Kinnock suffered two setbacks during the summer. The first, at the end of June, was the loss of his voice due to acute laryngitis which had first developed during the general election. Only complete rest from public speaking would prevent permanent damage, he was told. He rested his voice for a month, even resorting to passing notes to members of his family, and was allowed one concession only by his doctor: taking part in the Queen's Speech debate at the opening of the new session of Parliament. Correspondents noted that his silence 'added humour to an otherwise uninteresting campaign'. The Queen's Speech seemed a good opportunity to demonstrate his ability as a parliamentarian, and Labour MPs crowded into the chamber to hear him: however, when he spoke it was with a scarcely audible croak. 'As he had nothing to offer in terms of policy, this was just as well,' wrote Drower. 'He got great credit for trying and general approval from Labour MPs for his attack on the Tory government.'

Kinnock had only just returned to the public speaking arena a month later when the second catastrophe struck. He was driving back home to London from South Wales one night after appearing as guest of honour at a school anniversary in Tredegar and addressing a meeting in Barry. The journey along the M4 was monotonous and he was playing a tape – Brahms' First Symphony – to pass the time, driving 'slightly in excess of 70 miles an hour', when his Ford Sierra suddenly swerved off the motorway, overturned several times as it hit the grass bank, bounced 100 yards and came to a halt upside-down, with Kinnock hanging by his seat belt. He crawled out, shaken but unhurt apart from a small cut on his head.

The car was a complete write-off; Kinnock says it was 'scrambled'. Passing motorists stopped to help; the police were called and a breathalyser test proved that Kinnock had not been drinking. There was no apparent reason for the crash. 'I'm lucky to be alive,' he told reporters. 'Someone up there likes me.' It was a remarkable escape from the sort of accident which would invariably have left its victim dead or badly injured. It also, as several commentators pointed out, seemed to sum up Kinnock's entire career. Drower wrote: 'That Kinnock had been able to survive such a horrific accident did indeed seem miraculous; it enabled him to acquire the aura of charismatic indestructability which emphasised his image of being a natural winner.'

For the rest of the campaign Kinnock was chauffeured around the country in a car provided by the TGWU. (A few years later when Kinnock was asked to choose eight records when a guest on *Desert Island Discs*, the final movement of the Brahms' Symphony No. 1 was an 'inevitable' choice. He said that on the day after the accident he had taken the tape out of the wrecked car and put it in the tape deck at home, 'and it played'. The tape itself was auctioned later that summer to raise funds for the leadership election campaign.)

By the time that nominations closed on 15 July, Kinnock was already looking certain to be the future leader of the Labour Party, even though the actual election was another two-and-a-half months away. His personal manifesto was published on 18 July, and was notable for the watering down of two previously hard-line policy beliefs. On nuclear disarmament he maintained his traditional opposition, but added that the British independently-controlled Polaris submarines would be out of date anyway by the end of the decade; their scrapping could then be seen as a practical rather than an ideological measure. And, contrary to his stance to date, Kinnock now allowed that it would not be rational to withdraw from the Common Market. In other respects he stood by the status quo of Labour Party policy: changing the public's perception of Labour was the way to win the next election, he believed, rather than changing the party's policy. However he did allow that non-elected professional researchers employed at party headquarters might be given a wider brief in presenting the image of the party.

Image remained foremost in the minds of the candidates throughout the summer, with their electioneering deliberately and carefully considerate, with few lapses into personal attacks, mindful that another bout of internal bickering could lower Labour's respectability still further. Public confidence appeared to be ebbing even further away from them, as illustrated by the result of the Penrith by-election in July (caused by the elevation of William Whitelaw to the House of Lords). Labour's total of votes dropped from 6,612 a month earlier to just 2,834. Their candidate lost his deposit as the SDP surged into a very challenging second place. A month later a Gallup opinion poll showed that nationally Labour had slipped into third place behind the SDP.

Kinnock's campaigning was carried out at his usual frenetic pace, relieved only by a holiday in August, and one or two less serious public appearances, such as a fund-raising review which featured his daughter Rachel playing the guitar. The Kinnock family, who until then had played support roles firmly behind the scenes, now became the focus of media interest. Glenys Kinnock discovered the cost of fame when reporters and photographers descended on the school where she was teaching, and even followed her out shopping. They realized that she had more to offer than the role of housewife, mother and teacher, holding firm political convictions of her own.

That this should come as a surprise to commentators of the scene in the 1980s says a great deal about media reluctance to abandon stereotypical views. (Years later, with a varied and challenging career of her own, Glenys was still unable to escape this stereotype entirely. When asked by the chat show host Clive Anderson if she had been to Downing Street to measure for curtains, she cuttingly replied: 'I've never measured for curtains in my life and I'm not going to start now.') At the same time, the papers saw some novelty value in Glenys Kinnock's acknowledged intelligence and left-wing views, and began their attempt to cast her as the scheming wife. The old student newspaper label of 'the Power and the Glory' was dug out, only now the national press reversed the roles, and Glenys became the 'power'.

She and Neil arrived in Brighton on Saturday 1 October, the day before the leadership contest. The following morning they were asked to pose for the cameras on the beach, and in what was to become famous footage, they were filmed hand in hand, Neil inelegantly tripping as he pushed Glenys out of the way of a large wave. Contrary to popular mythology, Kinnock did not fall into the sea; he didn't even get wet. 'Neither – more to the point – did Glenys' new suede boots!' Nevertheless, the press photographers were delighted with the incident, and the Kinnocks realized the extent to which their lives would be under public scrutiny.

That afternoon the votes were cast: the result was even better than Kinnock had dared dream. Of the total, Kinnock won 71.3 per cent, with Hattersley taking 19.3 per cent, Heffer 6.3 and Shore 3.1. Kinnock's vote from the 40 per cent assigned to the trade union section was 29 per cent; he took 27 per cent of the 30 per cent in the constituency section, and nearly 15 per cent of the 30 per cent assigned to the Parliamentary Labour Party. Glenys was beckoned to join Neil on the platform and receive the applause of the conference delegates. It was not exactly a rapturous response: the outcome came as no surprise to anyone in the hall that day.

After the second count of the day, Hattersley joined Kinnock on the platform as his deputy. His success was a little less expected, although Michael Meacher's challenge had faded in the last two weeks of the campaign. Labour now had its 'dream ticket' team at the helm; the photograph of Kinnock and Hattersley, linked hands held high in triumph, is one of the most famous of all political pictures. (Years later Hattersley was to confess that as he was called to the platform, Gerald Kaufman whispered to him to take Kinnock's hand and raise it in the air, as George Brown had done with Harold Wilson, 'and Harold hated it. It made it look like joint leadership.' In fact, said Hattersley, there is no such thing as joint leadership. 'But Neil Kinnock and I worked in partnership. From then on whatever mistakes the party made were at least in part my responsibility.')

It was only when Kinnock began making his winner's speech that the sense of excitement spread through the crowd. According to habit, the speech had not been written in advance but scribbled on a piece of paper while the votes were being counted for the deputy leadership. Thanking Glenys and his family who 'tolerate me out of love, they raise my spirits,' he said:

> I look at the future of their generation, and it makes me determined that they must not know war. It makes me determined that they shall not live in a world of want. I look at those children of mine, and at other people's children, and I say that the new generation shall not inherit idleness, ugliness, or the prejudices of racism and sexism ... Here in this crowded, dangerous, beautiful world, there is only hope if there is hope together for all peoples. Our function, our mission, our objective as socialists is to see that we gain the power to achieve that and there is no other way to achieve it but by socialism, by the deliberate organisation of all the resources of humankind, all the talents of humankind.

He quoted Nye Bevan, with words which he commended as a maxim for a political movement:

> He who would lead must articulate the wants, the frustrations and the aspirations of the majority. Their hearts must be moved by his word, and so his words must be attuned to their realities. If he speaks in the old false categories, they will listen and at first nod their heads, for they hear a familiar echo from the past; but if he persists, they begin to appreciate that he is no longer with them. He must speak with the authentic accents of those who elected him. That means that he should share their values, that is, be in touch with their realities.

Kinnock added: 'If anyone wants to know the reasons why we must conduct ourselves in this fashion ... just remember how you felt on that dreadful morning of June 10th. Just remember how you felt then and think to yourselves, June 9th, 1983, never, ever again.' To loud applause Kinnock went on to call for unity:

> Not unity four weeks before the next general election, not unity before the local elections next year, but unity here and now, and from henceforth. Not a cosmetic disguise but living, working unity of people, of a

movement, of a party, of a belief, of a conviction that wants to win. We want to win to save our country, to save our world. That is the fight.

Robert Harris wrote that Kinnock's oratory was a triumph, both over the acoustics of the hall, and over the 'ingrained resistance of Labour activists to being impressed by their leaders'. Robin Day called it one of the finest speeches he had ever heard delivered from the platform at a Labour conference. 'That was a wee one,' Sam McCluskie, the conference chairman, told the applauding delegates. 'Wait till you hear him try.' There was a similarly ecstatic reception later in the week to Kinnock's main conference speech, which again had been jotted down at the last minute:

> When those who prate blimpish patriotism in the mode of Margaret Thatcher are also the ones who will take millions off the caring services of this country, I wonder they don't choke on the very word patriotism. They are the enemy, they must be defeated, and we must defeat them together. If we try by groups and factions we will not do it. If we give greater attention to arguments between ourselves than to our enmity against them we will not do it. If we give more attention to impressing each other than convincing the people we have to convince, we will not do it. They are the enemy, they must be defeated, and we must defeat them together. That is our purpose. There must be no activity in this Labour movement that is superior to that purpose. Now and for all time in the future that is our business. Let us get to it.

Michael Leapman, author of *Kinnock*, an analysis of the first few years of Kinnock's leadership, commented on the wild applause that greeted the new leader's call. 'Over the next four years some of the people in the hall that day, sharing in the excitement and enthusiasm, were to discover to their cost that he not only meant what he said but, to a greater extent than any other Labour leader in recent memory, he had the strength, skill and determination to act on it.' One man only, it seemed, was not sharing in that excitement and enthusiasm. Tony Benn recorded in his diary: 'In the afternoon Kinnock made his first speech as Leader. It was pretty vacuous, I thought, but he got a huge ovation.'

The accolades were not only for Kinnock personally. Labour had been in serious danger of becoming a fringe party, as the Liberals had done in the 1930s. The essential requirement for survival as a potent force, as many delegates no doubt realized, was a leadership team with the skill to steer all of the party, not just factions of it, into a challenging position. The 'dream ticket' alliance of left and right represented by Kinnock and Hattersley had considerable symbolic significance after the internal divisions which had cost Labour so dear – and contributed to their defeat at the 1983 election. Observers noted that the choice of two men with hitherto opposing factional connections, reflected the fact that parliamentarians, trade unionists and party members overwhelmingly desired party unity and a fresh political initiative.

A few weeks later Kinnock moved into the Opposition leader's suite of offices at the House of Commons. His new job carried a salary of £36,000 plus a chauffeur-driven car. At about the same time, Labour's showing in the opinion polls took a sudden and dramatic turn for the better, and by the end of the year they were only one percentage point behind the Conservatives. It semed as if Neil Kinnock's leadership might be the turning-point for the party. He had reason to be well pleased, but there was no complacency. The task ahead was described prophetically in a passage from C.S. Lewis's novel, *That Hideous Strength*, which Norman Willis, general secretary of the TUC, had framed and presented to Kinnock under the date of his election as leader: Sunday 2 Octobr 1983. It hangs in his office to this day:

> My dear young friend,
>
> The golden rule is very simple. There are only two errors which would be fatal to one placed in the peculiar situation which certain parts of your previous conduct have unfortunately created for you. On the one hand, anything like a lack of initiative or enterprise would be disastrous. On the other, the slightest approach to unauthorised action – anything which suggested that you were assuming a liberty of decision which, in all the circumstances, is not really yours – might have consequences from which even I could not protect you. But as long as you keep quite clear of these two extremes, there is no reason (speaking unofficially) why you should not be perfectly safe.

Nor was Kinnock ever allowed to forget the words of a county councillor from his constituency, Jim Winfield, who had told him when he was first elected to Westminster: 'Don't forget, boy, from now on all your successes will be written in sand, and all of your failures will be engraved in stone.' But he told reporters candidly: 'The day I start enjoying this Leader's job is the day I see the furniture van turning into Downing Street.'

4   Of Miners and Militants

The Labour Party which Neil Kinnock inherited in October 1983 was in a state of disarray, badly organized, badly run and beset with internal divisions. The June election had been lost following a campaign which was a shambles with a manifesto which was arguably both unreadable and unworkable. An intensive level of re-organization was necessary before the party could even begin to think about fighting – let alone winning – another election. Kinnock realized that in the field of policy making he had to avoid the mistake made by Callaghan of simply abandoning on principle anything of which he personally disapproved, and to avoid Foot's mistake of allowing virtually anything to stand. He saw too the need for a restructuring of the party's machinery.

Kinnock and his advisors set about reorganizing the Walworth Road headquarters in a way that gave the leadership more control over campaigning, presentation and co-ordination of party activity throughout the country. There would be a new, professional approach to public relations and campaigning. Kinnock also wanted to reduce the power of activists by challenging the outside left and through changing the constitution of the party.

One of his first tasks as leader was to make a combined assault on the party's problems. Abandoning the network of sub-committees of the NEC's Home Policy Committee, where politicians were outnumbered by party officials and drafted-on specialists and lobbyists – with varying degrees of expertise – in each field, he set up joint policy committees on which members of the NEC and the Parliamentary Labour Party were equally represented. Their role would be to formulate policy proposals in specific areas – defence, housing, for example – and they would then be disbanded once policy was agreed.

Kinnock also decided to take the chair of a Campaigns Strategy Committee, comprising members of the PLP, the NEC and the unions, whose task would be to choose the issues which the party should campaign for, and methods to be used. One of the first recommendations of this committee was the use of privately commissioned opinion polls to test public reaction to individual issues.

This was adopted and used with increasing regularity by the Labour Party, and its introduction was, perhaps, the first outward sign of the movement's new image consciousness.

Of all the policy matters requiring attention, none was more urgent then than defence. Confusion had reigned over the manifesto pledge to scrap nuclear weapons within the lifetime of the next Parliament, a commitment which was not wholeheartedly shared by members of the Shadow Cabinet, and other leading party figures. A cohesive defence policy was essential for Labour to look like a credible force. Unilateralism was not under threat at all at this stage, but the practicalities of abandoning nuclear weapons had to be considered more seriously.

Kinnock himself was a committed unilateralist: he and Glenys had been opposed to the use of nuclear weapons since their days at university. Glenys Kinnock was to make visits to the women's protest camp at the cruise missile base at Greenham Common (the missiles arrived in November 1983), and Kinnock had addressed a crowd of 200,000 at a cruise demonstration march in London, shortly after becoming leader. His first overseas visit as leader was to a meeting of the Socialist International in Brussels where he criticized the placement of American cruise missiles in Britain and nuclear weapons in Germany.

The first defence document of his leadership, *Defence and Security of Britain*, retained the firm commitment to remove all nuclear weapons from British soil, while remaining within NATO, and using savings on the nuclear arsenal for increased spending on conventional arms. It was to be overwhelmingly approved at the 1984 conference: meanwhile other, potentially destructive, battles were about to be waged.

A local industrial dispute in the Manchester area surrounding the *Stockport Messenger* group of newspapers escalated in November 1983 and spread to Fleet Street. At issue was the proposal to introduce new print technology, ending the closed shop – and effectively the power – of the National Graphical Association. Picket line violence outside the *Messenger* group's print works in Warrington led to allegations against the police, while the entrepreneur proprietor Eddy Shah took out injunctions against the unions under new anti-picketing legislation.

Once the dispute had spread to Fleet Street – with national newspapers on strike for four days – Kinnock called for Government intervention, blaming the dispute entirely on the new laws. The Government response was a call upon him to denounce the picket line violence. Whatever his feelings about the legislation, Kinnock has always insisted that protests of any nature should be kept within the confines of the law. Parliamentary democracy was the way forward, while violent law breaking would always be a barrier to the prospects of a Labour

Government being elected. Equally, and particularly with any industrial dispute, he has found it necessary to voice support for causes, while condemning tactics if violence is used.

This was a situation in which he would find himself placed regularly during the coming year. Now he issued a statement saying: 'I condemn without reservation the violence at Warrington whoever uses it and the union have already made it plain that they share this view.' Eventually the TUC withdrew its support for the illegal picketing and the NGA had to accept inevitable defeat. The British newspaper industry was about to make a massive lurch into new technology and would never look the same again, not least because of its drastically reduced workforce.

But the printworkers' case was merely a short introduction to the politics of industrial dispute for Kinnock; a greater and more damaging episode was just beginning. In the same month as Kinnock's election as leader of the Labour Party, the miners began an overtime ban in protest against pit closures planned by the new head of the National Coal Board (NCB), Ian MacGregor. The leader of the National Union of Mineworkers (NUM), Arthur Scargill, refused to discuss with management the closure schemes under which an estimated 20,000 miners would lose their jobs in the first year alone.

Kinnock had little time for Scargill, and the two men had clashed bitterly and notoriously during a BBC *Panorama* programme at the time of Tony Benn's challenge for deputy leader of the Labour Party. But shortly after the leadership contest they arranged to meet, both of them knowing that a strike could be in the offing. According to Martin Adeney and John Lloyd, authors of *The Miners' Strike: Loss Without Limit*, the Labour leader wanted to offer counsel that any strike must be the last resort and that all strategy must be properly prepared for, and played long. Public opinion had to be brought on to the miners' side: the Surrey housewife had to be made to feel sympathetic, as well as support maintained in the coalfields.

Scargill agreed. But in March 1984, with more pit closures and job losses announced, Yorkshire miners were called out on strike, and other areas soon followed. This was done under NUM rules which allowed the National Executive to call local strikes. While, under the same rules, a national strike needed the vote of a majority of the members in a national ballot, no such vote was called. Scargill's hope was that a series of locally called strikes would halt the industry nationwide without recourse to a ballot – and possible defeat.

Coming from a mining family and a mining community, Kinnock was well versed in every argument of the case for coal. He was as convinced then as he is now that the future demand for coal as an energy source was drastically underestimated by the Conservative Government, and he

– along with the entire Labour movement – saw the Government's policy as a threat not just to jobs but to entire communities. He saw that a major reason for the miners' victories in 1972 and 1974 was that national ballots did take place. Now, without a strike ballot, and in the atmosphere of violence which was breaking out on the picket lines, Kinnock's support for the way in which the cause was being fought could not be wholehearted.

Scargill's tactics were fundamentally opposite to his own belief in democracy as the essential basis for industrial action, and respect for the law as a virtue in its own terms, as well as a vital ingredient of successful industrial action. It was a belief which he found himself forced to repeat throughout the duration of the dispute. Scargill was the kind of socialist that the Labour leader instinctively mistrusted, according to Michael Leapman's analysis of the first few years of Kinnock's leadership. Scargill was, says Leapman,

> the impossibilist who will not give an inch on ideology, who will lead his followers to defeat rather than compromise on any one of his demands. The accepted technique of labour negotiation is, in the event of winning one concession, to use it as a basis for a negotiated settlement. That is not Scargill's way: instead he will instantly and intractably move on to the next, more improbable demand ... He seeks the support of others on the left as a matter of moral duty ... He convinces them that the politics of the streets and the picket lines are more likely to bring victory in the class struggle than the (to his mind) discredited methods of Parliamentary democracy.

Scargill knew he could not count on winning a ballot, so he never called one. And so he could never count on Kinnock's unqualified support. Kinnock believed that a ballot was vital, and he also thought that by late April 1984 there would have been a majority of miners' votes for a strike, but he said little in public during the early days of the dispute. His apparent reticence naturally led to attacks from the left in his own party, while in the Commons he was regularly attacked by the Government for not condemning the picket line violence strongly enough. Throughout the strike the NEC voted unanimously to give unequivocal support to the miners, but the Shadow Cabinet 'dithered' on the issue, according to observers at the time.

Kinnock only occasionally – and discreetly – visited picket lines. He went to the Wylfa power station in North Wales where his brother-in-law – Labour's parliamentary candidate – was taking a leading part in organizing support for the pickets. He found there that lorry driver members of the TGWU (Kinnock's own union) were less than anxious to support the miners' cause because there had been no ballot. But his criticism was muted and, according to Adeney and Lloyd, at meetings of the Shadow Cabinet, 'he found himself doing what he hated most – back pedalling, excusing. His overriding imperative was: don't give Scargill an alibi; don't pull the plug on him in a way that would enable the miners' president to blame Kinnock and the parliamentary party, for the strike's failure (which Kinnock saw as inevitable from an early stage).'

Michael Leapman says that Kinnock held back for months from voicing his criticism of Scargill's leadership to avoid accusations of damaging the cause of striking workers. But he continually attacked the Government for the policy that led to the strike and with Stan Orme, the Shadow Energy Secretary, made efforts to encourage the two sides in the dispute to negotiate a settlement. But at the end of May a series of violent clashes between pickets and police came to a head at the Orgreave coke depot near Sheffield, and once again Kinnock found himself urged to condemn the violence.

'There is no place in any industrial dispute in Britain for missiles, battering rams or any other implement or act of violence,' he said. 'The miners, like all other British trade unionists, realise that their strength comes from peaceful organisation, peaceful protest and peaceful picketing. Other methods give succour and advantage to the enemies of the trade union movement and do nothing to advance the cause of the workers in the dispute.'

A resolution on the strike was eventually tabled in the Commons in June 1984, proposed by Stan Orme, condemning the Government's handling of the dispute and calling for a negotiated settlement. Kinnock did not take part, neither did he attend a rally of 20,000 miners who marched the same day through Fleet Street to Jubilee Gardens. But a few weeks later he shared a platform with Scargill at the annual Durham Miners' Gala, an occasion when he did express unqualified support for the cause in his own terms:

> Here in this mining industry you have said: No more obedience, no more compliance, no more acceptance. No more rip-off, no more rundown. Here in this mining industry you have said you won't take the bribes and you will not take bullying. People who do not know this industry, people who do not know miners and miners' families and communities ask why you put up such a fight. The answer is a single phrase: There is no alternative.

But his speech was received coolly by the crowds of miners and their families who saved their ovations for Scargill and left-wing MP Dennis Skinner.

When the TUC debated the dispute at its annual conference in

Brighton in September, Kinnock once again had to restate his principles
in the light of further fighting on the picket lines: 'We must put that case
without violence,' he said.

> Our asset is reason. Our strength is the rationality of the case for coal.
> Violence distracts attention from the central issues of the dispute. It
> obscures the justice and validity of the miners' case. Violence has given
> the Government its only bone of excuse to gnaw on. It has enabled them
> to evade their central responsibility for promoting a settlement of the
> dispute. It has provided them with the opportunity which they have long
> sought to introduce politically motivated change in the methods of British
> policing. Violence provides opportunities to our enemies, whose lurid
> imaginations are bigger than their brains, to pretend that trade unionists
> are trying to secure power by means other than those of Parliamentary
> democracy.

There was heckling and shouts of 'whose side are you on?'

To be on the miners' side, says Michael Leapman, meant accepting
the way the dispute was being conducted and laying the blame for all the
clashes at the door of the police. Kinnock could not do that. Nor were
the miners and their supporters too pleased about the reference to the
underlying motive for the strike. Scargill had repeated his theme that it
was as much against the Government's anti-union legislation as about
pit closures, a crusade for the entire working-class movement. Kinnock
was forced again to defend his principles: 'General elections – and only
general elections – are for changing governments. British trade
unionism has never in its 116 years of history preached or practised any
other creed. And it never will.'

A month after the TUC congress, came the Labour Party
Conference, this year in Blackpool, and inevitably the week was
dominated by the miners' strike. The conference passed a resolution
offering support as wholeheartedly as the TUC had, blaming all the
violence on the police. Scargill called it 'state violence against the
miners'.

In his speech the next day Kinnock responded with an attack on the
pit closures policy combined with a denunciation of violence from either
side:

> The Government creates the climate of confrontation, the conditions of
> conflict. It speaks only the language of conquest. And in the midst of all
> that chaos, in the midst of all that assault on the essentials of civilised life
> in this country and of the values of this country, they call for
> condemnation of violence. I do not respond to that because it is a taunt, a
> call to forswear intimidation from a Government that bases its whole
> policy on intimidation. I do condemn violence. I condemn the violence of

despair ... of long term unemployment ... of loneliness, decay and ugliness. I condemn the violence done to hope ... to talent ... to family security and family unite. I condemn the violence done to civil and personal rights in this country. I condemn the violence too of the stone-throwers and the battering-ram carriers. I condemn the violence of the cavalry charges, the truncheon groups and the shield bangers. I condemn violence ... all violence, without fear or favour. That is what makes me different from Margaret Thatcher. I don't have her double standards. I do not take her selective and blinkered view of conflict.

He added:

Democracy is the first premise of socialism. It is a matter of principle, not of convenience. It is a matter of common sense, not of tactics. We are upholding the only system which can give us power. The only system that we want to give us power. And the only system that we are prepared to wield when we have that power.

In speeches throughout the dispute Kinnock attacked the Government for the policy that led to the strike. He called for a development plan for the coal industry that recognized that the cost of keeping 70,000 miners out of work was greater than the cost of investment and subsidy needed to keep most of them at work producing coal. But he could never escape the concern that Labour supporters would be exploited and the party persuaded to endorse Scargill's extremism because of their solidarity with workers in conflict. Kinnock desperately needed to win the middle ground support before fighting another election and these were the very people who would be alienated by extreme views and actions.

He refused to attend a series of rallies in November which had been planned to gather fresh support for the flagging strike. Naturally this refusal was criticized by the left-wing MPs, and at a meeting of the PLP Kinnock said he would have no part in leading the miners to glorious defeat. Miners in his own constituency wanted him to go to a rally in Aberavon; instead it was Norman Willis, new general secretary of the TUC, who went to the Aberavon rally, spoke out against violence and was jeered. Kinnock couldn't win: Mrs Thatcher praised Willis's speech and declared that Kinnock did not have the guts to face striking miners and condemn violence.

He did appear with Scargill at one rally, and that was the one organized by the Labour Party itself, in Stoke on Trent on 30 November. That same morning a taxi driver taking a Welsh miner to work had been killed by a concrete block which was thrown through the roof of his minicab. Kinnock said: 'We meet here tonight in the shadow of an outrage.' He was heckled but most of his speech was well-prepared, aimed at rehabilitating the struggle within the bounds of normal industrial relations. The dispute, he said,

> does not originate in any political motives. It is not fuelled by any ambition to harm democracy in this country. British democracy is strong. Its values and institutions have never been threatened from below by any social mood, industrial dispute or political movement, for it has always been the subject of democracy that has advanced liberty and tried to sustain that achievement.

Michael Leapman relates an anecdote about this rally:

> The police received a warning that someone was going to throw a hand grenade on to the platform. They were unsure if it was a hoax. When Kinnock was told he refused to have the meeting halted but suggested that people on the platform should be discreetly asked to step down from it, starting with the women. One by one they retreated, until only Kinnock, Scargill and a handful of others were left. A police officer pleaded with Kinnock to leave for the sake of his safety but he refused. He joked: 'Just at this moment I can think of worse last glimpses of this earth than Arthur going with me.'

Towards the end of the year striking miners were returning to work individually as the financial hardship endured so far took its toll. On the left of the Labour Party, Tony Benn (who was back at Westminster having won the Chesterfield by-election in March), Dennis Skinner and Audrey Wise were calling for a general strike: Kinnock retorted that such a move would put an end to all chances of negotiating any case for the coal industry. (There had been reports in the press that Kinnock was involved in a campaign to stop Benn gaining the selection for Chesterfield, which Kinnock denied at a meeting of the NEC. During Benn's campaign for the seat Kinnock joined him for a day in Chesterfield, and Benn recorded in his diary: 'For the purpose of the battle you have to be seen side by side, and he played it very well ... Kinnock performed his part excellently. At the public meeting we held up our hands together and I called it "The Return Ticket", a comment on the so-called "Dream Ticket." ')

In his own Islwyn constituency, Kinnock received a standing ovation when he addressed a meeting of striking miners there. Within the NEC opinion was polarized, with Kinnock always criticized for apparently not doing enough for the miners' cause; likewise at meetings of the PLP. When a group of left-wing MPs began disrupting Parliamentary business – notably when the Government refused an emergency debate on the strike – Kinnock's anger rose. He told them:

If you actually persuade yourselves that activities like today's enhance the miners' case, then there's nothing I can do in the world to prevent you. But remember as you talk of people in the coalfields and as you look into the newspapers tomorrow and search your consciences, it doesn't help their case by half a millimetre, or our prospects of getting into power.

Tony Benn was constantly on the attack. In one of his diary entries during the miners' strike he records:

Heard Neil Kinnock on the one o'clock news. His interviews are like processed cheese coming out of a mincing machine – nothing meaty, just one mass of meaningless rhetoric that defuses and anaesthetises the listener. The last thing we want is a row with him because he is still on his honeymoon, but the fact is that the Labour leadership has totally failed to support the working class when in struggle.

Benn found some rare praise for Kinnock, though, on one occasion after Prime Minister's questions in the Commons. He wrote: 'Kinnock really managed to do damage to Thatcher by asking straightforward factual questions about Government policy on cutbacks and closures in the coal industry. She couldn't answer and kept referring back, and the Tories sat silent.'

Kinnock, meanwhile, in a radio interview, said that MPs of any party who broke the rules of the House of Commons should be suspended. A Commons debate, he said, would not help the miners at all. Kinnock was only too aware that he would have little or no influence on the NUM. With more and more miners drifting back to work, and after a few more feeble negotiation attempts, the strike ended on 5 March 1985 with no agreement.

As Adeney and Lloyd maintain, the miners' strike had an effect far greater than any event since the war on the Labour Party and its leader.

Frozen during the strike in a posture of support which varied from the very grudging to the very gung ho, Labour since has had to reassess and come to terms with the ambiguity in the party, one which has run through it from its earliest days: is it a party of revolt or of reform? Does it overthrow the existing order, or amend it?

Realistically, Kinnock foresaw the outcome of the dispute, tainted as it was by the lack of a ballot and the picket line violence which served only to alienate public opinion. But it was the worst possible start to his stewardship of the Labour Party. Denis Healey wrote in his memoirs, *The Time of My Life*, that the whole affair was a 'godsend' for Mrs Thatcher.

She described it as fighting the 'enemy within' after defeating the 'enemy without' in the Falklands ... In the end Mrs Thatcher was able to impose an unconditional surrender on the hapless miners. It was regarded as a triumph of Falklands dimensions by the majority of the public.

Kinnock was to stress repeatedly that to call the miners' strike a distraction during his early days as leader was a huge understatement. 'It was a very large diversion. It totally preoccupied the Labour movement and the general public.'

'The problem that I confronted was that I couldn't say as clearly and publicly as I wanted to that there had to be a ballot,' he said years later. 'It was my first and biggest failure – the ballot was essential and I hesitated, and that was a gross mistake.'

There were further problems for Kinnock to encounter before he could effectively launch his attempt to make the Labour Party electable. And, according to the opinion polls, things had gone from bad to worse since the election of June 1983 when Labour's share of the votes was just 28 per cent. Three months after the election a Gallup poll indicated the Labour share down to 24.5 per cent. But there was one opportunity during the throes of the miners' strike to parade the Labour Party as a major force in British politics once again – the elections to the European Parliament.

There was no clearly defined policy towards Europe at the time. Kinnock himself had campaigned for a 'no' vote in the 1975 referendum when the official party line was to back membership of the EEC. In 1983 he had gone along with the policy which committed a Labour Government to withdrawing Britain from the Community, in spite of private opposition to such a policy. He thought that withdrawal was so absurd that no one would ever carry it out anyway. When he was elected leader he campaigned on the need to get 'A new square deal for Europe and a square deal for Britain.' The 1984 Euro-elections were seen as a test of Labour's strength. Even anti-Marketeers saw it as an opportunity to re-establish the party's position as the only feasible alternative to the Conservatives, in the face of the threat from the Liberal/SDP Alliance.

The party did well, nearly doubling Labour's seats from 17 to 32, with 15 straight gains from the Tories. And their share of the poll also rose. Some saw this as a national vote of no-confidence in the Thatcher administration, and indeed there was a great deal of emphasis on domestic issues in the Labour campaign: Tony Benn claimed it was an opportunity to vote 'for the miners'.

(Incidentally, it was during the campaign for these elections that Kinnock quietly replaced the traditional red flag party symbol with the red rose, which was later to be adopted on a large scale when Labour launched its new image.)

The Euro-elections provided a brief moment of glory. While Labour was evidently back in contention as a political force, there was for Kinnock no escaping the ramifications of the miners' strike. And he had yet to establish his own force as leader, within a party which was desperately divided. It was also likely to be desperately short of money, in the light of new industrial relations legislation which meant that trades unions could only levy their members for a political fund on the approval of the membership in a secret ballot. The Labour Party relied heavily on union contributions for its finance. Luckily the unions themselves saw the process as a means of voicing their opposition to the Tory legislation, particularly after the Government had decided to ban unions at GCHQ, the high security communications centre at Cheltenham. The political funds were all maintained.

With the appointment of Larry Whitty as new general secretary of the Labour Party in 1985, Kinnock was able to lead a period of streamlining and efficiency at Walworth Road. (Whitty, formerly a union research officer, was closer to Kinnock in both age and political philosophy than his predecessor Jim Mortimer.) Attempts to remodel the party had begun soon after Kinnock's election as party leader and he had been thwarted at the 1984 conference in his efforts to reduce activists' powers in parliamentary selection and reselection contests by shifting the decision from delegates to individual members. It was to take another four years before the principle of individual membership participation in party decision-making was accepted, while Kinnock's efforts at democratizing the party machinery have continued beyond his period as leader. When Peter Mandelson, a former television producer, became the party's director of campaigns and communications in 1985, Kinnock had the assistance he needed to set about improving the image of the Labour movement.

But there was another 'distraction', an issue which came to a head due to the Conservative Government's legislation setting a legal limit on the rates to be collected by councils which persistently spent above their guidelines. In Liverpool the city council was dominated by the Militant tendency. The group insisted that they were not a movement within the Labour Party, which would have been outlawed, but merely supporters of the newspaper *Militant*. At no time did they admit that the paper was, in reality, the organ of a separate political organization, the Revolutionary Socialist League.

Liverpool's Militant-led council had chosen to set no rate at all for 1984, sending the city into heavy debt. Other 'rate-capped' councils were urged to follow this example by way of protest by the leader of Lambeth Council in London, Ted Knight. Knight, a former Trotskyite, had once been expelled from the Labour Party for his extreme left-wing connections. Now he advocated mass defiance, believing that it would lead to a defeat for the Government. The action would also lead to personal fines on councillors involved, and subsequent disqualification from office.

Such law-breaking was anathema to Kinnock's philosophy, and in a speech to Labour councillors in Birmingham in February 1985, he urged them not to resort to gesture politics and risk losing office:

> Better a dented shield than no shield at all. Better a Labour council doing its best to help than Government placemen extending the full force of Government policy. We don't want to weaken the broad coalition by wrangles over legality or public dramas or exciting excursions. Our basic concern is – and must remain – jobs, services and democracy.

He found a surprising ally in Ken Livingstone, former leader of the abolished Greater London Council and a prospective parliamentary candidate, who urged the councillors to stay in power and fight their battles from within. The rebel councils gave way and set a legal rate, with the exception of Lambeth, who held out for long enough for fines to be imposed on individual councillors, and Liverpool.

The Labour Party then came under pressure to agree to pay back this money when it came to power. The miners, too, were demanding that a future Labour Government should repay the fines incurred by the NUM for contempt of court during their strike: Scargill also wanted an amnesty for men convicted and jailed after violence on the picket lines. Such calls, along with a private members' bill drafted by Tony Benn which called for a free pardon for miners convicted of violence, did more than raise Kinnock's wrath. It is widely held that they had an adverse effect on public opinion which culminated in the narrow defeat of the Labour candidate in the Brecon and Radnor by-election in July 1985.

When Scargill's call was repeated at the TUC conference in September, Kinnock opposed it saying: 'Many people have suffered financial losses as a result of Mrs Thatcher's policies. I am thinking in particular of pensioners who have lost literally thousands of pounds. No one is suggesting we should reimburse them.'

Scargill won the TUC vote, but Kinnock stood firm and prepared to take him on again at the Labour Party conference in Bournemouth later that month. He was also prepared for battle with Militant councillors in Liverpool who had announced that they would be making 31,000 employees redundant because no money was left to pay them. (The council had to make sure that each worker received his redundancy notice – according to the law – and so they had hired a fleet of taxis to take the individual notices to each employee's home.)

Kinnock was presented with an opportunity to tackle Militant head on. He detested their policies, but more than that, according to Colin Hughes and Patrick Wintour, authors of *Labour Rebuilt*, he calculated that their defeat would display to voters his determination to take a grip on the party machine and erase left-wing extremism. And so, towards the end of the traditional Tuesday speech made by the leader of the party, Kinnock launched into his attack on extremist views: 'You start with far fetched resolutions. They are then pickled into a rigid dogma, a code, and you go through the years sticking to that, out-dated, misplaced, irrelevant to the real needs, and you end in the grotesque chaos of a Labour council – a LABOUR council – hiring taxis to scuttle around a city handing out redundancy notices to its own workers.' He added, emphatically, as uproar broke out in the hall: 'I'm telling you, no matter how entertaining, how fulfilling to short term egos, you can't play politics with people's jobs and with people's services or with people's lives.'

Barbara Castle, in her memoirs, *Fighting All the Way*, described this as 'the most courageous and effective speech I have heard a politician make'. She feared at first that Kinnock had gone too far. 'But I was wrong. He had broken the cobweb of sentimentality with which many in the party shrouded Militant.' She reports how the Bennites and the hard left watched with anxiety and accused Kinnock of autocratic leadership 'and in one sense they were right. I need not have feared that Neil would be a lightweight. He now moved in with a steely determination to get his own way.'

Kinnock knew that his speech would be greeted with delight by the press which hated Militant. Said Hughes and Wintour:

> He was more anxious about the reaction of those on the soft left on whom he still relied for his command over the executive and the party. If they backed him, the realignment into a majority alliance of the centre-left and the right wing would be complete. If they recoiled from scourging Militant, the unity which Kinnock sought would prove elusive.

There was certainly no hiding the delight of the party's right wing. Denis Healey said: 'I think Neil's speech was of historic importance. He has shifted the centre of gravity not just of the Labour Party but of the Labour movement as a whole, decisively.' Roy Hattersley said that it was the best speech he had heard in his twenty-seven years in the party. 'It was historic because it will change the country's perception of the Labour Party. We look like a party which is interested in the views of real people rather than people from caucuses.'

On the left, Eric Heffer MP, a member of the NEC, had walked off the platform in protest during the speech. John Hamilton and Derek Hatton, the leader and deputy leader of Liverpool Council, spoke of a 'disgrace and a travesty of justice'. But it was felt that the far left had been isolated and Kinnock's position strengthened. However, there was more melodrama to come over the Militant issue, not immediately after Kinnock's speech but the following day when the motion seeking reimbursement for the fined councillors was debated. Union leaders were angry at the treatment of council workers, to the extent that there was no doubt that the motion would be defeated, and Kinnock planned to follow that with moves to expel the Militants from the Labour Party.

But, as the debate drew to a close, David Blunkett, leader of Sheffield council and a member of the NEC, made an offer to Derek Hatton: would he withdraw his motion if the NEC set up an inquiry into Liverpool's cash crisis? Blunkett, who is blind, did not know where Hatton was sitting, and had to call out: 'Are you coming Derek? Will you do it?' Hatton shook him by the hand and agreed, in the cause of unity to defeat the Government, he said. To some extent Kinnock himself had been upstaged, but he was relieved later in the week when, although the motion to reimburse the miners was passed, the vote did not reach the two-thirds majority required to ensure that it was considered for inclusion in Labour's official programme. (Kinnock had been hard pressed for a majority on the NEC on this issue prior to the conference. It was only a literally last-minute change of heart by Michael Meacher which gave Kinnock his authority by fifteen votes to fourteen.)

In the event, Blunkett's olive branch over Liverpool merely postponed what Kinnock knew would be inevitable. When Liverpool councillors rejected the findings of an independent financial inquiry, Kinnock was able to convince the NEC that there could be no compromise with the Militants and their allies, and the Executive voted to go ahead with moves to rid the party in the city of its Militant domination. By this time, Blunkett and others of the soft left, having seen the gesture of conciliation refused, now fully supported Kinnock. Blunkett was to say later that destroying Militant's base was the bravest and most perceptive act of Kinnock's leadership.

The expulsion of the Militant members of the Labour Party in Liverpool was a long, drawn-out and infuriatingly bureaucratic affair, in which Kinnock played chief prosecutor at lengthy hearings, and it took even longer still to make the district and ward Labour parties recognize them. By 1986 only fourteen members of the Liverpool district party had actually been expelled, but the number is less significant than the ferocity of Kinnock's stand. It also meant that the leadership of Militant's organization in Liverpool had been expelled. Years later, reflecting on his determination, Kinnock was asked what would have happened to the Labour Party had he not taken such a stance.

> We would have been perpetually misrepresented. The ultra left would have gained more and more control, because they would have bred from success, and they had such a demoralising effect on the party. The effect on morale and on self confidence would have made us less of a fighting force. We would have lost a lot of ground, and there might have been further fragmentation amongst the democratic socialist element.

Kinnock's personal crusade against Militant was to be a long-term feature of his years in office, but his single-minded determination was already both conspicuous to the right and influential on the soft left: he was beginning to make headway in his bid for the holy grail of party unity.

5   Roses and Thorns

At the end of September 1986, Neil Kinnock had good reason to feel moderately optimistic. His first three years in office had been turbulent, but there was now considerably more harmony within the Labour Party, which was to be rewarded with an unbroken run of eight months leading the opinion polls over the Conservatives. The Thatcher administration had suffered as a result of the Westland affair and subsequent Cabinet resignations. The Tories had also lost the marginal Fulham seat to Labour in April 1986. The threat from the SDP/Liberal alliance also appeared to be waning. At the 1983 election Labour had gained only 27.6 per cent of the votes, just 2 per cent more than the Alliance, who had soon afterwards actually overtaken Labour in the opinion polls.

There had been a danger that Labour could slip into permanent third place among the major political parties of Britain. Kinnock always maintained that he would never enter into any deal or coalition. In 1985 the Alliance had another surge of support but afterwards fell victim to disarray within its own ranks and slipped from view as a major threat to Labour. Now Kinnock could look ahead with some deserved confidence to an election campaign.

The change in his fortunes, and those of the Labour Party, had begun the previous year at the Bournemouth conference. Differences of opinion from quite opposing sections of the party had been settled, rather surprisingly, as a result of Kinnock's action over Militant. The report by the inquiry team into the affairs of Liverpool city council was presented to the NEC in February 1986 and the recommendations were accepted by a comfortable majority. NEC member Tom Sawyer, the deputy general secretary of the National Union of Public Employees (NUPE), was a member of the inquiry committee and after hearing evidence he was one of the converts to the view that the expulsion of Militant members was essential. He told his union's conference how he had been shocked by the atmosphere of intimidation by security guards: 'Some of the things I saw have more in common with the extreme right in European politics than with the left.'

Sawyer says that until he visited Liverpool, he wondered what all the fuss was about over Militant.

> I had come from the North East where there was no Militant around. But when I saw them in power, I thought it was quite horrific. I had gone to Liverpool to visit the NUPE branch, and I was shocked when they gave me chapter and verse about what was going on, the sharp practices, the corruption, that affected members of my union.

Sawyer was to become one of Kinnock's most loyal allies on the NEC: other union representatives who were awarded with the chairs of NEC sub-committees also played a part in the stabilizing role. Hughes and Wintour, in *Labour Rebuilt*, say that Kinnock used his control to build a new relationship between the executive on one side, and the Shadow Cabinet and other front-benchers on the other, by replacing the 'ramshackle' collection of executive policy committees – largely ignored by frontbenchers – with joint policy teams. 'They later became the model on which the policy review groups were based.'

The process of expelling the Liverpool Militants took until after the party conference of 1986, and as Kinnock himself chaired the proceedings he was forced to spend an inordinate amount of precious time in dealing with the problem. But he was determined to see the resolution of the matter to its bitter end, convinced that unless he did there would be threats to his efforts at party unity.

Tony Benn, as always, saw things differently. He recorded in his diary:

> No Leader in the past – neither Gaitskell, Wilson nor Callaghan – has ever had the determination to remove a complete section of the Party: because it isn't just Militant, it's the people who support Militant in their advocacy of socialism at the height of the present crisis. Kinnock is a ruthless man who thinks this will benefit him politically with the media. It is the bicycle theory of expulsions – if you stop expelling, you fall off.

But Liverpool continued to cause Kinnock unrest. In Knowsley North, a safe Labour seat, a by-election was forced by the sudden resignation in July 1986 of Robert Kilroy-Silk. A right-winger who, with Kinnock's active support, had fought a year-long battle with Militant in his constituency in order to safeguard his own re-selection, he was lured by a new career as a TV chat show presenter. One potential candidate to take his place had been Tony Mulhearn, president of the Liverpool District Labour Party, but as one of the Militants recently expelled he was no longer eligible.

Fearing that the Knowsley North party was unlikely to select anyone acceptable, the NEC imposed their own candidate, George Howarth, a former deputy leader of Knowsley Council and a left-of-centre member of the right-wing Amalgamated Engineering Union (AEU). Some of the local party leaders decided that they would not work on behalf of a man who was not their choice, and so the campaign was in effect run under the leadership of Jack Straw, the Shadow local government spokesman and a trusted ally of Kinnock, who was sent to work full time in Knowsley.

The party leader was met with abuse and protests from Militant sympathizers when he went to Knowsley early in November 1986 to speak on Howarth's behalf. But on 13 November Labour held the seat in spite of the alienation of the local party, and a swing to the Liberals. Once again Kinnock had demonstrated his control over rebellion and strengthened his position against extremism.

Such episodes reflect the negative side of the period of entrenchment for Neil Kinnock. But in attempting to establish his credibility as a prospective Prime Minister, he used every contemporary ploy to promote a more positive image for Labour. And this meant venturing into pop culture in an effort to attract young voters to the Labour cause. Kinnock played a prominent role in the launch of a new pop group, Red Wedge, a combined force of already famous names in the music world (among them Billy Bragg and Spandau Ballet) who had offered their assistance. He was the host at a reception on the terrace of the House of Commons for the group's first appearance in November 1985. He also appeared on a pop video of Tracey Ullman's recording of 'My Guy'. Exposure such as this was criticized by traditionalists who felt that politicians should stick to politics, but others saw it as an emphasis on the youth of the new party leader, contrasting him with his ageing predecessor, Michael Foot.

Image and presentation were to become keywords of this early period in office, but Kinnock soon demonstrated that, contrary to his victory speech in 1983, Labour's policies as well as their presentation had to be altered. For example, Labour Party opposition to the sale of council houses was recognized as a stumbling block, and out of place in the 1980s when a substantial number of homes in Britain were owner-occupied. Kinnock personally favoured the right to buy. As he explained at the time: 'I'm the first party leader to be brought up in a council house – I know how much people who've always paid their rent would value a choice.' In May 1985 following the report of a sub-committee led by Jeff Rooker, the Shadow Housing Minister, it was announced that council tenants would be allowed to buy their homes under a future Labour administration.

There was, too, the perpetual problem over industrial relations. Behind the scenes, Kinnock devoted considerable time during the first two years of his leadership working with the TUC and union leaders to develop a new blueprint for relations between the trade unions and a future Labour Government. They used the TUC–Labour Party liaison committee for this purpose, and their first publication was a document called *A New Partnership, A New Britain*, which was presented to the TUC Congress at Blackpool in September 1985. It included a promise to repeal the Conservative trade union laws and introduce instead a new basis for partnership between unions and management.

A key feature was to provide workers with positive rights to information, consultation and representation in company decisions. Its aim was to widen the collective bargaining agenda beyond wages to crucial investment decisions, and to see 'new rights for workers as a catalyst for the extension of democratic involvement and accountability not just within the enterprise but also beyond it in sector and national planning'.

When the document was published Kinnock was tackled on the level of future co-operation with the unions. He insisted that they would not be allowed to dominate a Labour Government, or to dictate management policy. NEC members on the left of the party complained that it did not go far enough (Tony Benn called it 'violently anti-socialist'); the Conservatives maintained that it would put a Labour Government at the mercy of the unions by going too far. The plan was accepted by the TUC. At their congress the following year they also approved, more crucially, proposals for the rights of trade unions under a Labour Government and in particular, the use of pre-strike ballots.

Kinnock himself was not likely to advocate the repeal of the Conservative-introduced law on balloting. As Michael Leapman wrote: 'The strongest and most consistent thread running through his political philosophy is that legitimacy can only be conferred through the ballot box.' But he assured union leaders that no Labour Government would legislate to prevent an instant strike in the face of 'intolerable provocation' by management, as long as a ballot was held on whether that action should continue. And it would not be necessary to ballot members in the case of overtime bans.

The document containing these proposals, *People At Work: New Rights, New Responsibilities*, said that an incoming Labour Government would place strong emphasis on assisting trade unions in the development of membership involvement and participation in union decisions, 'including the use of balloting.' But in stark contrast to the Tory Government's approach:

> the new framework would in no way give employers, or their customers or suppliers, any opportunity to seek injunctions and damages against a union. This new statutory framework will also entail laying down general

principles for inclusion in union rule books based on a right for union members to have a secret ballot on decisions relating to strikes and the method of election of union executives to be based on a system of secret ballots.

Union leaders did not automatically endorse the proposals wholeheartedly, but the air of realism of the time – and the recognition that rank-and-file union members wanted ballots – led to its acceptance. Also on Kinnock's side was the fact that, as Michael Leapman said, the unions and the party get on better when Labour is out of office, when they sink their differences and work towards the aim of winning the next election:

> Kinnock inherited the leadership at a time that, though inauspicious for the party as a whole, placed him in the strongest possible position vis a vis the unions ... They were demoralised. The new leader represented the only hope of a Labour victory. If the unions withheld support from him, they would be consigning themselves to a long exile in the political wilderness. So he was not in their pockets. They needed him rather more than he needed them.

But proposals relating to the activities of a future Labour Government were of little relevance during the actual industrial disputes of the present. One such was the Wapping affair, precipitated by newspaper proprietor Rupert Murdoch when he moved his four publications – *The Sun, The Times*, the *Sunday Times* and the *News of the World* – to a new, purpose-built complex at Wapping, near the Tower of London. The move was made without any negotiation with the two print unions, SOGAT and the NGA, whose skills were deemed obsolete by the introduction of new technology. Journalists using word-processors typed their copy directly into a computer system which bypassed a series of traditional press trades, and the new printing machines were operated by members of the electricians' union, the EETPU.

SOGAT and NGA members picketed the Wapping site in an attempt to win back their jobs, and they were joined each week by bus loads of sympathizers for regular Saturday night demonstrations outside the plant. It was a lost cause. The papers continued to appear, and the Wapping demonstrations were marred by violence, injuries and arrests. As a result Kinnock was a reluctant supporter of the cause, although in fairness there was little that the Labour leader could do practically to help.

He was able to make one individual stand of protest, and that was to refuse to answer questions from the lobby correspondents of the Murdoch papers. The lobby, who are the Westminster-based political reporters of the national press, were accustomed to meeting the leader of the opposition each week in the press gallery. They would not agree to restrictions imposed on any of their own members, so Kinnock refused to go to the 'weekly lobby' any more, and instead he announced that he would hold a weekly press conference in his own offices at the Commons, to which staff from the Murdoch papers would not be invited. The ban on them was lifted when the Wapping dispute ended, but Kinnock retained the new arrangement, keeping control of his relationship with political journalists.

From the start of his leadership Kinnock had also taken care to foster his image abroad, something which Michael Foot had never considered important. Early in 1984 he made two trips, the first to Greece on the invitation of the socialist Prime Minister Andreas Papandreou, and then to Washington. Kinnock likes the USA and the openness of the American people. More importantly, any Labour Government led by Kinnock would retain the alliance with the United States, in spite of a defence policy which demanded the removal of US nuclear weapons from British soil. So his first visit was an exploratory one, where he met President Ronald Reagan and other White House officials but made efforts to avoid contentious discussion.

At the end of that year Kinnock, with Glenys, and Shadow Foreign Secretary Denis Healey, visited Moscow. Far from finding a socialist's spiritual home, Kinnock had always been a firm critic of Soviet communism and, in personal terms, he found the USSR to be uncomfortable, its atmosphere stifling. He objected to the near-religious devotion to Lenin, and made representations on behalf of political prisoners and 'dissidents' to the Soviet leadership. Glenys, on one occasion, was mistaken for Margaret Thatcher.

In January 1985 Kinnock went to Nicaragua as a guest of the Sandinista Government, which was under constant threat from the right-wing, US-backed Contra rebels, and while there he openly criticized the USA for its support for the Contras. In the summer of 1985 he and Glenys went to East Africa, where famine in Ethiopia was beginning to give rise to worldwide concern. They also visited Tanzania and Kenya.

In a visit to NATO headquarters in Brussels he insisted that a future Labour Government would expel all cruise missiles, but that such action was not a threat to membership of NATO. In Paris, also in 1985, Kinnock met President Alfonsin of Argentina who was in the French capital at the same time. This meeting was certain to attract criticism at home, no matter what transpired, because Argentina had not formally ended its state of war with Britain after the Falklands crisis. Kinnock, in fact, had suggested ways in which relations between the two countries could be improved, and there were sections of the Conservative press which gave some support to his initiative.

In 1986 there were further European trips along with visits to India and Jamaica, all of which helped to establish Kinnock in the eyes of the international community. But on the domestic front, he lost some valuable opportunities to undermine the credibility of the Government which could have been rocked by political scandal. Instead the turbulence affecting the Conservative administration was minimal, although there were individual victims on the Government front bench. In January 1986 Michael Heseltine, the Defence Secretary, and Leon Brittan, the Trade and Industry Secretary, both resigned during the row over the future of the Westland helicopter company. Heseltine's stance was a matter of principle, a protest at Westland's acceptance of an American takeover bid rather than a European one. Brittan's resignation was more expedient: the leak of a letter criticizing Heseltine was traced back to his office.

Labour MPs were optimistic that these two would ultimately be seen as scapegoats, with blame attached firmly to the Prime Minister herself. Kinnock made one strong speech attacking Mrs Thatcher, but when the affair was debated again at the end of January, and with the chance of causing both Mrs Thatcher and her Government considerable embarrassment, he effectively let them off the hook with a poor performance. Hugo Young in *The Guardian* wrote that Kinnock made a speech 'of almost superhuman incompetence'. The Tories were waiting for a drubbing which never came, said Young. 'Suddenly it became apparent that he had nothing to say. He stood on his feet for his allotted span circling with ceaseless verbosity round the same few points about the Prime Minister's incompetence and dishonesty and ruthlessness, not bothering for a moment to render these tedious generalities precise or freshly lethal.'

It was one of those occasions which brought out the 'windbag' epithet again or, as one lobby correspondent said: 'He became a victim of his own articulacy.' (With hindsight Kinnock acknowledged his mistake. Parliamentary responses, as with most Kinnock speeches, were seldom prepared long in advance. On this occasion, Kinnock said, he had the 'luxury' of having prepared his speech a couple of hours beforehand, and he added an extra page at the beginning. 'It doomed my speech,' he said. 'I was too clever by half.')

Security rows were dogging the Conservative administration repeatedly. The previous year had seen Kinnock and Mrs Thatcher snapping at one another across the despatch box over the Belgrano affair and the prosecution of Clive Ponting. Ponting, a defence ministry civil servant, had been charged with leaking documents about the sinking of the Argentine cruiser *Belgrano* in May 1982 during the Falklands War, and had been acquitted. In the Commons in February 1985 Kinnock accused Thatcher of lying about her involvement in the decision to prosecute Ponting under the Official Secrets Act. They exchanged angry letters as he refused to withdraw his accusation. Then he attacked her over the decision to sink the *Belgrano*, and whether she had misled the Commons at the time. But Mrs Thatcher survived the assault.

In another security row, the Government bungled their attempt to suppress a story written by Duncan Campbell in the *New Statesman* about a British communications satellite, Zircon. Campbell had made a programme for the BBC, who then chose not to screen it, but the *New Statesman* publication went ahead. Kinnock pedalled softly, pointing out that if the revelation was really damaging to national security there had been plenty of time to suppress it earlier. His critics on the left would have preferred an attack on the satellite project and all credit for Campbell's efforts. However, the Labour Party united to criticize the Government when Special Branch raided the BBC in Glasgow and took away files, tapes and films relating to the programme.

Michael Leapman wrote at the time that Kinnock never enjoyed Prime Minister's questions in the Commons: he entered into the spirit of the occasion because it was required of him, but found the procedure pointless and not enjoyable. 'This accounts for his variable effectiveness … Sometimes he lets himself become too shrill, either because of his genuine concern about the topic under discussion – perhaps health, education or some aspect of welfare – or due to his frustration at Thatcher's refusal to give what he considers a straight answer.'

If he occasionally lost opportunities to damage the image of the Government, Kinnock was ever mindful of the image of his own party, and the damage that extremist attitudes could have on chances of electoral success. And while he was able to exert influence directly on both the Parliamentary Labour Party and the NEC, the behaviour of Labour activists on local councils still gave cause for concern. Liverpool had been tamed, but in London particularly, left-wing councillors attracted the attention of the press, who labelled them the 'loony left'. It was one thing for the Labour Party to be aware of the needs of minority groups, but quite another to be ridiculed in the tabloids on the 'gays and lesbians issue'.

Kinnock knew that prejudice inflamed like this could lose votes later. A case in point was the Broadwater Farm riots, when a policeman, Keith Blakelock, was killed during clashes on a council estate in Tottenham. Some local councillors in neighbouring boroughs – and notably Bernie Grant, now MP for Tottenham but at the time leader of Haringey Council – appeared to be over-sympathetic to the rioters' cause.

Kinnock was quick to condemn the killing of PC Blakelock, and later
went to Tottenham to unveil a memorial to him.

In 1986 Kinnock saw the publication of his first book, *Making Our
Way*, a critique of Britain's declining manufacturing industry and a call
for major development in industry to secure economic and social
stability. Its appeal was probably limited to students of politics and
economics, which is unfortunate, for a wider audience might have
appreciated its clarion calls to the faithful as well as texts designed to
convert the agnostic.

And it carries a perfect summary of Kinnock's own philosophy:

> I am a democratic socialist because I believe that a commitment to the
> freedom and dignity of the individual, to the construction of a society
> which is compassionate and fair, in which people are judged on their
> merit and are enabled to develop their abilities to the full, requires the
> control of the forces of production, distribution, exchange and
> communication by that society through a variety of democratic means.
> The belief started as an instinct; it was moulded into a political conviction
> by the knowledge that an economy that was not subject to democracy was
> an open season for the few who were already strong and powerful, or the
> few who could get to be so by exploitation, and a democracy not subject to
> the requirements of efficient production and fair distribution was little
> more than a pleasant adornment.

The tone of the book is unmistakably Kinnock throughout, each
chapter reading like the text of a conference speech. For example: 'Why,
in 1986, after seven years of Tory policies, is the rate of increase in
unemployment accelerating? Margaret Thatcher finds unemployment a
mystery because the central point in Tory monetarist philosophy is that
the operation of free markets will *automatically* adjust the level of
demand to the number of workers available.' And: 'The objectives of
choice, standards and relevance must be central themes of education.
They have been debased by the present government in order to mobilise
prejudice, feed propaganda and provide excuses for narrowing and
reducing provision – and therefore choice, standards and relevance – for
the great majority of school children.'

He concluded:

> Faced with the inherited condition and extent of need, the path towards
> the industrial, economic and social recovery which is a matter of survival
> for our country and essential to the future of ourselves and our children is
> very tough. But we will tread it with determination and, because the
> course is so necessary, we will keep on pursuing it. The alternatives are
> misery for Britain and powerless opposition for our Movement. That is
> why I believe that it is better to get on with the job than to be paralysed by

the size of it. Better to work for decisive victories of socialism than wait for some interminable date when they can be universal. Better to light a candle, than curse the darkness.'

Listen carefully and you can almost hear the applause from a crowded conference hall.

But Kinnock's appeal for Labour voters lay not so much in his skill in written economic theory, or in his performance in parliamentary debate. Each year the Labour Party Conference was proving to be his natural platform where his oratorial skills could be best employed, and 1986 in Blackpool witnessed more moments of glory. There was a general air of optimism and even of peace within the party, with few vitriolic attacks on one another by the right and left wings of the party. Kinnock saw his policy recommendations broadly accepted and his leadership barely criticized. The Militant left were emphatically denounced, even if the process of expelling Militant members other than in Liverpool was only just under way. The one significant note of trouble ahead was over defence – of which more later – but in other respects Kinnock had good reason to feel satisfied.

Within the space of three years he had welded together the 'soft left' of the party and those on the right, isolating the hard left. Three figures on the national executive played a key role in forging the new, centrist unity in the party: Tom Sawyer of NUPE, David Blunkett, who was then leader of Sheffield city council, and Michael Meacher, the defeated candidate in the deputy leadership election. Hughes and Wintour wrote that Kinnock attempted little without first obtaining their prior support, usually by speaking to them himself before crucial executive and committee meetings. 'The understanding between that triumvirate and Kinnock was finally sealed in the battle to expel the leading members of Militant.'

Tom Sawyer says that when Kinnock first became leader there were still a number of people on the NEC who would not automatically support him.

We three [he and Blunkett and Meacher] were among them. But we felt that the time had come to draw a line on this factionalisation, and that if Labour was ever to win an election again we had to work together. He was the first leader to be elected by the whole movement – the party, the unions, not just the MPs, and we felt that made a big difference. And of course we did have to start winning elections again. We broke away from the Bennites. We became the first Kinnockites.

He was a very charismatic leader. His ability to motivate and enthuse people was great. People felt excited by him and ready to work for him if they shared his values.

Tony Benn, leader of that isolated group on the hard left, as usual
expressed a different viewpoint after the 1986 conference. He recorded
in his diary that the leader's speech 'lasted interminably. I had my usual
agonies on whether to join in the standing ovation at the end. But I came
to the conclusion that it was part of the eve of election game you had to
play.'

In Benn's eyes, the Labour Party was beginning to look
unrecognizable. In the eyes of the public – the television-viewing public,
at any rate – it was beginning to look recognizably a smarter outfit. Back
in October 1985, when the former television producer Peter Mandelson
had been appointed director of communications, his brief was to update
the party's image. There were already cosmetic changes in evidence at
that conference, such as on the platform, where a background colour
scheme had been carefully thought out by designers. As if reflecting the
new image consciousness, the hall appeared to contain a far higher
proportion of smart suits than was traditionally seen at a Labour
conference. But the most dynamic and potent change was in the party's
symbol. The old red flag of traditional British socialism had been
replaced with a delicate red rose.

Credit for this belongs to Kinnock initially; he borrowed the idea from
the Socialist International organization and felt that its simplicity would
appeal more widely than the billowing flag. He had used the rose on his
own campaign literature during the leadership election, and it had also
appeared on Labour material during the Euro elections of 1984. But it
was Mandelson who commissioned the design of this particular rose,
which adorned lapel badges, carrier bags and ties in the conference shop
at Blackpool that week. And it was Mandelson who carried a large box of
red roses on to the platform on the final day of the conference, and
handed them to Neil and Glenys Kinnock who tossed the roses out into
the audience. It was a flourish of style which belonged firmly to the new
regime: it would have been unimaginable, said observers, for Harold
Wilson, James Callaghan or Michael Foot to behave so.

Style, image, first impressions: Kinnock has always been aware of the
importance of appearance in public perception of the Labour Party and
its elected representatives. He has never needed to adopt the dishevelled
'uniform' of the political activist, chosen (often by those from
middle-class backgrounds) to represent rebellion or to mimic the dress
of the working man. Kinnock's own working-class credentials are as
impeccable as his pressed suits and polished shoes. Yet suits and ties
had not always been popular with Labour Party conference delegates.

If the new look reflected the new leader, then it might also have been
influenced by the leader's wife. Glenys Kinnock dazzled the platform at
Blackpool in a Chinese silk dress. Her own image, both real and

perceived, had changed considerably since Neil became leader, according to Fiona Millar in a *Daily Express* profile in October 1986. She noted that seats at the conference which were once occupied by dungarees and woolly jumpers now seemed to be filled by smartly dressed men and women. Glenys's impeccable standards of dress – 'she loathes creases and has all her clothes transported on a hanger to avoid them' – seemed to have filtered down through the Party, Millar wrote:

> In appearance she has blossomed from an attractive, modestly dressed wife and teacher into a dazzling star. Her hair has got lighter and shorter, her make-up more professional and her clothes more eyecatching ... Moreover, no one who has witnessed Neil Kinnock dragging the Labour Party screaming into the 1980s seriously believes the old stereotype of Glenys as a bossy wife who nags her husband over tea into pursuing policies which interest her.

Glenys Kinnock insisted that she was not part of any consultation team. 'When there are issues which need to be discussed, he has a wide range of advisers and the Shadow Cabinet to do that. We are much more likely to be talking about Stephen's rugby kit or Rachel's homework – just like any other couple.'

But Glenys was far from being just a glossy accessory at conference time, Millar stressed. 'She sits on the Labour platform even when Neil is not there, to listen to debates which interest her ... She has addressed fringe meetings, plugged the causes which concern her, and attended eight or nine receptions a night.' Those causes are the ones still pursued by Glenys Kinnock, from the One World organization devoted to the needs of developing countries which she still chairs to nursery care for the under-fives. 'I only take on the things which are of a special interest to me,' she told Millar at the time. 'The things which millions of women like me are concerned about, for example, health, education, the problems of looking after elderly or disabled relatives ... I don't speak on behalf of the Labour Party but as an individual who is political, and as a wife and mother I see many problems in society which I want to do my little bit to help.' Millar concluded: 'That "little bit" involves being Labour's stunning rose that helps to hide the party's thorny reality.' The thorniest question of all that autumn was defence.

6 On the Defensive

The concept of unilateral nuclear disarmament had been a strong feature of Neil – and Glenys – Kinnock's philosophy since their first political awareness. It was a cause championed by a great many members of the Labour Party, some of them also members of CND. But it appeared as official Labour Party policy in an election manifesto for the first time in 1983. Michael Foot had promised that 'we will, after consultation, carry through in the lifetime of the next Parliament, our non-nuclear defence policy'. This meant scrapping the British-controlled Polaris submarines, and the closure of all United States nuclear weapons bases in Britain.

But even among those who opposed nuclear warfare in principle there was a fear that to be the first to abandon the weapons, with no guarantees that other nations would do likewise, would leave Britain isolated and exposed. The unilateral view held by Kinnock at the time was one of example: while the weapons existed anywhere, the world was a more dangerous place, but even if just one country lay them aside voluntarily then others might do likewise in time.

He saw nuclear weapons as either pointless or self-destructive, or both. As nuclear war kills indiscriminately, and particularly in a small island country, the effects on the environment would be devastating. The unilateralists also argued that Britain's own independent nuclear weapons – as opposed to the American ones based on British soil – were outdated and insignificant, making a mockery of the Conservatives' concept of Britain as a world power.

However, the 'Falklands factor' was still playing a critical role in public perception; defence loomed large on the voters' agenda, and they wanted a strong and powerful security force. Irrespective of the nuclear debate, Labour was seen as being weak on defence. Political opponents portrayed Kinnock as, at worst, being in league with the KGB or, at best, misunderstanding the threatening nature of the Soviet Union and the hostility of international politics.

The first sign of Kinnock's review of policy was an NEC document in 1984, *Defence and Security for Britain*. The unilateralist position was maintained: American bases would go, British weapons would be scrapped. But there was a distinct emphasis on the need for investment in conventional weapons, which would be met from the savings on the nuclear budget, and there was a definite commitment to Britain's continued membership of NATO.

The first American cruise nuclear missiles had arrived in Britain at the end of 1983, and a campaign against their presence started at once, gaining force through 1984, especially with prolonged demonstrations at Greenham Common in Berkshire and Molesworth near Cambridge. The protestors were predominantly women, many of whom set up semi-permanent homes in makeshift tents outside the perimeter fences. Glenys Kinnock visited the peace camps outside both bases and gave moral support to the cause. Their argument was with the concept of deterrence: if the very existence of nuclear weapons was a sufficient threat to a potential enemy, then why was it not enough to have the US missiles stationed on US territory and on American vessels? Their detractors claimed that this was hypocrisy, using the protection of America's 'nuclear umbrella'.

Neil Kinnock's view was that he would not ask the USA to use nuclear weapons to defend Britain, but in this he did not have the agreement of his foreign affairs spokesman, Denis Healey. Nor, it seemed, was unilateralism widely popular throughout Britain beyond the confines of the Labour Party. As the party conference got under way in October 1986, US defence spokesmen were quoted on British television claiming that Labour's defence proposals would destroy NATO. Healey was heard to imply that the US might persuade Labour to allow its nuclear bases to remain.

In the conference hall Kinnock insisted that Polaris, and the Trident nuclear submarines would be scrapped, although in an attempt to defuse the discord, he made no reference to Healey's remarks. In a typically rousing speech he left defence matters to the end: 'We are the first generation in history to have to deal with the existence of weapons of obliteration,' he said. 'I face it as the leader of this party who works to become the democratically elected leader of our country. I face it as an adult, as a citizen, as a father. And I tell you in no casual spirit that, like most of my fellow citizens, I would if necessary fight and give my life for my country. I would die for my country. But I could never allow my country to die for me.'

His words won an enthusiastic standing ovation. Inevitably the reaction from the Conservatives was to highlight just how totally and generally defenceless Britain would be under Labour. It was, of course, a debate in which all the arguments are theoretical and cannot be tested. Michael Leapman wrote:

What sways voters finally is not the detailed argument of options for action in scarcely imaginable circumstances, but the overall impression of competence in defence and commitment to it – and that can be built or destroyed with a single word ... Kinnock could see that, even ignoring his own firm convictions, it would be impossible to unite the party around anything but a non-nuclear policy.

Tony Benn, meanwhile, was typically sceptical. In his diary he recorded that the high point of Kinnock's 'I would rather die for my country' speech was 'the most crude demagoguery, which will satisfy people that he is in favour of defence, but I thought it poor stuff.'

It was more than unfortunate that the thorny issue of defence was raised that autumn; not only did it focus on the one item of policy over which Kinnock had notably failed so far to unite the party, but it brought to public attention the subject over which the party had failed to win credibility. It took the edge off Kinnock's optimism and was to take Labour away from election victory the following year. Instead of maintaining a steady upward climb towards the general election summit, wrote Hughes and Wintour in *Labour Rebuilt*, 'Labour's hopes of preventing a third term of Conservative Government tumbled away. The speed with which the party's fortunes crumbled demonstrated how fragile and restrained the Kinnock reformation had been to that point.'

At the end of 1986 Kinnock made another visit to the USA, with the aim of impressing voters back home. It was time to spell out more fully how Labour's defence policy would not threaten the British-American alliance. This time he did not meet President Reagan, but delivered a lengthy speech at the Kennedy School of Government in Massachusetts, in which he set out his view of the alliance between the US and a future Labour Government on defence matters. He insisted that Labour would keep Britain in NATO, but that 'the size and location of our country means that using nuclear weapons would always be either pointless or self destructive or both.' Some American bases in Britain would be closed, others would switch to a non-nuclear role.

Two days after he returned from America, Labour launched the defence policy document *Modern Britain in a Modern World: The Power to Defend Our Country*. This carried Kinnock's speech theme in greater detail, although there was still no definite timescale for the removal of American missiles from British soil. The savings made by abandoning the nuclear programme would be transferred to building up conventional weapons systems, which would be of benefit to NATO – a benefit which would not exist if all British resources went on Trident. The public appeared to be unimpressed. Labour's two-point lead in the opinion polls early in the autumn was, within a matter of weeks, turned into an eight point deficit.

Kinnock was already well aware that a unilateral policy on nuclear weapons was not likely to be widely popular with the electorate, in spite of party conference decisions. His job was to find ways of explaining the unilateralist logic to the voters while avoiding any damaging splits within the Shadow Cabinet during the run up to the next election. The problem was that Kinnock was undergoing a personal change of heart which would not be translated into political action until after the 1987 election. But changes of heart or of policy would be no easy matter for a man who had voiced strong objections to nuclear weapons throughout his political career so far.

Hughes and Wintour maintain that the defence document, *Modern Britain*, ultimately served only to underline Labour's lack of either clarity or unity on nuclear defence. 'It was hopeless to imagine that the party could successfully campaign on a non-nuclear policy, when that policy itself was internally inconsistent, and evidently self-evasive. The leadership's own lack of faith was transparent.'

If Kinnock did indeed already lack faith, he had very good reasons for concealing the fact at this stage, as he was to explain much later. Some time after his resignation as party leader in 1992 he was asked by David Dimbleby on BBC TV how he had conducted a campaign defending policies which in his heart he no longer believed in. 'You've got to be convinced there's a greater purpose. If you try to short circuit the process the fuse will be blown.' Kinnock smiled and added: 'You give very long answers and try to get round it.'

He said further: 'I knew that the defence policy was at the very least unconvincing and inconsistent.' He would have loved to make changes much more quickly: 'But to try to proceed at speed would have wrecked the Labour Party. And that would have destroyed the whole purpose I had of promoting unity.' He enlarged on that belief in a subsequent BBC Radio Four discussion with John Humphrys:

> Whatever my instincts might have been in 1985 about the credibility of our defence policy, if I had tried to bring in the changes which we did eventually secure there would have been schism, there's no doubt about that. My calculation at the time was that the best that could happen was that I would be defeated, and in the circumstances I didn't think anybody else could have made a better fist of it.
>
> My position was to persist and bring people round, and to take advantage of events. I would have loved to have done it earlier but the risk of dividing the party was so great, it was a risk I didn't think I could take.

As it was, Kinnock had to spend the period prior to the 1987 election clarifying Labour's defence policy. In March he went back to the United States, and this time he did meet President Reagan. It was to some extent in fulfilment of a vow he had made when questioned at the end of his earlier visit on why he had not met the President. It was not on the schedule, said Kinnock, 'but I will be going back to see him before the election'. His advisers thought the trip could only serve to highlight differences of opinion and Labour's already unpopular defence policy; others said that to back out would be even more damaging.

'Kinnock himself decided that there was no choice but to press ahead,' wrote Hughes and Wintour. 'Typically, he abhorred the prospect of being accused of cowardice. That Reagan gave Kinnock less than the allotted half hour was only one of many petty humiliations ... The President's press staff gave a dismissive briefing afterwards, conveying a powerful impression of Kinnock's irrelevance on the world stage.'

He returned home to celebrate his forty-fifth birthday, and to a row over the reporting of the meeting. Denis Healey, who had been with him on the American visit, told reporters that the White House spokesman, Marlin Fitzwater, had given a distorted view of the event. According to reports, Fitzwater said that Kinnock had raised the subject of unilateral disarmament and had been told that Labour policy was a danger to arms reduction talks. Healey denied this: he said that Kinnock had not mentioned the unilateralist stance, that he had stressed Labour's commitment to NATO and spending on conventional arms rather than Trident; and that Reagan did not allege that Labour policy would undercut the forthcoming Geneva arms talks. 'What does seem to be the case is that some of President Reagan's advisers thought it would be a good idea to try and help Mrs Thatcher in her election battle by being unkind to the Labour Party,' Healey said on BBC 1's *This Week Next Week*.

This was precisely the kind of controversy which Labour needed least. Early in the year Kinnock had admitted that Labour still needed an additional surge in public support to put it on course for election victory. The polls at the beginning of 1987 suggested that Labour was failing to make sufficient headway in the marginal seats it had to win to prevent Mrs Thatcher securing a third term for the Conservatives. Kinnock had to accept that Labour did not yet have victory in its grasp. 'In the last three years we have secured a significant turnround in support for the party,' he said in a BBC interview. 'We have been persuading people. We need that additional surge.' He said that the choice facing Britain was 'whether we are going to be a manufacturing economy, making and selling our way in the world, or a warehouse economy in perpetual decline.'

In another interview, in February, Kinnock insisted that he would continue as leader of the Labour Party whether or not he won or lost the coming election. When it was suggested to him by a TV South reporter, that his party was likely to give him only one chance to lead them to victory, Kinnock replied that people who knew him would confirm that he was 'no easy push-over'. But a MORI opinion poll published in the *Sunday Times* demonstrated how far support was slipping away. Kinnock's personal rating was claimed to be below that of Michael Foot prior to the 1983 election: 26 per cent of those questioned believed that Kinnock understood the problems facing Britain, compared with 41 per cent for Foot when he was leader four years earlier.

The poll coincided with the publication, by Conservative Central Office, of a document on the Labour Party which aimed most of its fire at the leader. This claimed that Kinnock 'failed to demonstrate the calibre required of the Leader of the Opposition, let alone a potential prime minister'. Shortly afterwards, more than one hundred Tory MPs launched an even fiercer campaign against Kinnock, on the grounds that he was unsuitable to hold office. They signed three Commons motions denouncing, among other things, his lack of ministerial experience, his failure to condemn violence by miners' pickets, his blacking of journalists, and his endorsement of extreme left-wing council policies.

It was an astonishing tirade from a group of senior MPs, led by Sir Marcus Fox, who was vice-chairman of the influential 1922 Committee at the time. For example, they listed Kinnock's 'fundamental and longstanding hostility to the monarchy'. This emanated from a well-documented and photographed incident in which Kinnock and Dennis Skinner were seen sitting together in the chamber of the Commons in 'solitary protest', refusing to listen to the Queen's Speech at the opening of Parliament. In fact, most MPs – of all parties – don't get into the Lords to hear the Queen.

'It's true that I've never been a fan of the royals but, as it happens, I wasn't making a conscious gesture on this occasion,' says Kinnock. In any case, he had moved a considerable distance from extreme views in the course of the decade, and had been careful to avoid personal criticism of the monarchy. When asked once by David Frost if he supported the Royal Family, Kinnock replied: 'Yes, and every other family in Britain as well'. That had been the extent of his 'fundamental hostility' for a long time.

The Tories also cited Kinnock's 'approval of the anti-democratic Militant tendency within the Parliamentary Labour Party'. It was true that a handful of MPs had Militant leanings, but the determination with which Kinnock had launched his attack on Militant in Liverpool had them already wondering about their futures. The Conservatives further claimed that Kinnock had demonstrated 'his inability to exercise self control, illustrated by scuffles in the Commons Lobby and outside an

Indian restaurant' (two unfortunately well-documented incidents where Kinnock had been excessively provoked). And they stooped to ill-mannered insult describing Kinnock's 'manifest inability, recognised by colleagues in the PLP, to master information, thus finally proving his intellectual and administrative inadequacy for the highest elected office in the UK'.

Bryan Gould, who would head Labour's election campaign, said it was obvious that Mrs Thatcher and the Conservatives were panicking. Kinnock himself treated the motions with contempt. He said that the Tory onslaught was 'infantile'. 'This is evidence of the desperation by the Conservative Party being cornered by so many policy failures they have to resort to gutter-fighting.'

He was able to make a minor counter-attack during Prime Minister's question time when he scorned Mrs Thatcher's stance over President Reagan's Star Wars programme and labelled her the 'presidential doormat'. But Labour suspected a carefully planned demolition exercise, orchestrated by 10 Downing Street, as the comments came only days after an attack in the Commons by the junior health minister, Edwina Currie, in which she suggested that Glenys Kinnock was the real leader of the Labour Party. Morale in the Kinnock camp was inevitably lowered.

Charles Clarke, who was Kinnock's chief of staff from the mid-eighties until after the 1992 election, witnessed many such attacks on the Labour leader. The Conservatives, he says, were beginning to recognize that Kinnock was transforming the Labour Party and creating an electoral challenge to them. 'They were frightened of him,' he says. 'Their response was to denigrate him, and to try to weaken him because they were afraid of him.' Clarke says that Kinnock is a man of deep commitment and vision – a description which is not used lightly of anyone, but has been used by more than a few of Kinnock's contemporaries who admire him. 'He had a very clear idea of where it was that the Labour Party ought to go.'

But the Labour Party's moment had not yet arrived, and a foretaste of their election chances came when they lost a by-election at Greenwich early in March to the SDP by some 5,000 votes. The Labour candidate, Deirdre Wood, was a former councillor with a hard left reputation whose selection had angered Kinnock – and he was subsequently proved right. He issued a tough warning that the 'antics' of the hard left fringe would exercise no influence on policy, direction or leadership, but he admitted that they were causing an 'identifiable problem'.

His remarks followed the leaking of a confidential letter from his press secretary Patricia Hewitt to Labour MP Frank Dobson who had chaperoned Wood before the Greenwich vote. Hewitt's letter said that

'The "loony Labour left" is taking its toll; the gays and lesbians issue is costing us dear among the pensioners.' Labour's own polls at the time showed that support in London had slipped by as much as 8 per cent since 1983, and Kinnock called a meeting of local council leaders, prospective candidates and sitting MPs to plan a specific election campaign strategy for the capital. He was equally stern when internal arguments threatened harmony within the Shadow Cabinet.

On one occasion he told colleagues: 'Since becoming leader, I've set myself a code of self-discipline which is the only way for a voluntary movement such as this to obtain victory. The precondition of making ourselves credible, electable and victorious is self-discipline. The objective of winning is greater than ego, and any vanity, and shortage of memory can be no excuse.'

As speculation mounted on the date of an election, Kinnock went on the offensive. At a joint meeting of the Shadow Cabinet and the NEC in February, he spoke of how the party was geared for election victory. Tony Benn in his diary recorded how Kinnock said that 'unemployment is the key, and we must turn anxiety into support for us. We must get rid of surrender mentality, because submissiveness among the electorate is our greatest threat'. Kinnock called for change by collective action, democratically controlled through the community, and for an attack on Mrs Thatcher. 'She is hateful, but she is thought to be strong; therefore we must attack Thatcherism as weak and wrong.'

Now Kinnock began his public attacks on the Government, for example over their cuts of almost one-fifth in Britain's overseas aid programme since 1979. He pledged that a Labour Government would more than double Britain's contribution. 'A quarter of the world's population are living in absolute destitution with no hope of adequate food or shelter,' he said at the launch of his party's new Aid and Development Charter. He contrasted Tory spending cuts with the generous response of ordinary people to African famine appeals. 'As the people in Britain have turned outwards to help, their Government has turned inwards to selfishness and desertion of duty.'

At a rally in Northampton in April, awaiting a date for the general election, Kinnock launched Labour's attempt to regain power. Acknowledging the threat from the SDP/Liberal Alliance, he warned a 1,500-strong crowd against the gamble of tactical voting: 'Are you really willing to play such fruit machine politics just hoping that enough people in enough places will spontaneously, coincidentally, and in the secret of the ballot booth, vote together to turn out the Tories?' Labour were still ahead of the Alliance in the opinion polls, but were trailing a long way behind the Tories. By the time the election was called on Monday 2 May, the Conservatives stood at 44 per cent, Labour at 33 per cent and the Alliance at 21 per cent. The date named by Mrs Thatcher was 11 June.

Labour were ready and waiting to launch their campaign officially. The mistakes of 1983 would not be repeated: Peter Mandelson, the head of communications, and Kinnock's press secretary Patricia Hewitt were in control of an organizing team which was managed with exacting efficiency. Hewitt had alerted staff to the fact that this election would be the first in Britain to be covered by the recently introduced electronic news gathering technology for television news – small camera crews working with a reporter could have videotape back at TV centres quickly and repeatedly throughout the day. So more than ever before, the key characters in the campaign would be playing to the cameras. She advised Kinnock that his tour of the country should be organized to give good locations for television cameras, as well as plenty of opportunities for newspaper photographers.

Michael Hickling, who covered the Labour leader's tour for the *Yorkshire Post*, described how this operated in practice.

> The journalist no longer has to pursue. Insulated in an air-conditioned coach, with two press officers for companionship, Kinnock cruises to every venue in style. The passengers aboard fall into two distinct groups, the photo and TV journalists who count, and the writing journalists who do not. This pecking order can be established from the fact that most stops are arranged specially for the first group, where the latter can only stand around like spare parts. Example: Mr Kinnock boarded a grounded aircraft at British Aerospace at Hatfield at the weekend and got out again. That was it. But the pseudo-event took up 45 minutes while the snappers and the TV crews got their shots.

Hickling said that having been attached to the 'people's party' at the last election,

> one retained distinct memories of pursuing an old man with a stick and a dog around the countryside, from shambolic city walkabouts to noisy public meetings. Even finding out where he was supposed to be at an allotted time and place was an achievement. In the intervening period, the old man has been disposed of, along with other awkward impedimenta like red banners, by the image makers who felt that a blander, more homogenised product would look better on the shelves. What we have now, tastefully wrapped and served with a smile, is the polite people's party.

Kinnock's role, and Kinnock's personality, were at the very heart of Labour's presidential-style campaign. 'Never before had Labour allowed the presentation of its party platform to be overridden by purely

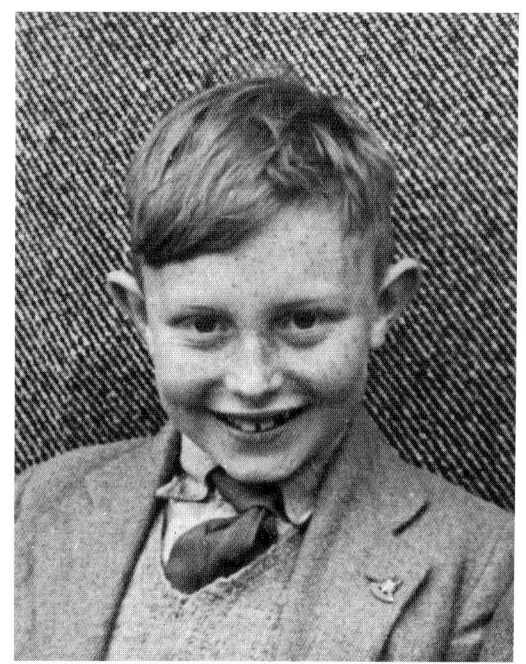

Freckle-faced Neil Kinnock, age 7

As a cub scout, age 9, in 1951

Neil, age 11, with his father, Gordon, on holiday at Southsea, 1953

Kinnock, age 17, in his final year at Lewis School, Pengam

Summer rehearsal camp for the Glamorgan Youth Choir and Orchestra at Ogmore by Sea, 1959. Kinnock is in the middle of the second row 'looking mean and moody'

Kinnock, age 18 (back row, fourth from right) with the Lewis School Choir

Kinnock, miraculously unhurt, and the wreckage of his car which crashed on the M4 in July 1983. 'Somebody up there likes me,' he said afterwards

Kinnock leaves home for Westminster for his first confrontation with the Prime Minister as Opposition Leader, 24 October 1983

The new Labour leader and his deputy at Brighton in October 1983.

Neil and Glenys Kinnock singing with the daughter of a striking Yorkshire miner at a Euro-election campaign rally in Leeds in 1984

Neil and Glenys with their children, Rachel and Stephen, leaving for Athens on an official visit to Greece in January 1984

Kinnock putting across the message of the new policy review following the 1987 election defeat

Kinnock in full voice at the controversial pre-election rally in Sheffield, April 1992

Appealing to the voters at Leeds Town Hall in June 1987

Kinnock on a visit to a Midland Bank staff nursery at the Arlington Business Centre in Yorkshire in June 1990

personal projection of the party leader,' wrote Hughes and Wintour. 'But Labour's new image making team knew that the Conservatives would aim to build up Thatcher's image as a world leader of post-war stature comparable only with Churchill; Labour had to respond by building up Kinnock.'

They did so with a remarkable party election broadcast made by Hugh Hudson who had directed the film *Chariots of Fire*. Titled simply *Kinnock* it had the dramatic force associated as much with winning an Oscar as winning an election. There were clips from Kinnock's most powerful speeches of the past few years, including his assault on the Liverpool Militants at the 1985 party conference; an excerpt from a recent speech made at the beginning of Labour's official campaign in Llandudno; quotes from members of his family in Wales; a memorable cliff-top sequence of Neil and Glenys walking hand in hand on the Welsh coast; and a soundtrack which included one of Kinnock's favourite pieces of music, the Brahms Symphony No. 1.

Broadcast on 21 May, it had a sensational impact on the viewing public – Kinnock's personal rating in the opinion polls went up by 16 per cent virtually overnight – although not everyone in the Labour Party approved of its presentation. At a Fabian Society conference later that year Peter Mandelson said that the '*Chariots of Fire*' broadcast had been 'the most effective piece of political communication in recent political history': someone in the audience shouted out – 'But it didn't work, did it?'

Predictably Tony Benn was also unimpressed. His own description of the broadcast is recorded in his diaries:

> It began with a bomber flying, then a bird flying, then Neil and Glenys on a mountain top, then Kinnock talking straight to camera about his inspiration, a woman from Wales saying, 'We always knew he would make it'; he talked about his parents and Glenys was brought in again. They showed speeches by Kinnock, with tremendous applause. The centre point was his attack on Militant at the Bournemouth Conference ... the high peak of his strength is that he attacked the Militant Tendency. It made my blood run cold.

The campaign trail was equally impressive to behold. Hickling's verdict: 'This product has clearly been well researched and the salesmen are enthusiastic but will they buy it out in the real world? If the election was to be decided by razzmatazz, then Labour must have won this one by a mile.'

Kinnock was to say later that he was not comfortable with the presidential style of the campaign, 'But in the absence of a better suggestion, I went along with it. I don't think I've got more or less modesty than anyone else, but this projection of Kinnock as President just didn't sit temperamentally with me.' In fact commentators at the time noticed that Kinnock appeared tired and drained at first from the long run-up to the announcing of the election, and that his speeches were lacking in their usual lustre; it was only when the campaign proper was under way that the adrenalin began to flow and the fire came back into his oratory.

His campaign schedule was a punishing one and reporters covering his tour marvelled at his energy and stamina. 'As one who has begun to curl at the edges after just four days on the road,' wrote Hickling,

> Kinnock's ability to turn up looking salad fresh to every engagement seems remarkable ... This public geniality is part of every politician's stock in trade. But the point about the Kinnocks is if you stick close by and watch carefully when the cameras are turned away the warmth and good humour remains and appears entirely genuine. Mr Kinnock seems to relish every encounter. His wife's smile occasionally seems glacial, especially during the numerous factory visits. This is understandable – after staggering out of yet another industrial estate a member of the Press groaned that when the election was over he never wanted to look at another lathe in his life.

Robin Oakley, then political editor of *The Times*, wrote in *The Times Guide to the House of Commons, 1987* that the tour of the provinces and the well-organized programme of speeches on jobs, health and education, showed the Labour machine back in fighting trim 'even if it did owe more to Madison Avenue this time than to Keir Hardie. Mr Kinnock made his mark as a man of vigour, confidence and passionate concern about the plight of the less well-off in society.' The '*Chariots of Fire*' broadcast he described as 'a hagiographical TV spectacular'.

So much for the image of the campaign, but what of the substance? Kinnock was always at his best on a party platform, and his first speech of the official campaign was on 15 May in Llandudno when he addressed the Welsh Labour Party Conference. It was an emotional speech in which he spelled out Labour's alternative to the 'wretched, squalid and brutal' regime of Mrs Thatcher. He said that the election had come just in time for those whose lives and skills were being wasted by unemployment, and warned of a third Conservative term of office: 'Britain cannot serve such a life sentence without it turning into a death sentence for more industries, more communities and more hopes, because unemployment and poverty are not just ailments and misfortunes, they are mortal afflictions.'

This speech also included the now famous – and completely

extemporized – lines which were to be incorporated in the *'Chariots of Fire'* broadcast:

> Why am I the first Kinnock in a thousand generations to be able to get to university? Why is Glenys the first woman in her family in a thousand generations to be able to get to university? Was it because all our predecessors were 'thick'? Did they lack talent, those people who could sing and play, and recite and write poetry, those people who could make wonderful, beautiful things with their hands; those people who could dream dreams, see visions … Were those people not university material? Couldn't they have knocked off all their 'A' levels in an afternoon? But why didn't they get it? Was it because they were weak? … Does anybody really think that they didn't get what we had because they didn't have the talent, or the strength, or the endurance, or the commitment? Of course not. It was because there was no platform upon which they could stand; no arrangement for their neighbours to subscribe to their welfare; no method by which the communities could translate their desires for those individuals into provision for those individuals.

Denis Healey, in his memoirs, *The Time of My Life*, saw this as the most powerful passage of a brilliant speech in which he believed Kinnock set the tone of the whole campaign: 'Incandescent oratory with an irresistible moral thrust'. Kinnock himself comments: 'The thing about Llandudno is that what's remembered are the parts I didn't write – I just said them "from the soul". It was good to get back to old habits!'

Labour's election manifesto was a moral crusade for job creation, health and education. They promised a £12 billion package to tackle unemployment, poverty and crime, with a pledge to reduce unemployment by one million in two years; a national minimum wage; an £8 a week rise in pensions for couples; and the borrowing of £3 billion more for spending on house building and the NHS.

Kinnock had confirmed his dominance of the policy-making machinery at a meeting of the Shadow Cabinet and the NEC on 12 May when this manifesto, seen by many as a move away from traditional left wing commitments, was adopted with little argument. Party conference calls for compensation to reimburse the miners fined during the pits strike and the local councillors who had been surcharged were dropped. Previous commitments to phase out nuclear power and to re-nationalize former State industries which the Tories had privatized were modified. The hard left were overwhelmingly defeated in their attempts to include a promise to withdraw from the EC, to remove all US military bases (not just nuclear ones) and to pull out of NATO and the Warsaw Pact.

But Kinnock and his team still had to convince the electorate of their most contentious policy item, unilateral disarmament, and they received a further blow when NATO's Supreme Allied Commander in Europe,

General Bernard Rogers, said that such a move would be the straw which broke the camel's back for the people of the United States and would lead to calls for their troops to be brought home. The campaign team were hoping that they would be able to maintain a low profile for the defence issue, but it was shoved to the top of the agenda following a TV interview with Kinnock by David Frost.

According to Hughes and Wintour, Frost took Kinnock

> steadily down the non-nuclear defence path until he arrived at a moment where Russian soldiers were ready to invade Britain. Instead of dismissing the scenario as preposterous, Kinnock ambled into a prolix reply, saying that at the last resort, defence would be guerrilla warfare. What he meant to convey was that there would, because of the inevitability of such resistance, be little for the Russians to gain by invading Britain. But the remark became a sore protrusion, as much because it was clearly ill-considered and confused as for its content.

The Tories picked up Kinnock's remarks a few days later, and subsequently ran a poster with the slogan 'Labour's defence policy' over a picture of a soldier with his arms up. 'But they were probably going to do that anyway,' says Kinnock. 'It's ironic, of course, that all of the European NATO powers had plans for guerrilla resistance built into their defence stategies.'

But would he have tackled the campaign any differently, with hindsight? 'By the time we got to 87 I don't think there was another way to face it. We had to make the best of what was becoming a less bad job but nevertheless was not a very good job.' It was not only defence which caused problems.

> The proposition for the reduction of unemployment was appealing, but not believable. On council house sales, we still had people saying, I'd like to vote for you but you won't let me buy my council house, and we had to say, no, we changed that three years ago. Our policy was not understood, it hadn't got through.

At the time, commentators assessing Labour's election chances focused on the way that the party had changed since Kinnock took control. A profile in *The Independent* pointed out that, 'one should never think that Kinnock simply fell into the job when Labour was going through a rough time and decided to skip a generation. He had been working very hard to get it. Once he had got it, he was just as calculating and determined about trying to reshape Labour into an election-winning machine.'

According to *The Independent*, the biggest change in the Labour Party since Kinnock succeeded Foot was that the leader 'always, but always, gets his own way'.

This realism, or ruthlessness, has naturally hurt some of Kinnock's most politically loyal supporters ... But even some of Kinnock's strongest enemies concede that it is precisely this quality which could make him a good prime minister. With the avalanche of poor polls, the cascade of hostile stories in the tabloid press portraying him as weak or silly and the poisonous trickle of innuendo that he is 'cracking up', it is all too easy to write off both Kinnock and his outside chance of succeeding Mrs Thatcher.

(The 'cracking up' reports had no substance; it was only Kinnock's vocal chords which came under strain again as election day neared.)

Kinnock admitted later that he believed Mrs Thatcher to be 'so profoundly wrong' that he did little further diagnosis of her character.

There was a popular sentiment that 'She's wrong but she's strong'. I found that deeply depressing. I think that people did believe I didn't have an innate strength. I had been wrestling with dissident elements in our party: that might be evidence of determination or a certain truculent toughness, but was it the strength they were looking for in a prime minister to lead the whole country?

As polling day drew near, the war of words between Kinnock and Thatcher grew savage. She painted a 'nightmare vision' of power restored to the union masters; he said that Mrs Thatcher's vision of a Britain in which personal security depended entirely on private affluence would be a nightmare vision for the entire nation. Kinnock insisted that 'We shall end the reign of those who use unemployment as a weapon, those who stain our country with their selfishness, those who divide Britain with their meanness.'

Kinnock's confidence towards the end of the campaign caused jitters among the Tory ranks. A week before voting day a Gallup poll in the *Daily Telegraph* suggested that the gap between the two main parties had narrowed to just 4 per cent. But Labour began to fade. Public confusion between Kinnock and Hattersley over the level at which Labour's tax and national insurance proposals would start to have effect appeared to unnerve prospective Labour converts.

New advertising posters were ordered, showing Kinnock in 'apocalyptic pose' against an electric storm background, with the slogan 'The Country's Crying Out For Labour' underneath. According to Hughes and Wintour, they achieved some impact – not least on Kinnock himself. 'The shadow agency had not dared show him the posters in advance, for fear that he would veto them – so the first Kinnock knew of his translation into a Nordic myth was when he saw one from the window of his campaign car.' Hughes and Wintour believe that the sequence of accidents and blunders in the run up to the 1987 election could not hide the underlying truth that the first phase of Kinnock's leadership had failed to drag the party out of its chronic malaise.

'After four years of Kinnock's "reforming" leadership, Labour had come full circle. There seemed once again, as there had in 1983, a real danger that the Alliance were set to become the main opposition party.' And it appears that, in retrospect, few within the Labour Party truly thought that victory was in their grasp in 1987. Their immediate concern was to re-establish the party as the major opposition force.

But on 11 June, television viewers watched Kinnock watching his party limp home. In a decision which he later decided was little short of crazy, he agreed to let a camera crew film the reactions of his family on polling night. They were all gathered at the home of Kinnock's agent Barry Moore, and were shown watching the election night special as the catastrophic news was delivered. The Conservatives swept back to power for a third successive term with an overall majority in the Commons of 101. Labour gained 27 new seats and lost 6, increasing its share of the vote where it had the least to gain – in Scotland, Wales and the North East, rather than eating into Conservative marginals. The threat from the Alliance failed to materialize.

But Labour, wrote Robin Oakley, was left to sort out a conundrum.

> In a society of owner occupiers, an increasing number of share owners and 40 per cent white collar workers, how does a party which is financed and dominated by the trades unions and which appeals largely to council tenants and the less well off build the support it needs to achieve the enormous swing required for it to regain power – especially if it remains wedded to a unilateralist defence policy which has twice been rejected conclusively by the British electorate?

On 12 June it looked as if Kinnock would have to start all over again.

7 Back to the Drawing-board

The scale of the defeat suffered by Labour on 11 June 1987 shocked the leadership and party members at all levels. No major political party enters an election campaign publicly acknowledging that it probably will not win. Labour realists had hoped for a considerable narrowing of the Conservative majority. They had hoped to curtail the ambitions of the SDP/Liberal Alliance; this at least was to prove the case thanks to internal bickering within the Alliance factions. Some might even have hoped for a miracle. Labour had fought an effective campaign. The party was better organized than ever before, they had made good use of the new technology available in presenting their message, and Kinnock had made a direct challenge to the dominant style of Margaret Thatcher.

But they lost, and lost heavily, and this time Labour did not have the excuses which they presented with justification in 1983. They had a new, professional leadership which had removed many of the more extreme policies from the manifesto; any internal divisions were certainly less apparent than they had been in 1983; and there was no 'Falklands factor' this time. According to Hughes and Wintour, Kinnock privately blamed the tax policy for the scale of Labour's defeat. Others saw the party as still trapped within the framework of 1983 and Kinnock's left-wing roots, notably in the persistent attachment to unilateral nuclear disarmament. In addition parts of the party, particularly in London, continued to be stuck with the 'loony left' label, and so the media constantly associated Labour with the hard left.

A week after the election, the Parliamentary Labour Party met to assess the damage. But first, Kinnock congratulated his colleagues on the success of the campaign. 'And if further proof were needed of that success we only have to observe the way that success is even now being dismissed by our opponents and by pundits – that is to say opponents who are paid to oppose us.' The campaign had been well organized in everything from the standard of the literature to the performances of spokespeople and candidates. 'And the most important ingredient was the fact that we were fighting on policies and for values that had the support of the whole Movement and we were fighting together.'

But the failure to win the general election offered little consolation, other than a better basis for building and lessons to be learned. 'There are no prizes in the result for the young, the old, the poor, the sick, the badly housed, the isolated or the frightened ... There are no defeats that are either glorious or gratifying. There are defeats that are challenging, defeats that can be turned into future victory. This defeat must be one of those.'

Any self-assessment, he said, must find ways of showing how the policies and the values of democratic socialism had 'utility for the breadth of people'. And the purpose of the analysis 'must be to further develop a consistent strategy for dealing with current and future changes in society, technology and the economy to the advantage of people of all classes and for the advancement of individual freedom'.

He stressed the need for unity of purpose. 'Unity is not an adornment. It is a vital instrument. It is not an afterthought. It is an essential. That unity does not require great sacrifice. No burying of principles, great or small. The demand for unity that I make ... is much more modest than that. It is to ensure that every word, every action, every statement and policy, everything we do is geared to victory.'

And a few days later Kinnock was given the kind of hero's welcome more usually accorded in victory. This was in the heart of Yorkshire's coalmining country at Barnsley, where he was a guest speaker at the centenary Yorkshire Miners' Gala. Also on the platform was NUM president Arthur Scargill, but it was Kinnock who won an ovation from the 30,000 strong crowd. He and Scargill had remained at odds since the 'lost year' of the miners' strike; now they were seen to shake hands curtly before heading a two-mile march through the town to a rally in Locke Park. They exchanged no further words or even glances, and Scargill's speech carried the kind of message which had distanced him from the Labour leader. He said that Labour could not afford to wait until the next election to help those in need. 'While we will do everything we can in Parliament, it will take the kind of extra-parliamentary activity that we sustained in the 1970s to oppose Tory government policies.'

The election-inquest meeting of Labour's NEC at the end of June was dominated by the need for a fundamental review of policy, although there was no decision about the form that review would take. A week later Kinnock repeated to a series of meetings at Westminster that Labour must shake off the shackles of outdated strategies. And he urged party organizers to think of voters as individuals rather than as blocks of trade unionists or members of other pressure groups. 'They have got to be told that socialism is the answer for them because socialism looks after the individual,' he said. Kinnock was aware that a good campaign would not be enough the next time round, if Labour was to be more than the natural party of opposition. What the party needed was a complete overhaul, a total reappraisal of its policies and beliefs on a scale never before considered. And it was Kinnock who set a two-year deadline for fundamental and far-reaching changes which he hoped would match Labour's policies with the needs of the electorate.

One of the key figures in the policy review was NUPE's Tom Sawyer, who had become chairman of the NEC's influential home policy committee before the general election. Sawyer, highly respected by Kinnock, was destined to play a major role in shaping the Labour Party of the future. It began, says Sawyer modestly, with himself and Adam Sharples, NUPE's head of research, 'knocking a few ideas about' as the basis of a plan of strategy from the 1987 defeat to a victory in 1992.

> We wrote a short paper, took it to Neil and he said it was a good idea. My job was to try and make sure it all worked. I didn't make policy, but I kept in touch with the key people – Whitty, Clarke, Mandelson, Hewitt – helping to resolve conflicts. It was a good team. They were all very talented people. If the policy review proved not to be good enough, then they weren't to blame.

By September, as a result of Sawyer's 'good idea', he, together with Neil Kinnock and Charles Clarke, Patricia Hewitt and Peter Mandelson, and working with NEC members, had set up seven policy groups, each with a convenor from both the Shadow Cabinet and the NEC. These groups had a brief to assess the policy issues and opportunities in the 1990s; make an assessment of the relevance and credibility of existing party policy matched against the need and concerns of groups of voters; and to recommend broad themes of political strategy as well as policy areas in which more detailed examination was required.

The immediate task was to propel Labour's vision towards the future rather than spending excessive time and energy in analysing past mistakes. In other words, Labour needed new policies and a new image. Central to the building of that new image was the shadow communications agency, led by Mandelson and another former advertising executive, Philip Gould. They worked alongside Larry Whitty, the party's general secretary, Patricia Hewitt, policy co-ordinator, and Kinnock's chief of staff Charles Clarke. But there was no question, insist Hughes and Wintour, of the party being hijacked by a veiled conspiracy of advertising executives and market researchers. 'The agency could not have carried the concept which lay behind the review unless it precisely fitted Neil Kinnock's personal leadership vision ...

Without Kinnock's active engagement, no project would long survive public scrutiny.'

Tom Sawyer describes their role as filling in the gaps left by the politicians who, he says kindly, 'are not very good at making policy. They are good at dealing with short term problems. They are the fire fighters on the front line, but they are not by training or experience strategic thinkers.' Apart from Neil Kinnock. Sawyer says that the Labour leader was exceptional in that respect. 'He had great qualities of strategic thinking. I would go as far as to use the word "visionary". I don't think he always communicated it effectively but he certainly had it. When you had the privilege of hearing him, you could see that he was a long way ahead of everyone around him.'

Kinnock, says Sawyer, is a man of high intellect with an eye for detail. 'He knows all the big issues, plus the long term perspective. He is an exceptional man in many ways.' One other attribute would also prove to be useful – as well as an eye for detail, Kinnock has a photographic memory. 'At least, that's what they say. I can certainly recall details like statements from meetings and references in books and papers long after I've heard or read material,' he says.

Kinnock's position in the review process was strengthened by the realization that Labour could not afford a fourth electoral defeat. Also, many members of the hard left who had been prominent during the past four years – among them Margaret Beckett and Michael Meacher – now joined the Kinnock camp. The policy review groups, with Kinnock's office co-ordinating the entire process, set about a task that would take at least two years, before the period of amendments and revisions began.

Meanwhile the Labour leader had a new Shadow Cabinet. The elections for the opposition front-bench posts early in July saw some of Labour's most senior politicians squeezed out, among them Giles Radice, Peter Shore, Peter Archer and Barry Jones. They – and Denis Healey who had decided not to stand – were seen as standing on the right of the party. In their place came members of the pro-Kinnock Tribune group – Frank Dobson, Robin Cook, Jack Straw, Gordon Brown, Jo Richardson – who represented the 'soft left'.

At the top of the poll was Kinnock's election campaign manager, Bryan Gould, followed by John Prescott and Michael Meacher, left-wingers, and Gerald Kaufman and John Smith from the right of the party. The new intake were described as the YAKS – young, able and Kinnockite. But they were not allowed to let power go to their heads, and it was the right-wingers who were given the top posts: Smith as Shadow Chancellor, Kaufman at Foreign Affairs, and deputy leader Hattersley, who became Shadow Home Secretary.

Light relief in the summer of election defeat came at a variety show organized by the Confederation of Health Service Employees when Kinnock put on a star performance as a comedian. The highlight of his turn on stage was a joke about a Common Market summit aimed at finding out whether Adam and Eve were French, German or British. Mimicking President Mitterand, Kinnock argued that as Adam and Eve were lovers and wore no clothes they must be French. Switching to heavy Teutonic tones he declared that as Adam and Eve were traditionally tall and blond they must be German. The punchline was made impersonating Mrs Thatcher: 'Two young people, obviously very little to wear, hardly anything to eat, nowhere to live, and they think they are in paradise – it must be Britain.'

In September the Kinnocks went on holiday to Corfu, and found themselves involved in the rescue of a group of holidaymakers from Nottinghamshire adrift at sea. The group were towed to safety by Neil and Glenys Kinnock when their outboard motor failed and water had started to lap over into their boat. 'It was great how they mucked in and helped us out,' one of the party told reporters. 'They threw us a line and towed us to a bay, and then helped pull the boat up onto the beach and bale out.' One of the group maintained that he would ever after vote Labour out of gratitude, and the incident inevitably gave rise to newspaper headlines about the rescue of 'floating voters'.

Back home at Labour's annual conference in Brighton at the end of September, Kinnock made it clear that the policy review would be the biggest shake-up of strategy for years, with a hint that the non-nuclear defence stance might be put to the test along with everything else. With the review process backed by delegates, Kinnock said that after losing three general elections, 'any serious political party which did not undertake the assessment, that did not undertake the review, and did not undertake the examination and do it honestly – that party would be betraying its principles, its policies and its people.'

He gave a clear warning to those on the left, and any party members attracting adverse publicity, that Labour would be judged on its public conduct over the next four years as much as on its policies and campaigns. But he also promised that in seeking change there would not be a 'bonfire' of everything that Labour stood for at the June election, nor would there be any pandering to 'yuppies'. (The 'yuppie' theme was taken up by Neil and Glenys Kinnock during their bill-topping act at the Red Review, one of the lighter moments of conference week. Their act included waving a Filofax and a portable phone, the props of the so-called yuppies whom Labour had been accused of trying to attract.)

But Labour did have to seek the votes of those who did not back them last time or the time before, and quoting the TGWU leader Ron Todd, Kinnock asked during his keynote speech: 'What do you say to a docker who earns 400 quid a week, owns his house, a new car, microwave and video, as well as a small place near Marbella? You do not say, Let me take you out of your misery, brother.'

It has been reported on many occasions that Kinnock the orator was at his sparkling best on a conference platform. It was only much later, after the 1992 election defeat, that he confessed: 'The only single reason why I'm relieved not to be party leader now is that I don't have to go through that hell of writing my speeches.' But surely there had been an element of fun, compared with the constraints of Prime Minister's question time? 'It was appalling. It was purgatory. They generally came out right in the end but fun it wasn't.'

At conference time, he says, he was faced with two frustrations.

> In a serious political party that was unanimously intent upon appealing to the nation and winning the election, putting a speech together would have been easy. But in the Labour Party, where that intensity of political purpose is not always evident, there was a hell of a lot that I had to do that I shouldn't have had to do. There had to be particular constructions of phrases and sentences and arguments that would maximise support for what I was trying to do, without giving the other side, as it were, ammunition. So there was a balance, a delicacy about the operation that was very trying. And the second thing was that there had to be a constant effort to invigorate and inspire. I find that quite easy if I've just got to get up and do it, but if you have to construct it beforehand at two o'clock in the morning in a dusty office, pacing round a desk ... well, there are other ways to enjoy your life.

While the 1987 conference overwhelmingly voted for the non-nuclear unilateral position to be maintained, commentators noted that Kinnock himself had steered clear of the word 'unilateral', and had pointed out that the review process was as applicable in the defence sphere as everywhere else. 'We will work to ensure that we have policies that are capable of dealing with the changed conditions of the 1990s, in a way that will enhance the prospect of removing reliance on nuclear weapons of any description.' Delegates at Brighton also backed Kinnock's plans for reforming the ways in which parliamentary candidates would be selected and reselected, opting for an electoral college system, seen as a half-way house to one member, one vote democracy.

When the new session of Parliament opened on 21 October, Kinnock used rugby terminology to warn that Labour would 'go in very hard and stay in pushing' against the Conservatives. Promising a lively term ahead, he foresaw trouble in the Government ranks: 'Mrs Thatcher's path is far from the triumphal progress she would like. Her arrogance which stems from that is causing a certain amount of resentment in the Conservative Party, too.'

Questioned for BBC news, he denied that Labour was too absorbed in its own policy review to be aware of problems facing the whole country. 'It would be a foolish and bereft Government that continually challenged the Opposition on what its alternatives were to their own policies.' It would not be credible for an opposition to have a complete and precise alternative to these policies so early on in a Parliament, said Kinnock. 'What we have to do is to try to block and stop and mitigate large amounts of what the Government is proposing.'

But Kinnock was not yet the spokesman for a united Labour Party, even if the majority of party members recognized that fundamental changes were necessary. MPs and others of the hard left persuasion, and notably the Campaign Group, organized their own conference at the end of October to debate the future of party policy. They were alarmed that the review process was abandoning Labour's traditional aims and values, with concern about the prospect of accepting privatization and share ownership as well as nuclear defence. In speeches by Eric Heffer, Tony Benn and Ken Livingstone – with the backing of Arthur Scargill – Kinnock's leadership came under repeated attack.

His regime was condemned as 'disciplinary' by Scargill, who maintained that the Labour leader had abandoned fundamental socialist principles. Heffer accused Kinnock of 'peddling second hand Thatcherism' and 'creating an SDP Mark II'. Livingstone asked how many of the defeats of the last ten years would have happened if Tony Benn had been elected Prime Minister back in 1976, and dismissing appeals not to indulge in personality politics he declared: 'Leadership at crucial times does matter.'

A challenge to the Kinnock and Hattersley 'dream ticket' partnership was beginning to build up. When John Prescott stated in December that he might have to oppose Hattersley on principle as deputy leader, Kinnock warned that such a move would be an 'inexcusable distraction' from the main business of fighting the poll tax (or community charge) – Mrs Thatcher's ill-considered replacement for the rating system – saving the health service and education, and saving the future for pensioners. 'In these circumstances it would be a distraction that simply will not be acceptable to the movement,' he said.

Kinnock's fear was well founded; the 'distraction' of the miners' strike had, in his eyes, done untold damage to Labour's credibility and to his own efforts at presenting a united front. Distractions of any kind only helped deflect his challenges to the Thatcher Government. One such challenge came at the end of the year when, in a row over funding for the health service, Kinnock told Thatcher: 'You are making a fool of yourself.'

The Government was resisting mounting pressure for a massive injection of cash into the NHS, and in what was described as the noisiest Commons confrontation for years, the Prime Minister stuck rigidly to her repeated assertions that no government had spent more on the NHS than hers. Kinnock said that 'the blood was showing through the bandages' of Government arguments about the quality of health care; and, as the Speaker struggled to maintain order in the debate, Kinnock told Thatcher: 'You are showing a complete determination not to respond to what the highest authorities and most expert opinions are calling the crisis in the health service.'

But as the year ended Kinnock was facing yet another crisis of his own, an attack on his position by a prominent trade unionist. David Warburton, the principal national officer of the GMB, Britain's second largest union, accused Kinnock of lethargy and of 'basking in the satisfaction of a new image'. Writing in the *Forward Labour* magazine, he said that since the general election Kinnock had made no major speech and taken no initiatives on a whole range of targets. 'The distance between the leadership and the rest of the movement is at best rather sad, even surprising. At worst it is demoralising.' But allies rushed to Kinnock's defence, concerned to avoid re-opening the wounds which had damaged the party after the previous two election defeats. Barry Jones, the former spokesman on Welsh affairs who had lost his Shadow Cabinet place in the summer, said that criticism of Kinnock was unjust and unreasonable. 'His achievements have been considerable, and Labour's prospects are the better for his 1987 actions and his consequential command of the party. The General Election campaign, the policy review, the emergence of sane and regular majorities on the NEC, and the spirited Commons opposition augur well for Labour in 1988.'

Certainly, by the beginning of the new year Labour's fortunes appeared to be in the ascendent. An opinion poll early in February put Labour just one point behind the Tories, the party's best position for a couple of years. Kinnock launched the first in a series of regional events under the title *Labour Listens*, which were designed to give rank and file supporters throughout the country the opportunity to present their own views and suggestions for the policy review process. These were large-venue, open-entry meetings, usually held during the day, midweek, at regional venues, to which Labour Party members were invited and given the opportunity to put their viewpoints to the politicians in the chair. Critics saw this as merely a public relations exercise to give the party a caring image, but they were intended seriously as part of the need to widen the debate about Labour's future.

As the Kinnocks prepared to fly to the Middle East for talks with President Mubarak of Egypt, the Labour leader stressed the need for self-discipline in his team if upward progress in the polls was to be sustained. Speaking on BBC Radio, he said:

> I think I am probably in the situation of a captain or a coach of a team who says to his players, we have got an important game and have got a really tough season ahead. I don't want anybody going out on Friday night on the pop, and if you do and you are not fully fit tomorrow morning when the whistle goes, then don't look for your name on the team list next year or next week.

He was aware of the possible challenge to the leadership from the left and commented: 'I think it is the sound from a grouping that's trying to mobilise a certain amount of distrust, and won't take up the challenges of policy review and of listening to people, because it wants its own way.' In one sense, Kinnock said, he would appreciate a leadership contest because 'temperamentally I like challenges. Set against that is the distraction for the party.'

But in March the distraction became a reality when Tony Benn officially launched his campaign to challenge for the leadership of the party, with Eric Heffer declaring that he would stand against Roy Hattersley as deputy. Kinnock's response was to label them as 'absurd' and uncaring about Labour's election prospects. With six months to go before voting at the annual conference, many in the party saw another futile period of time wasted. Kinnock insisted that he would not be taking time off from tackling the real issues of the moment – the health service and the poll tax – to run a leadership campaign.

And, as if to demonstrate that determination, in April he launched a new offensive against the community charge proposals. The poll tax, he said, was a tax on existing: 'If you live, you give, whether you can afford it or not.' He also attacked the Government's social security and housing benefit changes which would, he said, deprive millions in or near poverty already and thrust them further into the abyss.

The Government's persistence with proposals for the poll tax was having an effect on opinion polls which indicated that loyalty to Mrs Thatcher was crumbling away. Labour's one point lead over the Tories in April was not statistically significant, but Mrs Thatcher's own 'unpopularity' rating was now higher than Kinnock's. Even so, only 39 per cent of respondents in the Gallup poll saw Kinnock as a 'good' Labour leader, with 50 per cent dissatisfied.

And it appeared that Margaret Thatcher still had a psychological edge over Neil Kinnock. Her television interview performances were analysed by two specialists at York University, who claimed that she won sympathy by seeming to be excessively interrupted. Dr Peter Bull, who studied interviews with the two political leaders conducted by Sir Robin

Day, Jonathan Dimbleby, David Dimbleby and David Frost, found that there was no significant difference between the number of times that each was interrupted, but Mrs Thatcher showed skill at wrong-footing interviewers. 'While she gets interrupted just as much as Mr Kinnock, she makes a fuss about it, giving the impression that she is excessively interrupted and badly treated, which helps to win viewers' sympathy.'

The voters' sympathy, however, continued to ebb away from Mrs Thatcher, largely because of her intransigence over the poll tax. *A People's Petition Against the Community Charge*, launched by Kinnock, gathered 100,000 signatures in less than two months. But Kinnock seemed unable to capitalize on the Government's temporary unpopularity as he was constantly under personal attack – and not only on the political front. In April he and Glenys narrowly escaped injury when two men hurled a brick and a lump of concrete through the window of their house in South Ealing. The couple were showered with broken glass; Kinnock ran outside to chase after the attackers, but they got away. Glenys Kinnock had just returned home from a visit to famine-stricken Eritrea on behalf of War on Want. Stephen and Rachel were also at home at the time. Security at the house was tightened immediately afterwards.

That spring Kinnock was a guest on Radio Four's *Desert Island Discs*. His choice of records included, inevitably, a Welsh choir, some opera – for he and Glenys attend opera and theatre performances as often as time allows – and of course the Brahms Symphony No. 1. His favourite pop singer, Paul Simon, was there, so was John Lennon. But there were some unpredictable numbers, whose inclusions reflected the importance of his family life. One was a song by Dory Previn, 'Yada Yada La Scala', a song which Kinnock confessed he did not particularly like, but it was one which Glenys would choose during the quiet half-hour before guests arrived for supper on a Saturday night. ('The first to the tape deck determines what it will be. If it's me, it will be Beethoven or Haydn, perhaps Chopin.')

The other was singled out as the one which above all others he would take with him to the imaginary island – a recording of his daughter Rachel, at two-and-a-half years of age, singing *Horace the Horse*. Were it not for Horace, he says today, the top of his list would be probably a snatch of opera. 'It varies. "E Lucevan le Stella" from *Tosca* was a favourite for some time, so was "Di quella pira" (*Il Trovatore*). For about a year "The Romance" from Shostakovitch's *Gadfly Suite* was tops – it still is, in some ways. I play the Beethoven Violin Concerto, Bruch's Violin Concerto No. 1, and Bruckner's Symphony No. 4 – "*The Romantic*" – continually.'

The romantically inclined politician claimed he would be an unwilling castaway, too gregarious for island life. 'I can take a day, maybe a bit more, on my own.' Not that he would miss speaking. 'I have no passion for speaking,' he told interviewer Sue Lawley. 'I look forward to the day when I don't ever have to make another public speech.' And yet, Lawley tackled him, he had a reputation for speaking excessively, for being a 'windbag'. That accusation, said Kinnock, 'comes from people who have never been confronted with the requirement to make a real speech in their life'.

He was expected 'to really take issues head on, and to have nothing but words and commitment to try and convince others'. The other often-used description of Kinnock, said Lawley, was that he was ruthless. 'Only to the extent that there are objectives that need to be achieved, to make our country more just and more productive.' And did he not need a great degree of patience, when his tendency would be to get angry and exasperated? 'The problem with this job is that I have had to exercise a degree of patience that I have never had to exercise in my life before. The patience is needed in order to ensure that when a purpose is set, it is actually achieved.'

His job was not a series of 'death and glory rides', much as the press would like to believe. 'Life to them is a series of gunfights at the OK Corral. But life isn't like that.' His objectives were set patiently, and prudently, rather than 'drawing my sword and rushing at it, which is what, temperamentally, I would rather do'. Lawley reminded Kinnock that he once said he would only be happy as leader of the Labour Party when he saw the furniture van moving into Downing Street. Did he think that would ever happen? 'Oh, very definitely, for an assortment of reasons. It will happen.' And will you be able to bear it if it never happens, Lawley asked. Kinnock replied: 'I don't think that the possibility arises.'

But by early summer in 1988, that ambition was looking remote. Labour's brief and tentative ascent in the opinion polls dropped away alarmingly to become a ten-point deficit, and it became clear that the 'distraction' of the leadership challenge was taking its toll on Kinnock personally. As he had feared, much time and energy had to be spent in deflecting criticism from within his own party, and that criticism mounted when he appeared to be moving away from a unilateral position on nuclear disarmament to one of multilateralism – and then back again. This led to the resignation of Denzil Davies as Shadow Defence Secretary, who revealed his decision to the Press Association before he told his own leader.

'I am fed up with being humiliated by Mr Kinnock,' Davies said. 'He never consults me on anything. He goes on TV and talks about defence, but he never talks to his defence spokesman. I do not want to be defence spokesman any longer because he is clearly his own spokesman.' Davies also accused Kinnock of ignoring the policy review body. Much of the trouble lay in Kinnock's declaration on a BBC TV interview that: 'There is no need now for a something for nothing unilateralism. The idea that there is a something for nothing thrust that can be made is redundant.'

Few were clear about what these words meant exactly; most saw them as an attempt to modify if not change a policy which until then had been wholeheartedly backed by the Labour movement. Davies' resignation was followed by further attacks from the left. As Hughes and Wintour state, in *Labour Rebuilt*: 'The clouds of confusion were rolling in over an already morose and ill-disciplined parliamentary party.' They describe how the harder Kinnock tried to stay on top of the situation, the faster he sank down. Though the timing was wrong for signalling a defence shift, retracting earlier statements weakened Kinnock's authority, while any sign of backing down would be viewed as weakness.

That was exactly what happened after an on-the-record lunch with journalists from *The Independent*. Kinnock, in a poor temper and suffering with toothache, according to Hughes and Wintour was 'a tired man involved in a disjointed discussion with mostly antagonistic journalists'. The paper reported that the Labour leader had indeed retracted the earlier suggestion of a shift in defence policy. Kinnock was forced on to the defensive himself: he accused cynics on the left of trying to undermine progress, and refuted accusations that he was attempting to steamroller through policy changes.

The review process was the widest consultation in the history of the party, he insisted. By now there were reports that Kinnock was suffering from depression, that he was on the brink of resigning over the furore caused by his defence remarks, that he was temperamentally unreliable, that he might be replaced as leader, not by Tony Benn but by John Smith. They were all rumours of the type rife at Westminster every session. But commentators at the time saw the defence issue in particular as crystallizing the unpredictability which some members of the PLP found in Kinnock. Others, expecting a degree of camaraderie from their leader, complained that he had become remote and inaccessible.

One other argument levelled against Kinnock was his supposed intellectual inadequacy. This charge came from an Oxford academic who based his view on the undisputed fact that Kinnock did not benefit from an Oxbridge education. Further, he maintained that Labour's overall lack of success in recent years could be attributed to the desertion of the Oxbridge intelligentsia to the Social Democrats. Defending Kinnock, Ian Aitken in *The Guardian* pointed out that as a piece of reasoning this suffered from the self-evident truth that the SDP had hardly prospered for all its Oxbridge support.

'But the mere fact that some people can advance the argument in these terms probably accounts for the reluctance of many of Mr Kinnock's critics to come into the open: to repeat this sort of thing would seem to raise doubts about the very idea of a working class lad becoming leader of the people's party.' Aitken went on to say that critics who accused Kinnock of authoritarianism might be on stronger ground. There was something in Kinnock's manner which invited the feeling that he was a

> tough guy spoiling for a fight. Yet I strongly suspect that, far from coming naturally, this is a manner which Mr Kinnock has deliberately developed in the effort to present himself as a strong and decisive leader.
>
> All that strutting and shouting is a natural response to the criticisms aimed at the public image of his predecessor, Michael Foot. If this is so, it is something he should put right as quickly as he can. The real Neil Kinnock is a genuinely funny man, capable of shrivelling his opponents with wit rather than beating them into the ground with sheer volume.

As for the argument that he had cut himself off from former colleagues on the left, said Aitken, 'it would be easier to take this seriously if those colleagues had shown equal willingness to let bygones be bygones.'

If Kinnock had reacted to the strain caused by the events of the recent months, it would have been little wonder. His single-minded determination was to make Labour an electable party, and history had proved that any hint of disharmony was bound to damage that chance. He was already convinced privately that the defence policy had to be changed, while recognizing that the timing for such a move was crucial: hence his occasional displays of inconsistency.

Kinnock denies that he was ever depressed. Looking back on that period, he says that he became 'furious' with the fact that a lot of people appeared to be giving attention to issues which were not crucial to a future Labour victory. 'It was mainly to do with a lack of confidence in the review process. And there was a great focus on my performance.' He told David Dimbleby in a BBC TV interview that he had never considered standing down as leader.

> I had the belief that my replacement with anyone else would not have made an improvement, and that no one could do better. And I wasn't being arrogant in that. I don't think you would have found a combination that was sufficiently determined, willing to go into fine detail, expend the time and detail on endless discussions, and someone who could get up and light the Labour Party's touch paper when the occasion demanded.

One such occasion came at the end of June when Kinnock addressed the National Union of Mineworkers' conference in Great Yarmouth, a 'make or break' speech after weeks of confusion and doubt. Back on form, he told an enthusiastic crowd that socialist principles were not being abandoned in the review process. 'Reviewing is not shaping policy to suit the flavour of the day. It is relating policy to the facts of life. It isn't conforming to the latest opinion poll. It's recognizing the result of the only polls that count – elections.'

Labour, he said, would not 'cut and run' to some muddled middle ground; neither would it 'chase off to some ultra-Leftist Disneyland where insurrection and general strikes are supposed to bring capitalism crashing to the ground'. Addressing the NUM – who were mostly hostile to him – in this way was seen as a clear demonstration that Kinnock was strengthening his command of the Labour Party.

As a platform, such conferences suited Kinnock's style, of course. There remained criticism of his performances in the Commons. Political correspondent Phil Murphy wrote in the *Yorkshire Post* that faced with Mrs Thatcher Kinnock often proved frail.

> Too often ... his instincts in selecting a topic with which to harry the Prime Minister in their twice weekly Commons clashes have been awry. For a man compared throughout his development with the great Nye Bevan – one of the most consummate orators ever to grace the chamber – Mr Kinnock has been a disappointment.

It must have been a relief for Kinnock to leave behind domestic controversy when he and Glenys left for a ten-day tour of southern African states. He stressed throughout the tour his party's support for all-out economic sanctions against South Africa, attacking the white regime there for continuing to occupy Namibia, which Pretoria ruled in defiance of the United Nations. There was an embarrassing incident during the trip when the Kinnocks, travelling on a Zimbabwe Air Force plane to meet President Robert Mugabe, landed at an airstrip in the middle of a terrorist zone. Instead of the official welcoming party – who were waiting for them some twenty miles away – they were met by soldiers who held them at gunpoint for more than an hour.

Returning to Westminster, he put on one of his most effective performances in the Commons when he asked the Prime Minister if she was aware that since 1981 nearly 700,000 children in the front-line states had died and millions more suffered from hunger because of the actions by South Africa. 'Against that background can I ask the Prime Minister to increase support for the front-line states and also ensure that this is reinforced by using strong sanctions against South Africa?' Kinnock was cheered by colleagues. There had been few cheers during that session, and he was more than usually glad to wind down when the summer recess began. The Kinnocks – with Glenys' brother Colin, his wife Barbara and their children – escaped for a holiday in Portugal.

8   Meet the Challenge, Make the Change

There had never really been any doubt that Kinnock would win the 1988 leadership battle with Tony Benn – and win it comfortably. But the challenge had come not just to him but to his 'dream ticket' partner Hattersley who faced opposition not only from Benn's acolyte Eric Heffer, but also from John Prescott, MP for Hull East, whose bid had resurfaced at Easter. Prescott's motive was a desire to change the role of deputy leader of the Labour Party into a more campaigning post, working beyond Parliament to drum up support for a more substantial party membership.

The idea had some merit, and Prescott had equally admirable qualifications for the task, but Kinnock wanted no challenge at all to the leadership team. There was nothing sentimental in his defence of Hattersley. The two men were acknowledged to be utterly unalike. It was said that Hattersley viewed Kinnock as too brash, too matey, too fond of joking and clowning; that Kinnock saw Hattersley's intellectualism as slightly elitist. In fact, Kinnock says that he admired the self-confidence which Hattersley's 'intellectualism' gave him, 'and he could also be very funny because of it'.

Hughes and Wintour say that the two were, on a personal level, chemically incompatible: 'poured into the same test-tube and vigorously shaken, they would almost certainly detonate.' They also maintain that although Hattersley came to think that Kinnock was the better man for the particular task of reconstruction which confronted the party, he always thought he would have made a better Prime Minister.

> But he also knew throughout that he would never win the political battles necessary to win the war.
> In other words, Roy Hattersley took the view that, as Labour leader, he would probably never get to Number 10 Downing Street – whereas Neil Kinnock, for all his faults, very likely might.

Consequently Hattersley was utterly loyal to Kinnock publicly, as well as privately supportive, and certainly loyal to the cause of party unity. And the leader and his deputy had grown closer over the years as far as political principles were concerned, even if their respective pedigrees were from the left and right. The combination suited Kinnock, and he was keen to see that the stability at the top was not rocked to cause further turbulence elsewhere in the party.

Whatever the contemporary commentators might have surmised, after the election defeat in 1992 which led to the resignation of the leadership team, Kinnock spoke of Hattersley with praise and warmth. 'I have always admired his talents. He is enormously creative. But over those years he was absolutely loyal beyond the call of duty. It would have been so understandable for him to have been resentful, and detached, but he wasn't. He was the best deputy leader anybody could have hoped for. If you wanted anything at all, you only had to ask.'

One instance, Kinnock recalls, was when he had been trying for more than a year to get a statement of the party's beliefs written:

A couple of people had had a stab at it, and in the end I asked Roy. Within a fortnight he handed it in. We went through it, edited it, but it was Roy's document. But it wasn't just the fact that it was quality and that it had real idealism in it – for Roy is more of an idealist than I am – but he did it quickly, the job was done. I like people who deliver, and Roy always did.

Kinnock added: 'What Roy and I discovered over those years was the degree of agreement.' Charles Clarke had once said to him:

Neil, if you do ever become Prime Minister, you'll be the first Labour prime minister in history to have a deputy on whom you could absolutely depend. If you fell under a bus, he could run the country for you. And you're not going to have to select a government on the basis of 'one from the right, one from the left' simply because there's a different chemistry now, and Hattersley is part of that.

Says Kinnock of Hattersley: 'If you cut him open you would find the words "Labour Party" running right down the middle.'

The leadership election of 1988 was held at a special session of the electoral college before the main business of the annual conference began on the Monday morning in Blackpool. Constituencies had been 'advised' to ballot all their members, although they were not bound to do so. Benn and Heffer knew that where the choice was restricted to constituency party management committees, which tended to be strongholds of hard left activists, they would stand more chance of success.

As it turned out, just over 50 per cent of the constituencies who took part in the vote did hold ballots, but the result of the election was an overwhelming vote of confidence for both Kinnock and Hattersley which surprised supporters and critics alike. Kinnock won 88.6 per cent of the electoral college, and Benn only 11.4 per cent. In the contest for deputy leader, Hattersley took 66.8 per cent of the total to Prescott's 23.7, with Heffer taking only 9.5 per cent overall.

The result was a humiliating defeat for the left and a significant boost for the leadership – who had never wanted the contest in the first place. Tony Benn, in his diary, called the result 'appalling'. He wrote: 'I did my best to look impassive and cheerful on the platform. I just touched Neil Kinnock on the shoulder and smiled.' Finding the scale of defeat difficult to accept, he told a fringe meeting that he and Heffer actually had more support in the party than the voting figures suggested, and vowed that their fight would go on.

John Prescott was more gracious in defeat, but he could afford to be so: many of the proposals made by his campaign team were accepted, including a national membership list, and greater participation in local Labour parties. He promised: 'Now that the Labour movement has reached its decision, I will continue to devote all my efforts to helping Labour win the next election and make Neil Kinnock the next prime minister.' He declared that he would not challenge again for the post of deputy leader. In return, he was thanked for his 'honourable and clean campaign' by Kinnock's campaign manager Robin Cook who declared: 'I personally will be supporting him in his return to the Shadow Cabinet.'

Tony Benn, however, must have known that he had lost his last possible bid for power. When Kinnock made his keynote speech, he decided that he would stand during the traditional ovation: 'He had beaten me and that was the end of that. The first half of his speech was an attack on Thatcher and the second half was a vigorous defence of market forces. It just prepared the way for running the market economy better and for dropping our defence policy in the interest of "electability".'

He was alone in being so publicly dismissive. Virtually everyone else in Blackpool that week agreed that Kinnock's speech was one of his best as party leader. (He was widely popular in the seaside resort. Even a local police chief, whose responsibilities included security during political conferences, proved to be a fan. Kinnock, he said, was a good chap who always had some cans of lager for the team who made the safety searches of his hotel room!) Once again, the conference platform proved to be his ideal stage, and both confidence and authority were restored with the distracting leadership race now out of the way.

What is more, Kinnock made sure that such contests would not be so easy to stage against any leader in the future. A rule change passed that week meant that from now on any challenge to the leadership had to be backed by 20 per cent of the parliamentary party, rather than the previous 5 per cent. Now Kinnock told delegates firmly – and in spite of suffering with a sore throat – that Labour shared the principles and values of enough people in Britain to get back into power. The Tory market system could not produce either economic efficiency or social justice, he said. Labour would make a mixed economy work, combining public and private sectors.

> The day may come when this conference, this movement, is faced with a choice of socialist economies. The debate will be fascinating as the party conference chooses between the two but until that day comes when the choice of socialist economies is actually presented, actually in existence, the fact is that the kind of economy that we'll be faced with when we win the election will be a market economy. That's what we have to deal with and we will have to make it work better than the Tories do.

But the cheers were loudest for Kinnock's cutting dismissal of Mrs Thatcher and all that she stood for, after her remarks in a magazine interview:

> There is no such thing as society, she says. No obligation to the community.
>   No sense of solidarity.
>   No principles of sharing or caring.
>   'No such thing as society.'
>   No sisterhood, no brotherhood.
>   No neighbourhood.
>   No honouring other people's mothers and fathers.
>   No succouring other people's little children.
>   'No such thing as society.'
>   No number other than one.
>   No person other than me.
>   No time other than now.
>   No such thing as society, just 'me' and 'now'.
>   That is Margaret Thatcher's society.
>   I tell you, you cannot run a country on the basis of 'me' and 'now'.

Kinnock recalls that there were tears running down faces in the hall after he spoke. Peter Kellner, who wrote an introduction to a book of Kinnock's speeches, believes this was one of his most effective ever, a daring combination of repetition and mockery. 'That sequence, constructed almost as blank verse, was carefully written: it relied for its effect on precise rhythms.'

There were other triumphs for Kinnock that week. He won a clear endorsement of the party's broad economic strategy; a commitment to developing a detailed investment plan, encouraging modern innovative technology, controlling transnational companies, as well as restoring British Telecom to public ownership. But nationalization was no longer seen as the only model, and it was the vision of a mixed economy which roused the ire of the left. They put forward two motions – one calling for large scale renationalization of privatised industries, the other for the nationalization of banks and financial institutions. Both were defeated on a show of hands.

But it was not a totally victorious conference for Kinnock. On the evening following Kinnock's own speech, the TGWU chief Ron Todd warned a fringe meeting against the 'modernizers' in the movement who were 'all sharp suits and cordless telephones, clipboards and scientific samples'. They should not attempt to reform the basic values of the party, he said, and insisted that his union – Britain's biggest – would not stand by and watch policies such as unilateral nuclear disarmament thrown away.

And so it proved when defence was debated and delegates voted for a commitment by a future Labour Government to scrap all nuclear weapons quickly rather than bargain for trade-offs with other nations under bilateral or multilateral agreements. Observers reported that Kinnock sat 'glum-faced' on the platform, and he later insisted that: 'Today's votes were not conclusive. The policy review goes on ... It is our duty to secure a policy for defence and nuclear disarmament that can secure the support of the people of our country.'

One of his strongest allies, John Edmonds, general secretary of the General and Municipal Workers, told delegates:

> The electorate can see that there isn't much comfort in living in a non-nuclear Britain if they are surrounded by a Europe which is bristling with nuclear weapons. Some isolated gesture to disarm may be called noble ... but it is not useful when we can win so many more advantages and so much more disarmament simply by negotiation.

In radio and TV interviews after the closing debates, Kinnock admitted that the objective of projecting and promoting the Labour Party had been frustrated by the week's events. 'Anybody who is serious in the attempts they make to help their fellow men and women has just got to have that small requirement – self-discipline to shut up when he should shut up ... We are quite good at inflicting damage on ourselves. That, classically and tragically, has been the Labour Party.'

But while left-wingers were outraged at Kinnock's hint that the defence vote would not be binding, others thought that another year might make all the difference to the weight of opinion within the party. After Blackpool, Kinnock had his mandate for change: as Hughes and

Wintour saw it: ' ... The post election period of struggling for the party's soul – expressed as a contest for power among its leading individuals – was settled. Kinnock emerged incontestably sovereign.'

But although Kinnock was in firmer control of his own troops, he was no nearer to winning the crucial battle. Labour performed badly in two by-elections: at Govan, where they lost a 20,000 majority to the Scottish Nationalists, and at Epping, where they were beaten into third place behind the SDP. There were suggestions that Labour should make a deal with the Social Democrats in order to defeat Mrs Thatcher at the next general election but Kinnock's response to these was uncompromising.

'There is only one way to resolve the dilemma and defeat the Tories, and that is to fight in our own right, and to fight every seat everywhere for Labour votes.' Opinion polls gave no comfort, either. Just before Christmas Kinnock's personal rating, according to a Gallup poll, was at its lowest for five years, and the Tory Party was leading Labour by eleven points. This was demoralizing as the Opposition should have been riding high at the time, with Government popularity affected by rising inflation and the poll tax.

Then two of Kinnock's front-bench team, Clare Short and Andrew Bennett, resigned so that they could be free to vote against the Government's strengthening of the Prevention of Terrorism Act, when Labour MPs had been instructed to abstain. Hughes and Wintour maintain that as Kinnock left Westminster for the Christmas break, some of his closest staff feared once again that he might quit. He had appeared acutely depressed, but his temperament was notoriously volatile rising to great highs and then sinking low. Hughes and Wintour wrote: 'Kinnock's character was always self-fuelling. He could be dragged back by his own turbulence, or ride on his own adrenalin.'

Kinnock later told Fiona Millar of the *Daily Express* that thoughts of resigning had never crossed his mind: 'It's not in my temperament to give in. There isn't a surrender corpuscle in me. It's that, and a sense of humour, that keeps me going.' Millar reported that, over the years, 'Kinnock-watchers' had been convinced that a lack of confidence stopped him from doing the job as well as he might. There was a popular view, she wrote, that Kinnock tried too hard to be statesmanlike and heavyweight, boring many of his listeners and supporters in the process.

Julia Langdon, one of Britain's foremost political correspondents and a friend of the Kinnock family, believes that the mantle of leader had affected Neil Kinnock's personality. 'When he became leader, he was determined that he was not going to let the party down, and that he was not going to be patronised, not going to be laughed at,' she says. But in the event he lost touch with the Commons where he had been so popular until his election as leader. 'He threw away the common touch which made him so popular, in order to be taken seriously. He made himself be something other than he was. The real Neil Kinnock was jokey, jovial.'

Kinnock admitted at the time that his own image was not a very good one. 'I don't want to chatter on about how I feel personally,' he told Fiona Millar. 'Taking time off to be hurt is simply a luxury that, for a politician, can't be afforded.' He said that it was no more than he expected: 'Dora Gaitskell, Hugh's widow, said to me very early on, "You can expect a lot of attacks from the snobs". I did and I haven't been let down. It's part and parcel of being Labour leader.'

Charles Clarke, Kinnock's former chief of staff, denies emphatically that there was any possibility of Kinnock considering resignation at the time. Nor was he depressed: 'That suggests clinical connotations. He was very frustrated about the task that was ahead, and what was involved in bringing about the necessary changes.' Clarke says that whatever others might believe, Kinnock was not subject to emotional swings between high and low. 'What is striking about him is quite the contrary. He showed tremendous discipline all the time. People say that he is volatile but I don't think that is right. He is a very passionate man, and people may confuse that with volatility.'

If the Labour Party was going through a period of soul-searching over its leadership, then the leader himself had just cause to be equally irritated. As a leading article in *The Guardian* pointed out,

> a young, untried chap from Bedwellty inherited a party in an advanced state of nervous breakdown: broken morale, broken organisation, broken old policies. People who say he's had no experience of government should examine his six year governance of Walworth Road. He is a formidable in-fighter. The electoral spectre of the Left is washed away ... The front bench in the House is stuffed with bright, new debating talent. The policy cupboard is in the final throes of spring cleaning. Somebody (as even Lord James Callaghan may quietly admit) had to tackle the party head on after the collapse of the ancien regime. It's hard to think that anyone could have done it more diligently, more rigorously than Neil Kinnock.

Looking back on that period, Kinnock dismisses as nonsense his supposed 'depression'. 'My feeling in 1988 was one of frustration that you could push and shove as hard as you liked but we were not appearing to make much progress in politics generally or in terms of understanding in the party.' The chitchat had begun during the summer when people were gossiping over their gin and tonics, and there were a couple of newspapers 'who like that kind of copy written for them'.

'All this "depression" stuff emanates from just one or two journalists and one or two politicians who decided that because I wasn't singing and dancing, I must be going through a mid life crisis, which actually wasn't what was happening at all.' The tabloids saw the Christmas break as giving Kinnock the physical and mental respite to recharge his batteries. They went into some detail about how he relaxed, going to see some comedy at the theatre, decorating Rachel's bedroom at home.

'That fits in with the mould that they made,' he says, 'that Kinnock went into a terrible manic depression, he carried around this immense weight of troubles, that eventually he found the catharsis in decorating his daughter's bedroom – it is nonsense. If that's the mould that you have made, then everything has got to fit into it, including the conclusion: when does Kinnock come out of it? It's part of the mythology.' The same papers – and others – noted that, after Christmas, Kinnock returned to the Commons looking more self-confident and jocular, and his performances at Prime Minister's question time were said to have improved.

Kinnock's image had always been keenly scrutinized. In the early days of his leadership, critics maintained that he was too easy-going, too fond of a joke. Tom Sawyer says that he was occasionally guilty of silly behaviour, such as the time he was filmed walking through the wards of an empty hospital for a news item about hospital closures, and was seen to be laughing. 'It looked really out of place,' says Sawyer.

Kinnock heard what the critics said, and it may well be that during 1987 and 1988 he made such attempts to become the serious statesman that the appealing, lighter side of his personality was hidden. Certainly after the election defeat of 1987 he was accused of becoming withdrawn and remote.

Now some believed that he had taken the advice of columnists such as Stephen Fry, who wrote in the *Listener* that Kinnock should try to deflate his adversary Thatcher with mockery. She could be most wounded by humour, 'however monstrous Mr Kinnock may find the Prime Minister'. Kinnock's questions became shorter, wittier, and more authoritative. It was proof, wrote Hughes and Wintour, that the Commons was no sideshow. 'Such apparently small things as a brief exchange of maybe 100 or 200 words twice a week could alter the perception of a whole party, and even the national political mood.'

But there was little occasion for joviality as the crucial issue of defence loomed once again, and more particularly, what a future Labour Government would do about nuclear weapons. Having hedged and fudged over this for so long, Kinnock was about to find the timing right at last to clarify publicly what he believed. Activists in the Labour Party – among them Ron Todd of the TGWU – were still strongly unilateralist, and even though their majority had been reduced at the 1988 conference, they had still won the vote.

Kinnock himself had been one of the most passionate opponents of nuclear weapons for all of his political life so far. He had condemned his hero Bevan for advocating multilateralism, and one newspaper had claimed that he had even insisted that Glenys should walk out on him if he ever changed his own view. But Glenys Kinnock's own political interests and leanings had always been confined to her own activity, whatever the tabloid press tried to imply.

The couple are friends, soul mates and totally loyal to one another, but while Neil Kinnock makes no secret of his respect for his wife's political judgement, according to a profile in *The Observer*, 'he acts on it rather less often than is sometimes assumed'. The paper quoted a friend who said: 'He rails against her advice, because he knows she's always right.' While other politicians consulted their wives, it was usually in a 'What do you think, my dear?' capacity; Neil and Glenys Kinnock represented the first generation of political marriages whose partnership began and continued as that of equals.

It simply happened that about the same time the Kinnocks both began to review their beliefs on unilateralism. They were influenced, as were a great many people of all political shades, by the meeting between President Reagan and President Gorbachev at Reykjavik in October 1986 which heralded the first steps towards a global reduction of nuclear arms. According to Hughes and Wintour, Kinnock was enthralled and invigorated by the new era of disarmament Gorbachev offered. 'The summit opened up possibilities which would have seemed unimaginable only a year or two before.'

But the general election of 1987 illustrated Kinnock's difficulty: to demonstrate a change of heart at such a crucial time would have divided the party irrevocably; to go to the polls with a policy which did not reflect any substantial public support invited the inevitable consequence. Looking back on this period years later, Kinnock was to quote the economist Keynes: 'When I discover that I have been in error, I change my mind – what do you do?'

The time had arrived to make public that change of mind. There had been no discussion of defence during the first year of the policy review, as world events were changing the picture too rapidly. But Gerald Kaufman, the foreign affairs spokesman, had been working quietly behind the scenes, talking to political leaders in other countries, and assessing studies of public attitudes.

At the beginning of February 1989 Kaufman flew to Moscow, accompanied by Ron Todd, the arch-unilateralist member of the defence group on the policy review, whom Kinnock nevertheless wanted to be involved. Hughes and Wintour, who give a fascinating and detailed account of the whole defence episode in *Labour Rebuilt*, describe how

Kaufman 'buried Labour's unilateralism a few yards from Lenin's tomb'. The Russians insisted that they saw the next stage of disarmament 'as a process which should involve all five nuclear weapons states. France and China, as well as the USSR, the US and Britain, should be negotiating to rid the world of nuclear weapons by the year 2000'.

As a result of his trip Kaufman drafted a long statement for submission to the NEC. He stressed that the 'old Cold War thinking was now out of date. There was both a political and economic need for Russia to seek disarmament.' Kaufman, say Hughes and Wintour, tried to isolate Mrs Thatcher 'by showing the extent to which she alone in Europe, by continuing to argue that nuclear weapons should remain indefinitely in Europe, had failed to grasp the scale of change'.

While Kaufman was still busy putting his ideas down on paper, Kinnock went on television to announce that Labour would engage in multilateral disarmament talks with Russia and the US. He told ITV's *This Week* that as the world situation had radically changed, his views would not come as any surprise. 'The argument used to be that in pursuit of that objective (disarmament) you can only turn the key by the instance of disarmament undertaken by one individual nation regardless of whatever else happened. We are no longer in that situation because the change is well under way.'

His message inevitably angered the Labour left: it was, said one MP from the traditional left, 'a total sellout of Labour Party policy'. But Kinnock felt he was now fighting on safe territory and he responded at once, saying that it would be both foolish and stupid not to take account of the improvement in East-West relations.

'If the environment in which we are trying to make changes has itself changed, it would be stupid not to recognise the implications. The whole argument of the manifesto is to try to secure the greatest possible progress towards disarmament. No one is going to inflict 1,000 million Chernobyls on Europe.' Kinnock found a substantial ally in his predecessor, Michael Foot, a prominent anti-nuclear campaigner. 'I think it will be carried at the next conference, and people will see Neil Kinnock is right to go about it in this way. I think the vast majority of CND supporters will take the same view,' he said. The former chairman of CND, Joan Ruddock, now an MP and Labour spokesman on transport, refused to be drawn, and said that she would wait for the outcome of the policy review before making her views known.

Kinnock had yet to steer Kaufman's proposals through the NEC. But he was now so confident that the timing was right that he was able to make his views known with the utmost clarity. Until then, he had spent his time edging away from a policy in which he no longer wholly believed, an exercise which, he later admitted, demanded that 'you give very long answers and try to get round it'. Now, at a meeting in May, he told the members of the NEC:

> Many in this room have protested and marched in support of nuclear disarmament. I have done that. But I have done something else: I have gone to the White House, the Kremlin, the Elysée, and argued the line for unilateral nuclear disarmament. I knew they would disagree with the policy. But above that, they were totally uncomprehending that we should want to get rid of nuclear missile systems without getting elimination of nuclear weapons on other sides too – without getting anything for it in return. I argued for the policy because of the integrity of the objective of eliminating nuclear weapons. But I have to tell you that I am not going to make that tactical argument for the unilateral abandonment of nuclear weapons without getting anything in return ever again.

Kinnock said that he was aware some people were saying that they would not give up what they had thought to be right for the past thirty years, that they would not 'stand on their heads', and that they had to be true to themselves.

> I hear those things that people say in their sincerity. And I tell them now with equal sincerity, I'm not asking anyone to 'stand on their head'. I am asking everyone to stand up and face the future. I'm not asking anyone to give up what they have thought was right for the past 30 years. I am asking them to do what is right for the next 30 years. I'm not asking anyone not to be 'true to themselves'. I am saying that in the course of being true to yourself, be careful, be sure, that you are not being untrue to others.

It was a very powerful speech. Tom Sawyer, one of Kinnock's closest allies on the NEC, said that the leader's argument epitomized the problem: 'It was a policy which nobody else wanted, and Kinnock realised that he couldn't sell it to any other country. It might have been a nice thing to dream about, a good thing in a good world, but he couldn't sell it. And that had a big impact on him. He is a very practical man. When something needs doing he likes to get it done.'

Sawyer had been forced to vote against the proposals because of the unilateralist stance of his union, NUPE, but his members were shortly to vote in favour of the new options. He believes that Kinnock went about the process in the right way. 'The world was changing and he moved with the tide of world changes. But it was a change he had to make personally of mammoth proportions. He had to convince the party why change was needed and why he had changed.'

The NEC approved the switch by seventeen votes to eight. Most of those present applauded the leader's speech, say Hughes and Wintour.

'For the first time, they genuinely felt that Kinnock was not making the shift out of a cynical need to grab votes, but out of a real belief that the world had changed and that his former view was no longer tenable.' The policy endorsed would mean four moves to be taken on the first day of a Labour Government: the adoption of no-first-use of nuclear weapons until Britain was rid of that capability; an end to testing British nuclear devices; cancelling the fourth Trident submarine (in the knowledge that the first three would already be built or under construction by then); and cancelling increases in the number of nuclear warheads. US bases would remain on British soil for the time being, although the ultimate aim was a nuclear free country, indeed, a nuclear free planet.

The decision presented political correspondents with a key question for Kinnock: would he press the nuclear button in retaliation against a first strike on Britain? Kaufman gave the response: 'The question you have put is a question that no responsible Government would answer, since the answer of a responsible Government to that question would assist a potential adversary. It is a trap question and I am not going to fall into the trap.'

Kinnock himself later adopted the same line:

> We will negotiate with Trident and with the policy line that comes with all that operational weaponry, the policy line that never says yes or no to the question, will you press the nuclear button. That is the combination of nuclear weaponry and the doctrine of uncertainty that we shall inherit. And it is that combination, the whole package, that we shall use in negotiations to secure nuclear disarmament by ourselves and by others.

In October of that year, 1989, the new defence policy was accepted at Labour's annual conference, the culmination of what many saw as Kinnock's biggest U-turn. In interviews over the years since then he has repeated his conviction that to lead the party through the period of one election with a policy of which he personally disapproved was the only possible course. To push for change before the time was right would have caused schism in the party. 'The important thing to do is to announce clearly that a new course of action is being taken.' The public could accept changes of direction, 'But of course it depends how frequently you repeat U-turns', he later told a television discussion programme.

> If you do two U-turns, I suppose that's going in a circle and that's when things start to get difficult. The inconstancy comes by breaking away from policy and adopting a new policy, a clean break; the general public say, OK, we all make mistakes, but don't try and convince us that this is an absolutely consistent line with what went before, because we know better.

Kinnock's significant U-turn did his image more good than harm. Combined with his revived confidence and shorter, more direct speeches in the Commons, it helped his personal ratings and gave Labour a boost in the opinion polls. When Mrs Thatcher celebrated her tenth anniversary in power, her popularity was in sharp decline – and her relations with the Labour leader were at a low point, too. 'I've always been more than ready to acknowledge the fact that Mrs Thatcher secured a major achievement by becoming the first woman party leader and woman PM in Britain,' Kinnock told the *Daily Express*.

> But that contrasts with my deep concern about the fact that great opportunities coming from our oil revenue have been wasted, and in these ten years the Government has tried to run the country in the belief that the market system can best do things which market forces were not meant to do. The result is a country much more divided, more congested and dangerous than it needs to be, and in deep deficit.

The economic strategy emerging from Labour's policy review revealed how Kinnock hoped to exploit the market and make it work. In a series of speeches he explained about working with market mechanisms, intervening in the market, compensating for its failures and making it work better so that private companies and enterprises could compete more successfully to secure Britain's economic health and wealth. He also stressed that greater efficiency required greater economic and social fairness, which were interdependent and not contradictory concepts. And he argued that the impact of new technology and the changing demographic structure of Britain gave a new urgency to the expansion of equal opportunities at work.

The policy review documents, the product of eighteen months work, were published in May 1989 under the title, *Meet the Challenge, Make the Change*. The programme was hailed as probably the most comprehensive set of proposals ever assembled mid-term by any political party in Britain, and it put an end to the image of Labour as the irresponsible, high-spending party. It was a response to 'an oil rich decade under a wasteful, divisive and dogmatic Government that has refused to do its duty in preparing the country for the future,' said Kinnock. Labour's aims were to create conditions for economic success which would expand individual opportunity, foster equity and merit, and create a cleaner environment.

There was a clear move away from the dependency culture image of the party. Kinnock said: 'We do not work for dependence on the state. We work for dependable quality from the state. We want levels of contribution and provision that maximise the self-reliance which flourishes on opportunity and security, levels of contribution and provision that nourish the sense of responsibility which is essential to life in the modern community.'

The vocabulary was not that of traditional socialism; the substance was a realistic charter for the decade ahead. 'We have looked back, to gain inspiration from the great accomplishments of the past and to be instructed by the most successful,' said Kinnock in his introduction to *Meet the Challenge, Make the Change.*

> We have looked at the present in detail, intensifying our understanding of what needs to be done and of how Thatcherite rule has simultaneously increased social and economic needs and reduced the means of producing the wealth to meet those needs ... Most important of all, we have looked to the future ... Our emphasis on liberty, on freedom of enquiry and expression, freedom from fear, insecurity, preventable poverty and pain, is essential if change is to serve the human interest.

Among the proposals in the 88-page document were a charter of rights for employees; a new framework of industrial relations law; income tax starting below 20 per cent and ending at 50 per cent; increases in child benefit; new consumer laws; an elected chamber to replace the House of Lords; an environmental protection executive to act as a 'green' watchdog; a homes-for-all policy; and a new education standards council.

Two updated policy review documents appeared later, *Looking to the Future* (1990) and *Opportunity Britain* (1991), but all the significant features of the party's renewal strategy were contained in the first. Patrick Seyd, writing in *Britain at the Polls 1992*, saw that two major themes had emerged.

> First, intraparty political debate over the extent of public and private ownership was outdated; and second, the quality of public services should be improved by putting the needs of the user before those of the producer ... The report came down in favour of private ownership and affirmed that a Labour government's task would be to stimulate a successful market economy and that it would intervene only where that stimulation was not coming from market forces.

This wholehearted embrace of the market was something new. Says Seyd:

> In the past, the party had never wanted to eliminate private enterprise, but it had stressed its unpleasant characteristics ... Labour now adopted the 'responsible social market model' in which government would intervene only when provision was necessary but the market was not providing, such as in the areas of labour training or environmental protection or to

establish agencies to control exploitation of market power ... The document made clear that public ownership was not a fundamental priority. Some forms of common ownership were appropriate for the public utilities, particularly British Telecom and water, but what would be returned to public ownership would depend on the situation when the party was returned to office.

The policy review was a remarkable tribute to Kinnock's determination to achieve an objective. Remarkable, too, was the fact that it was received with little opposition. Eric Heffer did describe it as a 'retreat away from our basic socialist policies', but by the time it was published he was no longer on the NEC. Tony Benn and Dennis Skinner had refused to take part on any of the review groups, and they were critical of the result. But when the review was put to the 1989 conference, only three items were queried in debate: trade union rights, public ownership and defence. And all three were accepted, although with a small majority in the case of defence: there was still considerable hard-core support for unilateral nuclear disarmament.

Patrick Seyd says that the fact that Kinnock had succeeded in convincing the party's main deliberative body to affirm enormous changes in policy on nationalization, trade union laws, and unilateralism was extraordinary. 'Most people in the party faced up to the dilemma of reconciling deeply held beliefs and the need to win power by opting for the latter.' The 'Labour Listens' exercise, which had been designed to give the entire membership of the party an active role in the review process, was again criticized for being more of a public relations bid to make the democratic process seem as broad as possible. Grass-roots opinion, say those critics, was not seriously sought.

However Kinnock did hold a series of some twenty regional meetings with rank and file members, from 1988 to late 1991. Attendances ranged from 200 to 700, and every Constituency Labour Party and trade union in the region was invited to send four, or sometimes six, representatives. The 'Leader's receptions', as they were called, were two- or three-hour question and answer, no-holds-barred sessions. Kinnock began each one by saying: 'The doors are closed. There's only us here. And there are only two rules. Rule 1: you say exactly what you want to say. Rule 2: I say exactly what I want to say.'

The sessions were regarded, without exception, as great successes. 'Members told me that they found the exchanges informative and reassuring. They were certainly cathartic for me. And it's a tribute to the several thousand Party members who came to those evenings that, despite the great candour that we all showed, not a word ever appeared in the press – there were no distortions, no misrepresentations.'

The first-ever national poll of Labour Party members, to see where their real sentiments fell in line with the policy review conclusions, was carried out in 1990 at Sheffield University, where Patrick Seyd is a lecturer. This revealed a clear commitment among them to four socialist touchstones: public ownership, trade union legitimacy, non-nuclear defence, and high public expenditure.

> Members were attached to a number of distinct principles, which appeared to be at odds with the new model party.
>
> But it was also clear from the survey that members recognised the need to ensure that policies were electorally attractive, and a majority believed the party 'should adjust its policies to capture the middle ground of politics'.

Generally there was little support for the notion that Kinnock was too powerful in the party, although on the question whether Neil Kinnock would stick to his principles even if this meant losing a general election views were fairly evenly divided.

Their responses, says Seyd, were structured in such a way as to distinguish the 'modernisers', in favour of the party leadership's electoral strategy and its structural changes, from 'traditionalists' who were opposed to the strategy and changes. 'One in three of the members were modernisers, and only one in five were traditionalists', he concluded. 'Opponents of the modernisation strategy were a small minority of the membership closely associated with the party's hard left.'

At last, some six years after assuming the leadership, Kinnock could be confident that most of the party was united behind him.

9   Fit to be Prime Minister?

Labour's popularity ratings had been improving, slowly and unsteadily, since the 1987 election. With the publication of the policy review document *Meet the Challenge, Make the Change*, the party's support rose to over 40 per cent for only the second time in nearly a decade. The rejection of unilateralism and total nationalization, together with a newfound enthusiasm for Europe, heralded the return of Labour as a mainstream political force. Writing in *Britain at the Polls 1992*, David Sanders said that the policy review's success lay not just in the more moderate policy positions it proposed.

> Labour throughout the 1980s had been widely seen as extremist, irresponsible and disunited. The policy review and Kinnock's style of leadership generally reversed these perceptions. Within months of the review's publication, the widely felt sense that Labour 'had become too extreme' had all but disappeared.

Labour was able to highlight the party's revived popularity when launching the manifesto for the European elections, a vote which Kinnock hoped would become a referendum on ten years of Thatcherism. He had moved Labour away from its earlier reluctant attitude towards Europe: a coherent strategy for industry could help European-based companies compete with the USA and Japan, he believed. And co-operation between governments would ensure that multi-nationals would not play off one country against another, while benefiting from investment on education and training, and spending on transport and telecommunications.

But Kinnock opposed full-scale monetary union, and he was adamant that the European Community could only represent a positive force if it contained the social element protecting jobs and workers, which Mrs Thatcher saw as an impediment to competitiveness. 'We know that, if the completion of the single market is all market operation and no community obligation, then it will fail economically and socially. Europe and Britain will lose, not gain,' he said.

In an article for *The Guardian* in February 1988, Kinnock had acknowledged that few of the aspirations of the original architects of the European Community had been fulfilled, and that British membership had brought little of the benefit anticipated by its advocates. But the practical realities, he said, were that by 1990 Britain's integration with the other European economies 'will have proceeded so far that talk of economic withdrawal is both politically romantic and economically self defeating'. He argued that Labour's 'non-engagement' would give unimpeded movement 'to the complete economic and political domination of Western Europe by market power – with all of the effects on civil rights, environmental conditions, individual opportunities and collective provision which that implies'.

In April 1989, addressing the Welsh TUC, Kinnock said:

> We need a government in Britain that will participate in the development of Europe; that will play a direct, influential role in fashioning the institutions and relationships of the market within which our economy must work in order to prosper. Mrs Thatcher's failure to accept co-operation ... is creating the threat of a two tier Europe, with Britain firmly in the second rank ... a second speed Britain will not generate the wealth which is essential to sustain and enhance the prosperity and to expand the justice and freedom of the British people.

In a study of 'Labour and the European Community' by Stephen George and Ben Rosamond, which appeared in *The Changing Labour Party* (see *Bibliography*), the authors argue that in few areas can the change in policy have been as dramatic as that over the EC. 'The 1983 manifesto made a commitment to withdrawal from EC membership; the 87 manifesto said virtually nothing about the EC; by the 89 elections for the European parliament Labour was successfully presenting itself as the more pro-European of the two major parties.' They point to significant signs of the conversion: the party's embrace of the European social charter and its acceptance that sterling should be included in the exchange rate mechanism of the European monetary system. And they recall an article written by Kinnock in 1984, 'A New Deal For Europe', in which, while criticizing various aspects of the EC, he argued for its reform from within rather than reiterating the calls for withdrawal. 'It was really only after the 87 election, though, that rapid evolution began in the party's public attitude.'

The policy review developed the concern that Britain needed to be involved in the European decision making process, stressing the party's commitment to a socialist European Community in which environmental, women's, social and consumer rights would be protected. And certainly by the time the Labour manifesto for the EC elections appeared in May 1989, Kinnock was insisting that Labour were better Europeans than the Conservatives.

It was during the run-up to the European elections that senior Conservatives tried to stop Labour's revival with a determined attack on Kinnock following the Labour leader's argument with a BBC interviewer. Kinnock had made an angry tirade on the Government when questioned by James Naughtie, on BBC Radio Four's *World at One*, about Labour's answer to high interest rates. His outburst halted the recording, which was resumed shortly afterwards, but the unbroadcast material was published in London's *Evening Standard*.

The Local Government Minister, John Gummer, asked: 'Who could trust a man to talk to Gorbachev who could not keep his cool in talking to an interviewer?' And the Foreign Secretary, Sir Geoffrey Howe, said: 'The British people know that when it comes to ensuring its security, they want political leaders with heads on their shoulders, not hearts on their sleeves.' But defending Kinnock, Bryan Gould pointed out that there were Conservative politicians guilty of being aggressive or losing their tempers. He praised Kinnock's resolution and courage: 'No-one could have done the job he has done – infinitely the most difficult job in British politics – so successfully as he has done it for the past six years without having these immense qualities of self-possession, self-control, dedication and conviction.'

The attack backfired on the Conservatives; the public rather enjoyed the experience of television and radio interviewers being shouted down occasionally, and politicians were expected to raise their voices when necessary. A *Guardian* columnist, Sean French, revealed that he had a sneaking admiration for people who lost their temper in public. As for criticism that the outburst disqualified Kinnock from holding high office, French said that looking at the way real senior statesmen behaved, this claim was difficult to take seriously. 'President Reagan was once asked to test a microphone before delivering a radio talk and responded by announcing in jocular style that America was about to start bombing Russia.'

It was Mrs Thatcher's loss of personal popularity, along with Government failure to control the economy, that was assisting Labour's lead in the opinion polls. Hughes and Wintour, in *Labour Rebuilt*, wrote that Margaret Thatcher's tenth anniversary of accession to Prime Ministerial power had bored and irritated the public. 'At the moment when people were finally beginning to feel fed up with her reign, they were reminded that it had lasted a long decade.' The Prime Minister's opposition to greater economic and political unity within Europe had caused division in the Tory ranks. In fact, the unexpected success of the Green Party, splitting the Tory vote, was one of the factors which helped to give Labour a victory in the European elections in June.

The results were a spectacular success for Labour and, if translated into constituency results in a general election, would have given Kinnock a majority in the Commons of twenty-six seats. He was to confess later that the hours spent at Walworth Road watching those dramatic and satisfying results roll in were the best hours of the entire period of his leadership of the Labour Party.

It was a tremendous boost to confidence as far as the policy review was concerned, and Kinnock felt justified in pushing ahead with his planned – and drastic – changes to the Labour Party's structure, management and organization. His aim was to increase the power of individual members of the Labour Party at the expense of trade union and constituency party block votes. The role of the Parliamentary Labour Party had been losing status as a dominant force for a decade or so, and Kinnock himself had been a motivating force in one of the key changes: the electoral college for choosing party leader.

But although this had benefited his own career, he realized that the votes within that electoral system were held by influential activists and trade unionists. (He had been opposed to the other major change, that of reselection of candidates before each general election. This ruling had proved to be less controversial in practice than had been feared, and, prior to the 1987 election, only six sitting Labour MPs had in fact ben deselected by their constituencies.)

Kinnock's first attempt to introduce one member, one vote had been defeated back in 1984, but in 1987 a compromise solution had been accepted by the party conference. This, rather confusingly, set up another electoral college system at constituency level, in which trade unions would be restricted to a maximum of 40 per cent of the total vote. The remaining 60 per cent would be allocated to individual members, rather than delegates from branches. The aim of this move was to loosen the hold of the unions in choosing candidates. But it proved to be a system too complicated to be workable, and subsequent conference decisions agreed to the principle of one member, one vote at some time in the future.

Party membership, which had dropped by about 60,000 over a four-year period, to stand at around 266,000 in 1988, was also subjected to Kinnock's reform, with registration of members being centralized at Walworth Road national headquarters rather than operating only at local level. (There was never any attempt to centralize recruitment, and no power to recruit or record membership was ever taken away from local organizations.) This did lead to a rise in the numbers of people joining the Labour Party, but only for a year or so; membership then started to decline again. Says Patrick Seyd in *Britain at the Polls 1992*: 'Kinnock's determination to empower individual members was at the expense of both local party branches and union delegates. At the national level, his intention was more to reduce union influence than to eliminate it altogether.'

But his aim was also to increase his own power, says Seyd, and the conflict caused here was never quite resolved. 'What above all motivated the leadership was its desire to ensure that the party's image was as favourable as possible among voters, and this necessitated greater central control of both the message and the messengers.' Nevertheless, Kinnock deserves considerable credit for Labour's changes, says Seyd. 'Surrounded by a small group of personal supporters in his private political office, the party headquarters, the shadow cabinet, and the NEC, he displayed a clear and consistent drive towards office. He capitalised on the mood within the party to reverse its decline and to become again a governing party.' Leadership of the Labour Party was largely a thankless task; the party had never been an easy one to lead, and Kinnock had inherited extensive problems when he took charge. 'Yet by 1991 he had developed into the most powerful leader of the party since Clement Attlee. His goal was office, and the bulk of the party was willing to follow in his tracks.'

One area of concern where it was not at all certain that those tracks would be followed was the policy review's statement on trade unions. Within the party there existed conflicts of opinion between those demanding a complete repeal of the Conservatives' trade union legislation and those, including the leadership, who believed that statutory limitations on trade unions' actions were popular with the public and should not be repealed. The review document stated that trade unions had a central role to play in a successful economy, but there was no emphasis on the restoration and maintaining of collective rights for trade unions.

Instead there were proposals for guaranteed basic legal rights for individual workers, including their negotiation of decent wages and working conditions, their protection from discrimination for union activities and from unfair dismissal, their ability to take time off work for family care, and their entititlement to union representation. There was nothing to suggest that current laws regarding the closed shop and picketing would be repealed.

But after a summer of negotiation between the policy makers – in particular the employment spokesman, Tony Blair, and Charles Clarke – and leading trade unionists, agreement was reached over enforcing the law. New specialist labour courts would handle the issues of industrial relations, particularly over illegal disputes, and while sequestration of a union's entire assets was ruled out, union funds would be liable. As

Kinnock explained: 'The courts say to trade unions, "A corner of your union is involved in a dispute: we will put you, your pension fund, all your other work, all of your representation out of business." That cannot be accepted in a democratic society.'

Kinnock spent an untroubled summer in 1989 waiting for the conference which would put a seal – or otherwise – on his new look Labour Party. Untroubled, that is, except for an accident in which Neil and Glenys Kinnock were involved. They were on an official weekend visit to the Irish Republic early in September when the driver of the car taking them back to Dublin Airport suffered a heart attack at the wheel. The car crashed into the back of a lorry, and a third vehicle crashed into them. Kinnock, helped by a retired nurse who happened to be standing at the side of the road, used mouth-to-mouth resuscitation to try to revive the chauffeur, but he was dead by the time an ambulance arrived. Glenys Kinnock suffered quite a severe leg injury – her shin was scraped to the bone – but Neil was not hurt.

As the Labour Party prepared to gather in Brighton, a profile of Kinnock by Mary Ann Sieghart in *The Times* illustrated the upturn in his personal fortunes. The 'vicious spiral of confidence' which had dragged him down the previous autumn had turned virtuous. Having felt low enough to consider quitting, said Sieghart – reviving again the myth created by the press – Kinnock became more determined to be his own person, less desperate to prove himself, 'and as a result he is proving himself much better'. This happened once Kinnock realized that there was more to life than leading the Labour Party, she suggested, aided by Labour's improved performance in the opinion polls, and success in the European elections.

Now his elation was justified. 'Seldom has a Labour leader been so in control of his party.' Roy Hattersley was quoted as saying that Labour needed someone who would put the party right. 'That's what he does stupendously well and what he enjoys doing most.' So could the 'darling of the Labour Party' ever become the darling of the electorate, Sieghart mused.

In his favour, he is far more likeable than the Prime Minister, and the only people he really hates are journalists. Unlike Thatcher, Kinnock has not lost his common touch. He still goes to the London Welsh rugby club almost every Saturday during the season ... He shares Thatcher's extraordinary energy; being able to survive on half the sleep needed by ordinary people is probably a prerequisite for high office. But he still lacks what politicians inelegantly call 'bottom'. Kinnock just does not look weighty enough to face up to Gorbachev or talk economics with leaders of the world's biggest industrialised countries.

The judgement on journalists was one which had developed during the leadership years. In his early days in politics Kinnock had numbered quite a few columnists and lobby correspondents among his friends. Indeed, it was said that he often envied their relative power and relative freedom from responsibility, compared with the life of a politician. He would probably have made a good broadcast journalist himself, one producer said, having a natural flair for performing on screen together with the ability to know when to bow out of a discussion and let the interviewee take over. But the papers, and the tabloid papers in particular, had soured his relationship with the reporting profession. 'Hate' was a strong word to use, but certainly he was suspicious of most, apart from those with whom the degree of friendship was such that professional interests scarcely intervened.

Happily for Kinnock, the most immediate task was to face up to his own supporters in the arena which suited him best, the party conference. And he opened his key speech in a mood seen as upbeat and powerfully optimistic. 'The people of Britain know that we have worked for and earned our increased strength,' he told delegates. 'They respect us for the changes we have made and the changes we are making. Increasingly they know that we are attuned to the realities of our time. Increasingly they are prepared to trust us with the future.' He avoided any attacks on the left in the party and emphasized unity: 'We'll go on getting support – by continuing to construct strong unity of purpose; by our conduct as a serious, socialist, self disciplined party.'

It was a conference of progress and celebration. 'The great thing about that conference was that it was the first one at which I could concentrate entirely on the world outside the Labour Party because most of the nonsense had been stopped by then,' he recalls.

Kinnock's first triumph was on the defence issue when a significant majority gave backing to the multilateral strategy for nuclear disarmament. He then secured another victory, defeating a left-wing attempt to commit Labour to repealing Tory trade union laws. A future Labour Government would keep secret strike ballots, and ballots for the election of union officers, while curbs on secondary action would be ended. All this with the approval of most of the big unions. And in the elections to the NEC, Kinnock's outspoken critic Ken Livingstone lost his place. Finally, Kinnock's proposal to review the union block vote system was given overwhelming support.

On the final day of the conference, a national opinion poll gave Labour a nine point lead over the Conservatives, with Kinnock's own 'satisfaction' rating at long last ahead of that of Mrs Thatcher: 48 per cent to her 39 per cent. Asked by a television interviewer if he now felt fit to be Prime Minister, Kinnock replied:

Yes, partly because I love my country, but that would not be enough of itself. I'm fit to be prime minister because I truly represent the people of this country and their hopes for economic success and social justice and their aspirations because I'm from them. I'm not detached in the way that this government certainly has become. I know that I'm tough. I know that I can see objectives and drive after them. I think that kind of tenacity is required too, and I've got it.

But he stressed that Brighton in 1989 'is a real starting point and not the end of anything': they had still to fight and win an election.

Hughes and Wintour wrote in *Labour Rebuilt* that when Kinnock could say such things 'and be heard in earnest, it was clear the turnaround had been achieved'. The success of the review strategy, which had brought with it the realistic prospect of general election victory, tamed the party into acquiescence, they said. What's more, within a month of the end of that conference, the Government was 'ripped apart' by the Cabinet rift over European monetary co-operation and the intensifying pressure on sterling. Nigel Lawson, the Chancellor, insisted that Thatcher should sack her economic advisor Sir Alan Walters because of his comments against the European monetary system. Thatcher refused, Lawson resigned in protest, and Labour's lead jumped to fifteen points. Nearly half the population were willing to support Labour. 'Those fast-moving events swiftly proved that the review had enabled Labour to capitalise instantly on Government misfortune.'

With the believable prospect that Kinnock might be the next Prime Minister, the spotlight focused on Glenys Kinnock once again. She had continued to work part time as a teacher and to continue her own political activities. When Neil became leader of the party in 1983, he and Glenys talked about what role she could best play. Michael Leapman in his book *Kinnock* assessed that three considerations had to be balanced. She naturally wanted to help him become Prime Minister, but she was also anxious to pursue her own political and professional interests and not to function as a traditional politician's wife, the dutiful hostess occasionally let out on her own to open jumble sales. 'The third, and they both agreed the most important object was to ensure that they could enjoy as normal a family life as circumstances allowed. They were determined to protect the children from the circus of constant publicity.' This they had managed to do in spite of the ever-present interest of the media. A normal family life meant that Kinnock was prepared to miss occasional meetings to attend parents' evenings at his children's schools.

All Christmases and holidays were special times for the family. The Kinnocks, with Glenys' brother Colin Parry, his wife Barbara and their children had taken holidays together for years, renting villas in Greece or Spain. (In 1989 they had gone to Tuscany for the first time – without the children – an area of Italy which was to become a favourite haunt.) Kinnock enjoyed gardening and, according to Glenys, was always good with jobs around the house and would determinedly complete a task like redecorating the kitchen in just one weekend.

Stephen, a keen rugby player, had been a member of London Welsh junior rugby teams from the age of eight; his father had coached and refereed boys' rugby until the early eighties. Now Stephen was at Queen's College, Cambridge, in the second year of a degree course in modern languages – French and Spanish. Rachel, now seventeen, was at Hounslow Borough College studying for a BTEC in media studies.

Their lives were described by Martyn Harris in the *Sunday Telegraph* as 'slightly self-conscious normality, but quite genuine. You just can't fake the normality of people who fret over their fuchsias or who own a cat called Fluffy ... The Kinnocks are ordinary people with ordinary intellects and ordinary ambitions and ordinary children.'

When Neil became leader Glenys had stopped working full time and took a part-time job at Wykeham Junior and Infants School in Brent, and later at Viking Primary in Northolt. (She had joined colleagues on the picket lines during the teachers' dispute of 1985.) She began to receive invitations in her own right, independently of Neil, and is now an able and confident speaker. It wasn't always so; at first she relied on the advice of the American pioneer feminist Gloria Steinem who told her that 'in front of an audience, keep telling yourself, you won't *die*'.

The insinuations that Glenys Kinnock was the dominant force in the partnership had faded with time. Glenys had always been angry with the suggestion that 'you actually have to be an MP in order to have an opinion or to campaign for issues that concern you'. Glenys, of course, is now launched on a career of her own as Labour's candidate for South East Wales in the European Parliament election of 1994. She has long been active in a number of Third World charities and still chairs One World Action, a development charity which she founded to raise consciousness of issues relating to developing countries and to generate funds for self-help projects in the Third World.

But her independence has always been balanced by an impressive degree of loyalty which blends the personal and the political: 'I would be prepared to do everything I can to elect a Labour government, to help Neil or anyone else.' In an interview with Suzie Mackenzie in *The Guardian* she admitted to being an idealist. 'I believe that if you set your sights high enough, then you will work towards that. You won't always arrive.'

The Labour lead in the opinion polls was no brief illusion. Before the end of 1989 Ladbrokes bookmakers were offering Labour as odds-on favourites to win the next election. After the resignation of Nigel Lawson there was a new degree of confidence in the Opposition's concerted attack on the Government and Mrs Thatcher herself. Kinnock claimed that her 'monarchical delusions' lay at the root of the Tory crisis and described recent events as a shambles brought about by the conflict between collective cabinet government and a Prime Minister who has taken to calling herself 'we'. The result, he said, was that the Thatcher regime was now 'a medieval court operating under a system of rule of favourites'.

In his own time – and not at the bidding of radio interviewers – Kinnock revealed his solution to Britain's economic problems. In a speech to the Institute of Personnel Managers, he said that entry into the Exchange Rate Mechanism of the European Monetary System was necessary, as was a new relationship with the banks and financial institutions to secure co-operation for lending restrictions. And his familiar appeals for comprehensive strategies to improve industrial performance were backed with calls for an integrated transport system and a major boost to pure and applied science. 'Until Britain benefits from the employment of systematic and comprehensive strategies to improve industrial performance, all policies will, to a greater or lesser extent, be hand-to-mouth responses to pressure more than foundations for sustained competitiveness.'

He also reiterated his belief that education and training were the 'commanding heights of the modern economy'. But a new framework was required in which part-timers, temporary workers, older people, women – and especially mothers in need of child care facilities – would get the support, the training and the work that they needed, he said. 'There is only one thing more expensive than making proper provision for education and training, and that is not making it.'

When the Shadow Cabinet met for a special one-day strategy session, Kinnock announced: 'We know from the feelings that are coming from all quarters that the Tories have had the eighties and wasted their chance. We are equipped and fit for the nineties and deserve to get our chance.' A November opinion poll in *The Guardian* put Labour thirteen points ahead of the Tories, with Mrs Thatcher's style of government a focal point of objection. Kinnock dismissed any suggestions that the Tories' fortunes might improve under a different leader.

Oddly enough, when proceedings in the House of Commons were televised for the first time at the end of November 1989, it was Mrs Thatcher who made the better impression on viewers. Contrary to expectations – her combative style, it was suggested, would alienate rather than endear – the Prime Minister was judged to have performed better, according to an ICM (Independent Communications and

Marketing) poll. On the small screen, Mrs Thatcher had done more to please the party faithful and more to impress her political opponents. Ironically she had been a long-standing opponent of televised parliamentary proceedings, while Kinnock had always been in favour.

As 1989 drew to a close, details were revealed of Kinnock's next moves in his scheme for overhauling the Labour Party. Further changes in the democracy and structure of the party would be put to the next annual conference – including reducing the proportion of the unions' conference vote to as low as 50 per cent, and the reselection of MPs on a one member, one vote basis. Kinnock realized that the 1990 conference might be the last one before a general election and that proposing more controversial changes would be a risk.

But there was an air of confidence in the leader's office now, and an element of risk was no longer to be feared. In the new year Kinnock's confidence was boosted further by two opinion polls which gave Labour a lead of more than fifteen points over the Conservatives: the biggest lead since he became leader of the party. More than half of those likely to vote if a general election was called immediately said they would back Labour, and at last Kinnock passed Mrs Thatcher in voters' estimation as the leader best equipped to be Prime Minister. On most crucial issues Labour were judged to have the best policies, the exceptions being the economy, and the old stumbling block of nuclear weapons and defence.

But one issue above all others was contributing to the decline of Conservative support – the poll tax. Many Tories privately supported the view that the new community charge replacing the rates was 'a political cyanide pill' for them. Even before the charge was introduced, there were violent town-hall protests all over the country against the prospect of huge bills being drawn up. Public opinion was tested in March when Labour won its best by-election victory for 50 years, overturning a 14,000 Tory majority to take Mid Staffordshire. Only two days after the poll tax was officially introduced on 1 April, plans were announced for its reform. But that weekend saw the biggest – and most violent – of all the public protests in London, a protest which turned into a riot with battles between demonstrators and police.

Such action had always alarmed Kinnock. His insistent belief that political protest must stay within the bounds of the law meant that he was obliged to condemn those who rioted. But he was also angry because such events provided the distraction which Mrs Thatcher badly needed. In a heated exchange in the Commons he maintained that she delighted in the diversion. 'When it comes to extremists, the difference is this: I fight them, the Prime Minister needs them,' he said.

When Mrs Thatcher insisted that she had been deeply concerned, as she had been by attacks on the police during the coal dispute, and during the printworkers' strike at Wapping, Kinnock replied: 'You expose yourself even more. By dredging through all those past acts, you demonstrate exactly the truth of what I said earlier. Those who affect to despise your policies most, give the greatest comfort to you, but you deride that comfort and you encourage further uproar.'

The Government was forced into appeasement measures while the longer term future of the poll tax was considered, and by the summer the Environment Secretary Chris Patten had secured an extra £2.5 billion from the Treasury to try to hold bills down. As prime defender of the faith in the charge, Mrs Thatcher's leadership was increasingly questioned. And with the Conservative Party split by the kind of internal wrangling which had once beset Labour, there was further encouragement for Neil Kinnock: the SDP was wound up by its leader David Owen because it was no longer big enough to carry on as a national force. Had there been a general election in that summer of 1990 few doubted that Labour had a very strong chance of success.

Kinnock's certainty was absolute: 'We would have won,' he said later. 'We would have had a working majority. I think we would have won 326 seats, possibly 335. But it would have been the biggest turn round in British political history, and I think we would have done it.' He added: 'In fact, we would have done it whenever there was an election, provided Mrs Thatcher had remained as Prime Minister.'

10   Of Leaders and Leadership

Neil Kinnock was probably at the zenith of his career early in 1990. The electorate appeared, according to the opinion polls, to be firmly behind him, as they lost faith in Mrs Thatcher. Her status at the time was summarized by Denis Healey in his autobiography, *The Time of My Life*:

> The most striking feature of Mrs Thatcher's third term in power is that she seems to have lost that instinct for the popular mood which marked her first two terms. Every major item in her programme is now unpopular. All the opinion polls show large majorities in favour, not of her values, but of those which the Labour Party has traditionally represented ... Neil Kinnock spoke for many outside his own party when he condemned Thatcherism with the words: 'No obligation to the community, no sense of solidarity ... no neighbourhood, no number other than one, no time other than now, no such thing as society – just me! and now!'

The Labour Party, too, was both more popular and more united behind its leader than it had been for a decade or more. It was a party changed utterly in style, appearance and substance, with an updated version of the policy review highlighting those changes. Patrick Wintour wrote in *The Guardian* that the policy review did not offer a new definition of socialism.

> It did, however, supremely convey the more important truth that the party had changed the way it thinks and acts. For that Kinnock deserves lasting credit. There is probably no other leading figure who could have been so systematically successful, or so emphatically correct, in believing that rebuilding and re-educating the party were preconditions for lasting reform. Whatever happens from here on, that will be a lasting memorial.

The updated review, entitled *Looking to the Future*, appeared in May as a 'proto-manifesto', with Labour anticipating an early call for a general election. This document – 20,000 words on 51 pages – was to be the basis of a true election manifesto and an agenda for government, with promises to create a dynamic economy and a decent society. And it had a distinctly pro-European flavour. It aimed to shed Labour's image as the party of high taxation and spending, stating: 'We will not spend, nor will we promise to spend, more than Britain can afford.' Pledges to increase spending on social services were qualified with such phrases as 'where resources allow', and a commitment to full employment which was part of the 1987 election manifesto was dropped.

There would be a 'fair' tax system with income tax ranging from below 20 per cent to a maximum of 50 per cent, and the poll tax would be replaced by an ability-to-pay property tax. Britain would enter the European exchange rate mechanism at the earliest opportunity. Union rights to take sympathy action and to picket in limited numbers would be restored; the water industry would be returned to public ownership; a new green watchdog, the Environmental Protection Executive, would be created; and Scotland would have its own separate parliament.

The document was launched on a high note of positive expectancy but there were those who argued that it did not go far enough. Some still believed that Labour's links with the trade unions were still prohibitively tight; as Hugo Young in *The Guardian* wrote, 'Labour's past clings like plastic film to the packaging of its future.' Memories of previous Labour governments were not glorious ones, he said, and the deadliest reminiscence was called up by the party's continuing trade union connection. 'Although Mr Kinnock has presided over the decline in importance of block voting … Labour as the party of the individual member still has miles to go before emerging credibly into the light.' The unions, he said, were beginning to look like vultures on their prey's arrival. 'If the voters are prisoners of the past, it is that part of the past, from the winter of discontent backwards, which stands most in need of exorcism. Until Mr Kinnock takes another large stride towards it, the party will suffer.' Kinnock knew the move had to be made; he was still campaigning after the 1992 election defeat for it to be fulfilled.

At the time the Labour leadership was aware that the other item for which the public most needed reassurance was taxation, in spite of Kinnock's explanations about modest spending plans. Otherwise, research at the time appeared to suggest that the party's broad agenda was fairly close to the issues that most concerned the electorate. And that included defence, the topic which had caused the Labour Party such anguish during the eighties. Abandoning the commitment to unilateral nuclear disarmament appeared to have done all and more for Labour's popular appeal that Kinnock had hoped for.

He had been assisted, of course, by the collapse of communism in Eastern Europe, by President Gorbachev's efforts in defusing the Cold War and even by the symbolic dismantling of the Berlin Wall. Such world events had helped to convince former unilateralists that they no longer had a cause to pursue. But Kinnock deserved every credit for removing what had once been a significant domestic political issue. His critics could no longer claim that a Kinnock-led government would leave Britain defenceless.

Now the attacks concentrated on the vagueness of Labour's income tax proposals. So in June when Kinnock gave his first in-depth television interview for several months – on BBC's *Panorama* – he used the opportunity to assure middle-income earners that they would not be worse off under a Labour Government. It was an opportunity which misfired to some extent, as the tabloid press chose to misinterpret his remarks and portray Labour again as the party of high taxation. His message, that fourteen out of every fifteen basic rate taxpayers would not pay any more under Labour was repeated the following day by the Shadow Chancellor John Smith.

In fact, according to Hugo Young in *The Guardian*, the tabloids and Tory politicians 'hysterically misrepresented' what happened, and did so because Kinnock had come over so well, that he had proved he was not the 'gibbering nitwit' of Tory propaganda. 'This is a foretaste of what will probably be the most abrasive 18 months in modern politics,' wrote Young. 'Mr Kinnock had a bad enough time when he had no chance of winning. With Labour's victory a serious possibility, panic drives the assassin's hand to stop at nothing.' Of Kinnock's performance, Young wrote: 'There was less garrulity and more gravitas than usual. The years have aged and hardened him into a more credible figure. With grace and directness he conceded that he had changed, for example on nationalisation.'

In a less politically demanding interview shortly afterwards, with Terry Wogan, Kinnock praised the Conservatives for choosing a woman leader, and hoped that there would one day be a woman Labour Prime Minister. 'Reluctant though I am to give credit to enemies, I have to say that it is to the credit of the Conservative Party that they did elect a woman to be their leader when the cause of women was not quite as advanced as it is now,' he said. He spoke, too, of how he reacted to the demands he faced as opposition leader: 'The pressures that come on can be put into their proper perspective by having the kind of home and family relationship that I have. I use them as a reality, as an anchor. They are not a shell to creep into. They have got lives and they have a father. They want to raise things with him. It is not a kind of protective shell. It is a reality.' He added: 'Sometimes the best escape from politics is into reality.'

The two worlds overlapped that summer when Glenys Kinnock accompanied Neil on an official visit to the USA. This was not a family holiday: he was to meet President Bush, she had a separate programme of engagements which included talks about her work with Third World charities. Back in April Kinnock had pledged a firm commitment to the special relationship between Britain and the United States. His comments were prompted by the reported remarks of President Bush who said he was confident that good relations would continue if Labour were to replace the Conservatives. 'Those who say there is a dilemma about whether we should look across the Channel to Europe, or across the Atlantic to the United States, are not being realistic. Our place is in the whole world and the United States is a big partner in that world,' Kinnock said.

'It has been clear for some time that there is a natural relationship between the United States and Britain, as we have a natural relationship with the rest of NATO and the European Community. I look forward to that continuing to the mutual benefit of the world.' (Around the same time, Denis Healey, former deputy leader of the Labour Party, said on BBC Radio Four's *The World at One* that there had been a convergence of views between Labour and the Bush administration in recent years. 'Mrs Thatcher and President Reagan had a very odd personal relationship,' he said. 'He accepted almost anything she said. But she gets on badly with Bush, who represents the sort of upper-class wet she most dislikes in Britain.'

So when Kinnock arrived in Washington in mid-July it was to a very different sort of welcome from the cool reception he had received from Reagan three years earlier. According to newspaper reports, President Bush received him with a degree of style rarely accorded to a foreign politician, particularly one in opposition. The *New York Times* said that Bush treated Kinnock 'almost like a head of state', and spoke of Mrs Thatcher's 'fading political fortunes'. The US administration evidently recognized the possibility that Kinnock could be in Downing Street within two years' time, and that he was to be taken very seriously indeed. The two men talked for thirty-five minutes – more than the usual time allotted to foreign visitors of Kinnock's rank – and the Opposition leader's meetings with other members of the government and political figureheads all overran their time. In return, Kinnock spoke of a 'common agenda' between the Labour Party and the Bush administration.

'What underlines the distinctiveness of our view, and the closeness it has to the American presidential view is the eccentricity of Mrs Thatcher in terms of the European Community and NATO ... she is not in the same gear or looking for the same objectives with the same kind of pragmatic pace which is evident in the United States administration. We are.' Kinnock said that in the wake of the Cold War most Western governments – including that of the USA – had a forward looking attitude to change and a constructive desire to foster the liberation and modernization of Eastern Europe. 'The British Government is led by someone nostalgic for the Cold War and physically unwilling to undertake the co-operation necessary in these new times.'

In New York Kinnock addressed the Council on Foreign Relations, a private non-partisan organization whose members are leaders in the fields of government, business, research and the media: previous speakers had included Boris Yeltsin, Nelson Mandela and Jacques Delors. There his theme was how to improve security across Europe when security was becoming increasingly defined in economic as well as military terms. He also spoke of initiatives needed to ensure the rapid and manageable spread of the mixed economy in Eastern Europe and the promotion of comprehensive changes in the Soviet Union.

The whole visit was regarded as a triumph. In America a senior State Department official said that Kinnock had tried 'to demonstrate to us that he is not the radical some people have perceived him to be, which makes us pleased', while back in Britain the success of the trip was viewed as an enormous boost for the Labour Party and its leader.

Kinnock's next victory was with the trade unions, with them rather than over them, for the essence of the Trades Union Congress in September was of co-operation. On the eve of Congress the TUC general secretary Norman Willis told unions that they could not expect to instruct the Labour leader what to do as Prime Minister. 'We know that if we are to see the implementation of many of the policies we decide upon this week we need Neil Kinnock at No. 10,' he said. But he added that Kinnock would on occasion 'have to say No to many groups, and that includes us. But what we are confident of is that we will have a listening Government ... But we will all be clear from the outset that we are not in his pocket and he is not in ours.'

When Kinnock addressed Congress on its opening day he was given a standing ovation when he promised a balanced system of rights and responsibilities for trade unionists, guaranteed by law. 'A framework of law establishes positive rights, so it clearly brings commensurate responsibilities. In a democracy there cannot be one without the other,' he said. Labour would establish the right to take industrial action, subject to membership ballots, the right to picket peacefully and the right of access to fair and open court procedures whose decisions would be binding on both employers and the unions. Accusing the Government of presiding over eleven years of decline in Britain, Kinnock said to loud applause: 'Never had so much been taken from so many by so few, with so very little to show for it all.'

Kinnock's passage to power appeared to be progressing smoothly, but unpredictable diversions led to attention being suddenly focussed elsewhere. On 1 August, Saddam Hussein of Iraq had sent his troops into Kuwait; Britain responded by sending air and naval forces to the Gulf. And so began a series of events which would turn to war in the new year. On the home front, battle was under way in the Conservative Party as Mrs Thatcher's days in office appeared to be numbered. In July the Industry Secretary Nicholas Ridley told *The Spectator* that the Germans were trying to take over Europe. The furore which followed resulted in his resignation and the loss of Mrs Thatcher's closest ally in the Cabinet. In October, on the last day of the Labour Party Conference, the Government announced entry into the European Exchange Rate Mechanism, Mrs Thatcher having been persuaded that there was no alternative.

Meanwhile, the Labour conference in Blackpool had heard Neil Kinnock fire the starting gun to his party's election campaign with a call to loyalists to prepare for the fight of their lives. The emphasis of his plans for a Labour Government lay on a new deal for education: an improved supply of qualified teachers, guaranteed provision of essential books and learning materials, and up-to-date buildings and facilities. It was called getting back to basics, he said. And then, after what observers described as the most exultant response to a Kinnock conference speech since he became leader, he returned to the rostrum to plead: 'Save all the energy you have got to spare to fight and win the General Election.' And he averted a clash with the unions over proposals to weaken their power within the Labour movement. Plans would now go ahead to abolish the electoral college in local constituencies under which the trade unions had up to 40 per cent of the votes for selecting a parliamentary candidate. The unions and all other affiliated organizations would be allowed to retain the right to nominate candidates for consideration.

Kinnock then found defence souring the taste of conference victory as it had done often before. Delegates voted in favour of a left-wing demand for a huge cut in defence spending, down to a European average level, against the advice of the leader, and the policy review document. But because the motion was passed on a show of hands, there was no obligation to consider it as party policy, as Kinnock insisted afterwards. 'Labour Government policy will be one of providing effective defence for Britain in British interests and doing it on the basis of the funding that's necessary,' he said. His opponents were incensed, and, although only a small crack, party unity was seen to be impaired. Tony Benn's caustic view of the conference was recorded in his diary: 'October 3. The Party is just a machine for putting Kinnock into Number 10, and I would like to see him there rather than Thatcher, but there is no excitement, no sense of vision, no moral commitment.'

There was soon to be no lack of excitement on the political front but all of it centred on the Conservative camp. On 18 October the Tories, against all odds, lost the by-election at Eastbourne, the seat formerly held by Ian Gow who had been murdered by the IRA. With morale at rock bottom, two weeks later Sir Geoffrey Howe resigned as Leader of the Commons, infuriated by Mrs Thatcher's stance on Europe. The Prime Minister had been angered by a deadline of 1994 for the start of the second stage of monetary union, set by a European Council summit meeting in Rome. It was, she said, the back door to a federal Europe. When Sir Geoffrey made a devastatingly critical resignation speech it seemed as if he was inviting someone – anyone – to challenge the Thatcher leadership. The challenge was taken up, on 14 November, by Michael Heseltine.

In the first ballot, on 20 November, Mrs Thatcher polled 204 votes to Heseltine's 152, a margin insufficient under party rules for outright victory. At this stage, Neil Kinnock called for a general election, maintaining that the Government was deeply divided and incurably disabled. 'It is not fit to rule. If 40 per cent of your party votes against you, it is very clear that the Prime Minister figuratively speaking, politically speaking, and internationally speaking, limps in the councils of the world.' Kinnock had tabled a motion of no confidence in the Government shortly before the result of the first ballot was announced. There would now have to be a second vote, and although she insisted that she would fight on, Thatcher was eventually convinced that her moment had passed, and on the morning of 22 November she announced that she would resign.

It was the end of a formidable era in British politics. Margaret Thatcher's power and influence had been incomparable, and when Kinnock later admitted that he thought her so patently wrong that he made no further diagnosis of her character, he was confessing an error of judgement. Others saw her influence as far more reaching: one writer has suggested that the phenomenon of Thatcher's 'strong leadership' (the sentiment 'she's wrong but she's strong', which Kinnock found so depressing) was eventually adopted by both Labour and the SDP, having a profound effect on both Kinnock and David Owen. Ivor Crewe, in *Britain at the Polls 1992*, states that Thatcher's domination of the House of Commons fascinated them.

> It also appealed to the sizeable macho streak in their personalities. They were convinced that an image of decisiveness and toughness won votes and had been an important factor in the Conservatives' landslide election victory in 1983; and they blamed the internal troubles of their own parties on the feeble leadership of their predecessors. Their emulation of Thatcher's style came out in trivial ways, such as Neil Kinnock's

transparent efforts to assume a military bearing on public occasions, but also in more serious ways, such as their method of party management.

(Kinnock is angered by comments suggesting that he ever chose to dress the part for political purposes. He had never swapped casual sweaters for formal suits and 'regimental' ties; those were always the kind of suit and tie that he wore, and his shoes had always been polished.)

The serious ways, said Crewe, were how Kinnock and Owen in their respective parties chose to lead from the front.

> They confronted problems, set objectives, took clear positions and sidelined or bullied opponents. Both of them accumulated power in their own hands by building up their private offices and creating ad hoc committees of personal allies to bypass their parties' official decision-making structures. In Owen's case this approach eventually led to the disaster of the SDP split over the issue of merger with the Liberals. In Kinnock's case it was an almost unqualified success. By 1990 his leadership was unchallenged and his party had moved, institutionally and ideologically, in exactly the direction he wanted.

This does not tally exactly with Kinnock's view of events, of course. In 1992, in a televised discussion on leadership for *Behind the Headlines*, he explained:

> People who were reluctant allies came on board. Mostly it was done by persuasion and argument ... You have to believe sufficiently in your colleagues, to value their judgement, so that when you persuade them of your point of view they are not doing it as a result of 'suasion' but because they are in sufficiently broad agreement to be enthusiastic supporters of the line that's taken.

What Kinnock does admit is the inhibiting presence of Mrs Thatcher in the Commons – one reason for the adoption of his formal style which was neither entirely natural to him, nor always appreciated. The reason was a simple one, as he told Sarah Baxter of the *New Statesman*: 'It was difficult to make jokes against someone who has no conception of humour at all.' Also, it had been drummed into him at an early age to be respectful of older women. 'I was happier conforming to that than I would have been had I tried to break out and say some of the things I would have to a man or woman of my age.'

His new sparring partner was to be a man of his age – or rather, just one year younger. John Major entered the leadership contest at the second ballot, and defeated both Heseltine and Douglas Hurd who had also entered the fray. On 27 November he became the new Tory leader and Prime Minister.

No longer the Leader of the Opposition but still on the campaign trail. Here Kinnock visits a school in Clitheroe, Lancashire, prior to the county council elections in 1993

The Kinnock family's Victorian house in the Montpelier area of Ealing, to which they moved in the summer of 1992

Addressing supporters on the steps of Labour's Walworth Road headquarters in the early hours of the morning on 10 April 1992, after the election defeat

Listening to a speech with Tony Benn at the 1984 party conference in Blackpool

Relaxing with Glenys at the end of the 1984 conference week

Dealing with distractions – Kinnock at Labour Party Conference in Blackpool in 1988 after Tony Benn's challenge for the leadership had failed

All in a morning's work for a leading politician – breakfast at a scout camp in October 1991

Neil and Glenys with Rachel and Stephen in the spring of 1992

In retrospect it was easy to see how Margaret Thatcher had fallen increasingly out of touch with both parliamentary and public opinion – a remoteness that was symbolized by her insistence that the poll tax must be introduced in spite of all the opposition it engendered. The radical solution to her unpopularity – removal from office, followed quickly by the abandoning of her much-resented community charge, had an instantly unsettling effect on Labour. Kinnock derided Major as a 'no change, no majority Prime Minister' and repeated his calls for a general election even though he was aware that the Conservatives had thrown overboard one of the main impediments to their future success. 'John Major is a Thatcherette,' he said. 'That is how he sought election, that is how he has got election.' But senior Labour figures were already considering how they would have to adjust their strategy to match the new regime.

Kinnock has since admitted that Labour did not adjust very effectively to Major's leadership but, he explained to the *New Statesman*, he was stuck.

> We were faced with two options. One was to treat him as the product of Thatcherism, which he was, and the other was to say, 'Here's somebody different' and attack him on that basis. But of course the one thing he and the Tory party wanted more than anything else was for us to acknowledge his difference. So why should we do their job for them?

Kinnock has also stated, quite categorically, that 'We would have defeated Mrs Thatcher.' Major, he said, was a more difficult target to hit. 'He was new and, despite having been Chancellor for two years, relatively unknown and, extraordinarily, regarded to be innocent of any connection with the recession. Even by the 1992 General Election only about five per cent of respondents to polls thought that he was to blame for the slump.'

In fact, when Thatcher was replaced by Major, there was an immediate upturn in public opinion in the Tories' favour. In June 1990, according to a Gallup poll, Labour had the support of 49.5 per cent of voters, with the Conservatives way behind at 33.7 per cent. By December, Labour had slipped back into second place, 5.5 percentage points behind the Tories. At the beginning of November, polls indicated that 69 per cent of the electorate were dissatisfied with Thatcher as Prime Minister, and only 26 per cent satisfied. A month later, 50 per cent were satisfied with Major and only 28 per cent dissatisfied. Under Major's new regime, Heseltine announced the end of the poll tax, which Labour – with the agreement of most people in Britain – had called 'the world's worst idea'.

And yet Major inherited a party governing Britain which was slipping into recession. Opinion polls revealed that the Conservatives were widely thought to have failed on the issues of unemployment and inflation; that they had cut back too far on health and education; and that they were handling the economy badly. Kenneth Newton, in *Britain at the Polls 1992*, asked how, with the economy in a depression and public opinion figures of this sort, was Major able to turn around a Labour lead?

> The answer is that while expressing strong criticism of the Government's economic record and disapproval of many of its policies, a large section of the electorate believed that a Labour government would do even worse. Almost twice as many thought the Conservatives would handle Britain's economic difficulties better than Labour.

It was almost inevitable that some sectors of the Labour Party began to voice their question that perhaps they, too, should have a new leader. At the beginning of December an opinion poll suggested that Labour's deficit would become a lead over the Conservatives if John Smith were to take over as leader. The faithful rallied to Kinnock's defence. His deputy leader, Roy Hattersley, insisted that Kinnock would make a first-class Prime Minister and told a TV interviewer that: 'Nobody in their right mind would want to see at this minute John Smith or – since we do not want any misinterpretation – anybody replace Neil Kinnock.' He believed that Smith was 'too loyal and too sensible' to think that there was a real prospect of a leadership challenge. 'I have seen what he (Kinnock) has done to the Labour Party and its policies. He has carried the battle to the Tories in the most adverse circumstances.'

The Shadow Trade and Industry Secretary, Gordon Brown – mentioned as another possible leadership contender – insisted: 'My only ambition is to serve in a Labour government under Neil Kinnock.' And even the not-so-faithful rallied to the cause. Ken Livingstone, MP for Brent East and an adversary on the left, said: 'For years we have known the polls showing that John Smith is the most popular Labour figure. But I don't think there is any question but that Neil Kinnock will take us into the next election.'

Such speculation, said Hugo Young in *The Guardian*, defamed Kinnock's unquestionable talent and no doubt corroded his confidence. But even more, it was quite irrelevant: 'For what the Tories have signalled is that the uniqueness of the leader ... has ceased to be the issue.' The leader of any party, he said, must be competent, honest, copious with fact and swift with argument, possessing a modicum of moral fibre when the going gets tough. 'But the other credentials have been sharply lowered. He is no longer required to be mother, governess, harridan and all-purpose colossus. The job is reduced to human scale, in which other people play their part and other issues come into focus.' Heralding a new era of the politics of pragmatism and committee, in which the detail of policy and the management of public service far outdistanced personal charisma, Young admitted that the Tory party held a considerable advantage: 'It has replaced a leader whose mighty dominance in office redoubles the therapeutic possibilities inherent in her departure. When the giant is deposed, the pygmies can be believed when they promise a new world.'

However, according to a survey among Labour Party members carried out by Patrick Seyd and Paul Whiteley in late 1989/early 1990, the bulk of the membership at that time were strongly supportive of Kinnock as leader and appeared well satisfied with him. His personal ranking among members was high. They asked a wide range of questions about his qualities as party leader and the survey revealed considerable warmth of feelings towards him. More than three-quarters of the membership regarded him as likeable, caring, capable of being strong and good at getting things done. Less than one in ten regarded him as 'not likeable as a person'. The strongest criticism came from the 15 per cent who described him as 'bad at getting things done'. Kinnock's support was strongly related to members' own political views. Seyd and Whiteley state those on the left were thirteen times more likely to regard him with hostility. Those on the right of the party spectrum were twice as likely to feel very warmly disposed to Kinnock as those on the party left. In addition, the older the party member, the greater their support for him.

In the national eye, though, John Major had the dubious 'benefit' of the Gulf War starting within weeks of his becoming Prime Minister, early in January 1991. This was a stroke of luck for although Major had, as one observer put it, reduced the Government's unpopularity by virtue of the fact that he was not Thatcher, he still faced problems on almost every front. The war gave him the chance to avoid the difficult issues of domestic politics and to play the role of a national and world leader. On the other hand, the conflict in the Gulf merely added to Kinnock's own troubles. While he backed the Tories' stance in sending in the troops, a group on the left of the party, the 'Supper Club', decided to try and limit the leadership's approval of the Government line. It seemed as though defence – in one form or another – was to be the issue which once again would damage the unity of the Labour Party.

This time the divisions came into the open with the resignation of Clare Short from the Labour front bench after criticizing the party's support for the allied bombing campaign in Iraq. Kinnock asked her not to speak beyond the confines of her social security portfolio: Short chose the freedom offered by resigning to voice her opinion. 'It's the nature of the bombing that I'm worried about,' she said. 'People not having water and food; it's got nothing to do with the liberation of Kuwait.'

Kinnock's stated attitude was: 'Now that the engagement has been undertaken what is necessary is that we have the maximum possible unity and we seek the shortest possible conflict, with the minimum number of casualties both among our forces and amongst innocent Iraqi civilians and the people of Kuwait.' This was an obvious line to take, but one which some found hard to countenance in view of Labour's 'golden thread of loathing for war' as Edward Pearce called it in a critical analysis in *The Guardian*. He suggested that a wiser leader would have created a wider discretion in which individual members of the party could express their own consciences. 'As it is ... Neil Kinnock, for all his courage and decency, has tried so hard to look like a Prime Minister that he hardly now looks like the leader of the Opposition.'

Pearce took the opportunity to review Kinnock's wider vices and virtues. He took up the 'windbag' theme, interpreting this as Kinnock's 'touch of the inflationary condition in verbal terms, too many words chasing too little meaning. Control of the word supply has not been all that it might.' But, Pearce said, Kinnock also had courage, dogged purpose, and an unquestionable decency: 'I was best impressed by him in Bristol during the last election talking off camera to old people in a home. He spent much of his time on haunches or knees, talking softly, being kind, showing great sensitivity. Kinnock is entirely wholesome and decent.' But here too was comment that Kinnock had learned too much from Thatcher: 'He has renounced his humorous, anecdotal, unbuttoned private self for high recessed eminence, has abnegated his considerable wit for the stuffy Rotarian persona put on with the wrong, safe, identity-suppressing clothes.'

This apparent obsession with the Opposition leader's dress sense probably dates only from the early eighties and the furore over Michael Foot's appearance at the Cenotaph on Remembrance Sunday in an appropriately warm duffel-style coat. Foot eventually had the last word on that episode.

> They said it was a donkey jacket and of course it wasn't. Now, after the Cenotaph you cross the road and go into the Foreign Office for drinks, and as I went in the Queen Mother came up and said, 'Oh hello, Michael! That's a smart, sensible coat for a day like this.' Which it was, and d'you know, I'd far rather take the Queen Mother's opinion than that dreadful woman Thatcher's.

The Gulf War ended at the end of February with the rout of the Iraqi forces, and many thought that Major might call a general election at once to cash in on patriotic sentiment. Kinnock announced that Labour was ready and on the alert. He told Labour's local government conference in Nottingham:

> The fact remains that considerations of good taste and economic probity are not going to get in the way of a Tory Government that knows it's pushed Britain into a slump and will grab at any chance they think they can get, however slim, for avoiding defeat. Even in those circumstances, they won't save themselves. We are ready to take them on and ready to beat them on any date that they choose.

In his speech, Kinnock condemned the 'chronic complacency and congenital incompetence of Toryism'. He said: 'The head of Government who proclaims his belief in the "classless society" has been a social security minister and treasury minister during the years when the poor have been made poorer, the rich have been made richer and the millions in between have been made indebted and less secure all over our country.' In fact, Major later said that he would have considered such a move immoral; his decision was undoubtedly assisted early in March when the Tories lost the by-election at Ribble Valley, the tenth safest Tory seat, to the Liberal Democrats. The moment of truth was postponed.

11   Almost There

The Conservative Government had until June 1992 before its term came to an end and a general election had to be called. But in fact from the time that the Gulf War ended, speculation about an election date never abated. (The first hint came from the Tory Party chairman, Chris Patten, who said that the Government wanted to allow the economy to recover before calling an election, but at the same time he refused to rule out any options.) The period came to be seen as the 'phoney campaign', with the leaders of the two main parties in particular ever on the alert and acting as if the day of judgement was imminent.

Events in the Gulf faded quickly from public memory, and domestic issues once again dominated the clashes between John Major and Neil Kinnock. The first of a series of head-to-head debates came at the end of March 1991 when Labour tabled a motion of no confidence in the Government and Kinnock challenged the Prime Minister to call an election so that the voters could comment on the 'refusal to right the wrongs of the poll tax'. While preparing their plans for a speedy replacement of the ill-fated community charge, the Conservatives announced a cut of up to £140 in the current year's bill, which would benefit around half of all those who paid. Kinnock insisted: 'The poll tax is still alive and kicking the British people,' while the Tories promised that new local tax would be lower than old rate bills in real terms.

Kinnock accused the Government of conscience-less expediency and ineptitude, and declared that ministers would have to fight the forthcoming local elections on a manifesto called: 'Don't ask us, we're only the Government.' The latest panic decision, he said, would cost £200 million. 'And after all that, what we haven't got from all of the cost and chaos is a single additional home help, not a single extra police officer, not an extra teacher or road repair.'

Kinnock was seen as holding his own well against Mrs Thatcher's successor and, as one observer put it, 'the coming election will be fought between leaders who punch the same sort of weight'. (Kinnock was to say later that debating with Major was frustrating. 'You'd land a punch and it would go straight through him,' he told the *New Statesman*. 'In a sense, that was the secret of John Major's success.')

The following month, Labour again re-launched the policy review of 1989, this year's update being titled: *Labour's Better Way Forward for the 1990s*. Like its 1990 predecessor, the document aimed to be a mini-manifesto for a general election and while there was little new of substance, there was an air of confidence about its presentation. Neil Kinnock, in a foreword, said that the Conservatives had turned Britain into a nation of debt.

> If individuals are to flourish and society is to thrive in freedom, people need the means to develop their potential, economies need the vitality of competition that is fair and efficient, and countries need the practical advantages and self confidence that comes from a real sense of community. They need government that is accountable not arrogant, enabling not meddling.

Kinnock also foresaw moves by the Tories to revive defence as an election issue and he stated categorically that a Labour Government would not 'get rid of all nuclear weapons for as long as others have them'. That announcement was made at a press conference marking the launch of the programme for Labour's future; the Conservatives immediately maintained that this stance still amounted to unilateralism. It was a relatively feeble challenge, and one which Kinnock could confidently ignore as he was currently on the ascendant in public opinion during a year which resembled a very active seesaw for the fortunes of the Labour and Conservative leaders.

The continuing success of Kinnock's strategy to unite the Labour Party and bring it firmly under control was one reason. Patrick Seyd, writing in *Britain at the Polls 1992*, said that Kinnock had provided the drive, determination and direction of a move away from an unsuccessful past, 'and in so doing, he initiated reforms that went beyond what others originally envisaged so that by 1991 Labour had been moulded very much in his image.' Another popularity factor was undeniably the change of leadership in the Conservative Party.

As Ian Aitken wrote in *The Guardian*, Mrs Thatcher may not have been very nice, or even very admirable, but she was undoubtedly a colossus in much the same way as Saddam Hussein was a colossus in Iraqi terms. 'You needed a heavier punch than Mr Kinnock possessed to stand up to her week after week. Standing up to Mr Major may get more difficult as he gains experience, but it is never likely to be as hard as going two or three rounds twice a week with Mrs T.'

Both Kinnock and the Labour Party were looking alive and well as the local elections approached in May. Critics were beginning to look more kindly on the Opposition leader and even bury their former suggestions that he was not the man ever to be elected Prime Minister. There was less frequent reference to his 'famous wordiness' and one of his chief shortcomings – that of inexperience in Government – now appeared irrelevant beside his years of experience of parliamentary procedure, and his achievement in rescuing Labour from what had appeared to many as the brink of extinction as a political force. Correspondents were regularly looking ahead to possible outcomes of the election, whenever it might be, with a popular theme proving to be a small majority for Labour, or at least a hung Parliament; should Labour fail, there was already speculation as to the leader's personal responsibility for that failure, or whether the Labour Party itself was a spent force.

Of more immediate concern were the local elections where both Labour and the Liberal Democrats made widespread gains. And after analysing the share of the vote in 67 selected key marginal seats which showed Labour well in the lead with 43 per cent to the Tories' 37 per cent, the party claimed that such a swing would put Neil Kinnock into Downing Street with a 6-seat overall majority. May also saw a by-election in Monmouth, where the Conservatives were in danger of losing a seat which they had won with a 9,000 majority.

The biggest threat seemed to be from the Liberal Democrats who were enjoying a surge of popular support. Only days before the voting took place, Labour's chances appeared to be put at risk when *The Sun* published a story claiming that Neil Kinnock was linked to a Greek Cypriot tycoon whose business – and an alleged missing £10 million of company money – was being investigated by the Fraud Squad. The national press eagerly followed up the tale; it was, after all, the first ever whiff of scandal involving the Labour leader.

They found nothing of substance – and published it all. Neil and Glenys Kinnock were acquaintances of fashion manufacturer Charilaos Costa and his wife Chryssa. The two couples occasionally had dinner together; Costa had donated money to Labour Party funds; and one of his factory units was based in Kinnock's Welsh constituency. What seemed to fascinate the press most was that Glenys Kinnock had been given a few dresses as gifts from Costa's fashion house. But even the story which first broke in *The Sun* insisted: 'There is no suggestion of any impropriety involving Mr Kinnock, who has no business links with any of Costa's companies.'

Kinnock was quite unaware of inquiries into allegations of false accounting and obtaining property by deception until they appeared in *The Sun*. He said he was astounded by the news. Costa blamed the press for creating a political issue out of a group of companies going into receivership and said that the affair had developed into a smear campaign. Costa maintained that he had also made gifts of clothes to wives of Conservative MPs who had visited his factories.

The connection was an embarrassment, even though the press could not find anything even remotely improper with which to accuse Kinnock. *The Sun* published a full account from Kinnock's office answering every one of the points raised in the original story. This appeared on the paper's page three, and was said jokingly by a member of the Kinnock team to be 'one of the most literate pages *The Sun* has ever published'. Nevertheless, Labour feared that the damage had been done, that bad publicity would affect the party's chances with the voters. But in fact Labour won the Monmouth seat; Kinnock had ridden the storm-in-a-teacup and found by the end of the month that his party had an eight-point lead over the Tories in a national poll. Talk of a June election swiftly evaporated; even the autumn was looking unlikely.

Once again the public mood was swinging in Kinnock's favour and his personal credibility – and that of his party – was given a further boost by a surprising and unexpected tribute from a former Tory Cabinet Minister, John Biffen. In an interview certain to anger his own colleagues – who were determined to focus on Kinnock's alleged weaknesses – Biffen said that Kinnock had helped to make Labour 'distinctly electable'. 'I have no hesitation in saying that, when I think of Labour leaders, Neil Kinnock is outstanding,' Biffen said on Channel Four.

> He has done more to bring the Labour Party back to the centre ground of British politics than Hugh Gaitskell. When it comes to sheer political sensitivity, knowing where to apply the pressures, Neil Kinnock has been quite outstanding in putting the Labour Party into a better position politically than it has been in for decades. After so many years in the margins, Labour now looks distinctly electable.

Another by-election in July strengthened this view, and also marked a further significant victory for Kinnock in his battle to oust the Militant left. His vigilance in this crusade had never wavered, and now, at Walton on Merseyside – a seat that had become vacant on the death of Eric Heffer, a veteran left-winger – Militant had been forced into the open to fight the seat under their own banner. The 'Real Labour' candidate backed by Militant polled only 6.6 per cent of the vote, compared to the 54.6 per cent share for the official Labour candidate who won the seat with a majority of just under 7,000. The biggest swing was to the Liberal Democrats who took second place; the result emphatically killed off any prospect of an autumn general election.

Kinnock warned that party members who had backed the rebel candidate would be expelled, and there was also a hint that neighbouring Liverpool MP Terry Fields could be on the 'hit-list' for failing to support the official candidate during the campaign. The Conservative candidate polled just 2.9 per cent of the vote in the Tories' worst by-election result since 1918. Bookmakers were quoting Labour as odds-on favourites to win the next general election. Kinnock was actually hoping for a late autumn date. He believed that John Major would make a move before the implications of the council tax – the replacement for the poll tax – became widely known. And he maintained that as the year progressed, Major's prediction of an end to the recession would be shown as false. Kinnock wanted to trade on Labour's standing in the polls, which on current figures would give them an overall majority in the Commons.

Yet there were still occasional signals that Kinnock's transformation of the Labour Party was not wholeheartedly endorsed. In June the man who had taken over from Peter Mandelson as director of communications, John Underwood, resigned after only a year in the post. This followed a rift with his deputy, Colin Byrne, who had also been Mandelson's second in command. Underwood maintained that he had been unable to establish a relationship of trust with Byrne whom he wanted moved to another post. It was widely believed within the party that when internal disputes occurred, Byrne firmly favoured the leader's office and position. Critics argued that Byrne was employed to represent the party as a whole and not just the leader.

It appeared to be a relatively insignificant power struggle, and yet it undermined the stability and party unity for which Kinnock had devoted his entire leadership. One critic, the MP Clare Short, a member of the national executive, said that Underwood had operated fairly in the party's interests and that his position had been made intolerable. Kinnock, she said, had behaved in a 'very Thatcherite and undemocratic way'. Underwood's replacement was David Hill, a seasoned campaigner and long-time political 'minder' for Roy Hattersley, and his appointment was seen as a move to ease the internal tensions. It also strengthened a personal and political circle around the Labour leader: Colin Byrne shared a house with Julie Hall, Kinnock's press and broadcast secretary, and with Mandelson when he was in London, while David Hill lived with Hilary Coffman, Kinnock's press and broadcasting officer.

Then, just as internal troubles faded, the public mood started to shift again during the summer recess. It had little to do with Arthur Scargill's attack on Kinnock at the NUM conference in Blackpool; these days it was almost expected that he would charge Kinnock with abandoning socialist principles. If anything, it had more to do with events in Russia, and John Major's performance once again as a 'world statesman'. On 18 August President Gorbachev (one of Kinnock's heroes, incidentally) was toppled and held under house arrest in his holiday home after a coup led by Boris Yeltsin. He was reinstated after three days, but his return was merely a preparation for retirement a few months later.

Major flew to Washington for talks with President Bush about the Soviet situation, and then visited both Moscow and Peking. On his return his personal ratings soared and, coupled with a cut in interest rates, gave the Tories an unexpected surge ahead of Labour in the opinion polls. It was a lead won without any political risk, as Hugo Young described in *The Guardian*: Major 'has merely been required to say sensible things about events outside his control, which have ended by securing him an effortless political advantage'. And while Labour had gone back on to the offensive as if an election campaign was really under way, attacking the Conservatives' economic record, what Young called the 'infamous debate' about Kinnock's character and competence intervened again.

'No leader has been deconstructed more thoroughly,' wrote Young.

From the shape of his lips as seen by camera shots from the underside, to the ill-judged signals sent out by the quality of his neckties, and never forgetting the doubtful grammatical exactitude of some of his sentences, he has been subjected to more intensive critical scrutiny than any public figure in the western world.

Young believed that it was important to distinguish between Kinnock's capacity to be a decent Prime Minister,

and his capacity to win the election that would put him there. He's commonly described as a man who cannot win because he could not properly fill the job. Closer to the truth would be to say that, if he cannot win, the main reason is because it is so widely thought he cannot win.

In other words, Kinnock was suffering from public fatigue with his electoral failure. Young counselled that when the election campaign began in earnest, Labour should play up the Government's record, and play down the Kinnock image. But if Labour lost again, he said, the outcome should not be pinned on Kinnock alone. 'Although he will take the blame for not articulating a Labour alternative, that will be more a collective than an individual failure. Labour may ultimately deserve to lose, but not because Mr Kinnock is the leader.'

Another viewpoint, only whispered until after the 1992 election defeat, was that Kinnock had betrayed his roots, his party and socialism in pursuit of the goal of prime ministerial office. Two members of Labour's left wing, Richard Heffernan and Mike Marqusee, devoted an entire book to this theme (*Defeat from the Jaws of Victory – Inside Kinnock's Labour Party*), in which they said that Kinnock had turned himself into the archetype of everything the public hates about professional politicians.

> He was seen as a man who would do anything or say anything, repudiate any conviction or embrace any prejudice for the sake of a handful of votes. In the end it was hard for many people, in the privacy of the polling booth, to vote for a man whose sole ambition was apparently to become Prime Minister.

Such attacks ignore the basic, simple reality that without power Labour was unable to implement its policy. They also maintained that Kinnock had become increasingly isolated and remote in his pursuit of power. Kinnock is scathing about their assessment:

> It's obvious that they are wrong about most things and they are certainly wrong about 'isolation'. Like most other politicians I have very few really close friends among other politicians. That has always been the case. It remains so. My friends are from a cross-section of politics, journalism, the arts, sport, education and industry and, of course, South Wales. That's how it has always been. Those politicians who are friends but not all that close came and went with complete freedom and easy access when I was in the Leader's office. They still do. People called 'old friends' or calling themselves 'old friends' may not always be faithfully represented by writers, or they may not be quite as close as they like to think.

As the preliminaries to an election campaign continued, further opinion polls suggested that Labour's standing would be improved under a different leader. Kinnock was being criticized as much for what he didn't do as for what he did, for example over the Kremlin coup which happened while the Kinnocks had four days remaining of their family holiday in Tuscany. Should he have flown back to Britain rather than keeping in touch with the situation and making his comments by phone? It was not that Kinnock was in a position to take any action, but a question of image: would his hurried return, simply to be available for comments to television interviewers, have increased public confidence in his ability? Or would he have been derided by the tabloid press for playing the role of 'Prime Minister in waiting'?

Labour has been accused routinely of concentrating too much on image-making during the Kinnock years, and yet by the early nineties all politicians, of whatever persuasion, had become obsessed by public relations. Kinnock had actually spent the late summer and early autumn doing what he did best – and believed was most crucial: touring the country and speaking at public meetings. (In two separate weeks, in late July and in September, he visited Birmingham, Plymouth and Exeter, and then Sheffield, Scunthorpe, Aberdeen, Glasgow and Edinburgh.)

The criticism led to undercurrents in the parliamentary party and murmurings about a change of leadership. But Kinnock made his intentions quite clear when he wrote in the *Parliamentary House* magazine: 'I have never thought about quitting and can't afford to take notice of the attacks on me personally.' But he said he was saddened when his family became involved. The idea, circulating again, that Glenys pulled the strings was more than absurd, 'it is interesting as well because it says such a lot about the people who make those allegations. I think there must be some gap in their lives if they can't understand that two close and loving people can have a great relationship without determining the position of the other at all.' He said that in the thirty years since he had met Glenys, 'she has been absolutely basic to the enjoyment of my life … We didn't have what was called a perpetual courtship, but from day one we were very good friends and then loving friends.'

Evidence of Kinnock's determination to lead Labour into the election came in the autumn release of a party political broadcast which was dubbed as 'Kinnock: The Movie II'. Directed again by Hugh Hudson, it was an updated version of the celebrated 1987 election film, and opened with a montage of grim black-and-white pictures illustrating the accuracy of the Labour leader's warning not to become old, poor or sick in Britain under the Conservatives. In style it was less glamorous and certainly less presidential in tone. There were scenes from life in the Welsh valleys, choirs singing, and a relaxed interview with Neil and Glenys Kinnock. The aim was to illustrate an eight-year journey towards Downing Street, alongside the wasted opportunities of the eighties.

The film may have played down the Kinnock personality, but when Labour's annual conference opened in Brighton he was given a movie star reception. His keynote speech was greeted with the level of rapturous applause which delegates had awarded him year after year. This year there was confidence in the air, too, even without an election date in sight yet. (The Prime Minister had abandoned the prospect of going to the country in November, and the following spring was now the aim.)

Kinnock had his party firmly under control, disciplined and determined; the ousting of Militant was almost complete with the two hard left MPs, Dave Nellist and Terry Fields, under investigation and soon to be expelled from the Labour Party; and the leader had won a critical eve-of-conference vote at an NEC meeting over proposed reform of the reselection of MPs. This was designed to remove from sitting MPs the threat of deselection by small groups within a constituency. The new rules insisted on a one member, one vote mandate on whether to initiate a reselection process. The NEC decision was seen as a substantial vote of confidence for Kinnock following months of consultation with union leaders who were concerned at their prospective loss of power. The one member, one vote controversy has followed Labour way beyond the 1992 election defeat, of course.

Kinnock's conference speech was a serious delivery of the programme for a Labour Government rather than a rallying call to troops. He insisted that after twelve years the Tory Government was 'stale and sour' while he promised fresh direction and new approaches. He pointed to the monuments to Conservative rule: a million people on hospital waiting lists, 150,000 homeless families and the highest recorded crime rate in British history. Labour would release money from council house sales to help build more homes; public transport would be modernized; economic success would be built on converting scientific inventiveness into competitive industrial production. And Labour would modernize the NHS. 'The Tories would privatise the NHS. Of course, they protest that they won't. But that means they either don't understand or that they won't admit to understanding the dynamic of a process they have already started.'

At the next election people would be deciding whether they kept the NHS or lost it. 'Those who vote otherwise will be voting to allow the break-up of the NHS.' It was time to start transforming Britain, he concluded, from the country it had become 'into the country we know it can be'. As *The Guardian* commentator Hugo Young wrote, Kinnock did not make a great speech but he made it into a great occasion. And he laid to rest 'the search for a big new idea with the glaring discovery that new ideas do not exist – only old ideas whose time has come. This is the essence of Kinnock's vision and it is no small achievement to have made it believable.' He won the inevitable ovation, and more emotional applause when he returned to the rostrum to thank 'people like you' for their support during the recent weeks when his leadership had been under fire. Then he led the delegates in singing the civil rights anthem 'We Shall Overcome'.

There was also that week the now familiar setback over defence policy, the only sour note for Kinnock at a triumphant conference. A two-thirds majority voted in favour of cutting back UK defence spending to the Western European average. But as in the previous year the leadership immediately insisted that in government Labour would have to meet its obligations – even if they were out of line with conference decisions. It was further evidence that Kinnock's control over the party was such that he was intent on proceeding with a policy of negotiated disarmament at a pace dictated by international events and negotiating sessions rather than by party conference.

The heckling which resulted was forgotten the next day when the week ended with a party atmosphere. Breaking with conference tradition Kinnock made a second platform speech, surrounded by his 'government in waiting' who had been called individually to the stage in 'come on down' rally style. 'Victory is more than within our grasp,' he announced. 'When we next meet together we shall meet in government – government that will take our country, the whole of our country, to victories yet unseen.' And to the strains of the pop song 'We are the Champions', the members of the Shadow Cabinet swayed rather self-consciously as delegates cheered them loudly.

It was seen by many as Labour's most successful conference for years, largely due to a new mood of confidence which Kinnock endowed. Nicholas Timmins in *The Independent* described the week as a 'near replica' of Brighton a year earlier. 'The paradox is that Labour entered its last conference 19 points ahead in the polls, with Margaret Thatcher still in place, but with few delegates daring to believe they could win. This year they are back neck and neck with the Tories, but delegates now believe they have a fighting chance of victory.'

There was another vote of confidence for Kinnock later in October when Labour MPs re-elected the existing Shadow Cabinet and saved the leader from a difficult pre-election reshuffle. Among them were four women: Labour had introduced an element of positive discrimination in the elections three years earlier by making ballot papers valid only if MPs voted for at least three women. Kinnock also deliberately promoted women to the front bench. This in itself was evidence against those who claimed that Kinnock was a 'man's man', with too great a rugby-playing heritage to be aware of women's issues and women's problems. He does enjoy all-male company on occasions, but cannot be said to have ever deserved a 'macho' label.

Ask Kinnock whom he admires most, and among the famous he names the female Burmese opposition leader Aung San Suu Kyi, the winner of the 1991 Nobel Peace Prize, who has been under house arrest by Rangoon's military junta for more than three years. And the not-famous? 'Particularly some elderly working class women in my constituency. They have hell – and they are still generous and progressive.'

He is careful with his vocabulary and takes pains to change one of his favourite quotations: 'For evil to triumph it is only necessary for good men to do nothing' into 'good people to do nothing'. And he recounts with delight an incident at a conference of the Iron and Steel Trades Confederation, at which both he and Glenys spoke independently. He was pleased to note that Glenys was not introduced as 'Neil Kinnock's wife'; nevertheless she was welcomed by the previous speaker, Brian

Moore, as 'the lovely Glenys Kinnock'. Glenys stepped forward and told the almost totally male delegation that it was a pleasure to follow 'the lovely Brian Moore'. 'The steelmen rocked with laughter and poor Brian Moore is stuck for life with the nickname "Lovely".'

Such anecdotes are not necessarily of themselves evidence of feminist sympathy. Sebastian Faulks, who interviewed Kinnock for *The Guardian*, maintains that 'his age, background and exuberant personality make it impossible for him to stop calling women "my love" or buying them flowers'. Nevertheless, Kinnock had made the adjustment to feminism by strong declarations of support for his wife: he had elevated his affection into a political statement, and 'a feminism that begins at home is hard to dismiss'. Kinnock acknowledges that between them Glenys and Jan Royall, his personal assistant since the mid-eighties, have his life organized for him. And he talks with affection of 'all these terrific women', his good female friends and colleagues: they are, he says, using a term of masculine camaraderie, 'bloody good mates'. But most essentially, he never patronizes women. When he compliments his friend and NEC colleague Tom Sawyer on a rare ability to talk to women as easily and as equally as he does to men, he is overlooking the same quality in himself.

As the period of the phoney campaign continued into the autumn, Kinnock was again looking the popular voters' choice. In the Yorkshire constituency of Hemsworth his appearance gave a boost to the campaign of the official Labour candidate in the by-election there. Derek Enright, a former Euro MP, had been imposed as the official candidate by the NEC under the system agreed at conference. His opponent for selection was the regional vice chairman of the mineworkers' union, Ken Capstick. Enright went on to win the seat – in a strong mining constituency – and vindicate Kinnock's judgement.

While Kinnock's personal rating looked more positive, and the economy worsened towards the end of the year, Labour gained a small, fluctuating lead in the polls. But the Conservatives held on to their belief that recovery would begin in the new year, and from the end of October onwards there was little to choose between the two major parties in the Gallup poll – it was usually a matter of one percentage point. Without a date, but certain of a spring election, the campaign was to all intents and purposes already under way.

The Conservatives insisted that under Labour the country would only suffer further, that they had not the competence to handle the economy, to deal with inflation, unemployment, interest rates and so on. Kenneth Newton, in *Britain at the Polls 1992*, said:

Almost every Labour criticism of Conservative economic policy brought forth not a defence of the policy, but an attack on Labour's economic competence. For example, in reply to Kinnock's claim that 'this Government caused the recession, they continue the recession and now they haven't got a clue how to get out of it,' Major claimed that Kinnock was 'an economic illiterate' whose policies 'would mean perpetual recession for this country'.

And on a campaign visit to Aberdeen for the Kincardine and Deeside by-election, Kinnock told reporters that Labour stood by its pledge of borrowing for investment but not for consumption.

The Government approach to the public expenditure round is to undertake the biggest public sector borrowing requirement in history and to try and give the impression that they are being very tough. What they will do before the election is build up a set of promises which make people believe that Christmas has arrived.

Just before Christmas did arrive, on 11 December at a European summit meeting in Maastricht in the Netherlands, John Major brought off what was seen as a negotiating triumph when a treaty was agreed which allowed Britain an opt-out on the single currency. Delegates from the other EC countries also agreed to press ahead without Britain on the 'social chapter'. At the cost of alienating most of his European counterparts, Major had avoided a damaging split in the Conservative ranks. His success was such that it was only well after the election – and after a no vote in a Danish referendum – that Europe, and in particular, Maastricht, became an issue again.

Major's strength was illustrated again in the new year in a Harris poll for *The Observer*. One of the questions asked who was to blame for rising unemployment: 43 per cent named Margaret Thatcher, 28 per cent said the world recession, and only 9 per cent blamed the current Prime Minister. It seemed that on any issues surrounding the state of the economy, the public were placing the fault on policies established before Major took over.

Labour, meanwhile, made another final relaunch of the policy review entitled *Made in Britain*. At the same time, the Tories attacked Labour's tax plans, making capital of the proposals to abolish the upper limit on National Insurance contributions. Kinnock's response led to the sort of pre-election embarrassment which he and his team had been anxious to avoid this time. At an informal dinner with political correspondents at Luigi's Italian restaurant in London, Kinnock hinted that the National Insurance changes would be phased in, so that no one would feel the effect immediately. This appeared to contradict Shadow economic policy that the contributions limit would have to be removed at once if

Labour was to honour its promises to increase child benefit and pensions.

A damage limitation exercise followed, while the incident led Kinnock to reinforce his suspicions of the press. He was angered further by a series of two articles in the *Sunday Times* which maintained that he had contacts with the Kremlin at the height of the cold war. The paper reproduced details of private dialogues alleged to have taken place between Kinnock and other Labour leaders and Soviet officials, criticizing the Thatcher administration for allowing US nuclear bases in Britain. Leading Labour MPs insisted that the Tory 'dirty tricks' department had been involved in a conspiracy with newspapers to mount a campaign to blacken Kinnock's name in the run-up to the election. Government ministers maintained that the allegations did not cast doubt on Kinnock's patriotism, only on his judgement. But the row caused considerable ill-feeling and bitterness across the rival front benches.

The story was rapidly superseded on the front pages by a 'scandal' involving the Liberal Democrat leader, Paddy Ashdown, who admitted having had an affair with his secretary some five years earlier. This appeared to have, if anything, a positive effect on his party's standing in the opinion polls, while Labour and the Conservatives were now level with one another. By mid-February 1992 the prospect of a hung Parliament was being considered seriously.

In March, a MORI poll showed the Government leading Labour on the question of economic competence by 11 per cent; and 47 per cent considered John Major best equipped to handle the economy, compared with only 31 per cent who rated Kinnock best equipped. The Tories improved their image on Budget Day, 10 March, when taxes were reduced and government borrowing doubled. The following day John Major made the announcement for which the political world had been waiting for more than a year: the general election would be held on 9 April.

Peter Kellner, who introduced a book of Kinnock's speeches, *Thorns and Roses*, wrote at this stage the Labour Party was following its leader more obediently than at any time for at least half a century. The task had taken Kinnock eight years and his method had resembled that of a climber scaling an awkward rock face: 'Hammering pitons into tiny cracks, testing them for strength, and making sure of each foothold before climbing further. To any spectator hoping for a fast ascent, Kinnock's method was slow and sometimes tedious. Yet at least he can claim to have reached the summit.' One summit, at least. Another climb remained. Wrote Kellner: 'If Labour wins the coming election, its victory will be unusually sweet for its leader. Kinnock has spent eight years plucking thorns from his side, not all of them placed there by the

Conservatives or unfriendly newspapers. Triumph at the polls would vindicate his strategy since 1983 and, for the time being at least, provide a conclusive response to his detractors.'

12   The Last Rally

Labour went into the election campaign in a spirit of confidence and optimism, and Kinnock looked as though he was going to enjoy the contest. If his moment did not come now, then it never would; he was certainly ready for the fight. More than eight years of leading the Labour Party in opposition had not been an enjoyable or rewarding experience, but reward was in sight. In *The Guardian* Hugo Young said of Kinnock:

> He has grown leathery in the service of the Labour Party and possesses a carapace of experience that makes him impenetrable by even the most pointed attacks. This might have been one of his weaknesses, when he was so intent on remaking the Labour Party that he was unable to apply much great wisdom to the wider world outside it. But he is starting into the political moment he most enjoys, and for which life has prepared him more fiercely than any other man in the field.

Striving for office had matured Kinnock, according to the *Financial Times*: 'The leader of the Labour Party has spent eight years preparing for the forthcoming general election, and it shows.' Their reporters found him in control, not only of his party but also of his responses. 'The Labour leader will never be accused of pithiness. He is by nature loquacious. Yet he seems to be aware of the huge effort of self-mastery that he must undertake if he is to stand a chance of winning.' Kinnock gave full answers without rambling, avoided 'more than a modicum of sub-clauses and dialectical by-ways' and was judged to be no easy mark for the Conservatives. 'To the extent that they are banking on the windbag image to see them through the campaign they may be in for a surprise.'

In fact Kinnock was to play a mostly low-key role in the campaign, stressing time and again that he had the 'team' to win and presenting to the electorate his cabinet in waiting. Even the election issue of *Labour Party News* which, after all, was preaching to the converted, deliberately avoided the 'presidential' approach. In thirty-six pages, Kinnock's photograph appeared only twice: plus the cover picture, a line-up of the

172

entire shadow cabinet in which Kinnock appears dwarfed by John Smith on his right and Roy Hattersley on his left.

Hugo Young in *The Guardian* also noted the absence of 'verbosity and blether', and learned from Kinnock that the verbosity had been all to do with tactics. Obscurity was part of the act. 'I was never going to let the party down by making a direct answer when that would have generated confusion, slowed down the process of change,' he said. This led to 'longer sentences with more sub clauses than otherwise might have been the case'. The changes in policy since 1987 had made it easier for him to be direct, he explained. Young also accused him of changing his mind almost as radically as Mikhail Gorbachev

> but without Gorbachev's lengthy explanations to help his people account for what had happened. Kinnock's strength, however, is that he seems impervious, at quite a deep level, to these insinuations. They do not embarrass him. Being right now is what matters. The end justified everything: an end not scented for 18 years, since Labour was last elected to power.

As in 1987, Labour was doomed to win the campaign but lose the election. But, unlike 87, Labour entered the contest marginally in the lead in the opinion polls – 41 per cent to the Tories' 38 per cent – and appeared throughout to present a serious threat. Their strategy was to let the Conservative record speak for itself and in effect allow the Government to lose the election. Labour stressed the 'caring' values of its manifesto – on health, education and pensions – while pointing to the Government's failure to end the recession.

The Conservatives had launched their attack on Labour's tax plans earlier in the year, claiming that people would pay £1,000 a year more tax under Labour. The Labour proposals had been announced well before the election date was known, so that voters would have time to get accustomed to their implications. The finer details were added now, in an 'alternative budget' presented by Shadow Chancellor John Smith. He announced that Labour would raise the threshold below which no tax or National Insurance contributions were to be paid. At the other end of the income scale they would bring in a 50p tax rate for those earning £40,000 or more and abolish the National Insurance ceiling of £21,000. Child benefit and pensions would be increased.

The proposals were welcomed by the Tories: John Major said that they had effectively won the election for the Government, by hitting the middle classes. But on first appraisal the plans were received favourably. Most voters did earn less than £22,000 a year and would be marginally better off under the Labour scheme. The Conservatives were keen to insist otherwise.

Talking to John Humphrys on BBC Radio Four's *On the Ropes*, a year later, Kinnock agreed that removing the National Insurance ceiling and raising the higher tax rate had cost the party dear.

> We didn't leave ourselves enough time for explanation, not just about the redistributive effect or the amounts that would be involved, but about the fact that the increases in personal taxation would be applied to very, very few people. And the consequences of collecting that tax would be a general benefit to the whole country.

But would he have changed the proposals had he known what their effect would be?

> No, because none of our sums would have added up had we not been willing to make specific commitments for the raising of additional revenue. A lot of our programme could be financed from the improved growth record that we would have secured, but we had immediate obligations to higher pensions and increased child benefit, and it was essential that we had the resources for it. If we wanted to make new, modest but important investment in education and health, the money had to be found. But I hoped that the sense of public purpose and the frustration with low standards of public provision would be enough to offset that negative effect.

It was a gamble which the Labour Party is bound on principle to take, and it failed in spite of opinion poll evidence that the majority of voters were willing to pay higher taxes as long as they were spent in the right areas, such as education, health and social services. This raises the question of the veracity of opinion polls, and what Kenneth Newton (in *Britain at the Polls 1992*) calls the 'shame factor'. He wrote that whatever people tell opinion gatherers, they may still vote for tax cuts in the privacy of the polling booth. 'It has been suggested that a "shame-factor" (a reluctance to state a Conservative voting intention to pollsters) may have accounted for the fact that the polls underestimated the Conservative vote.'

In fact the Conservatives' claim that individuals would be worse off by £1,000 under Labour was later adjusted upwards to £1,250, a sum which, according to Newton, 'was calculated on the basis of some questionable assumptions; besides, it was an average figure that took no account of the incidence of taxation'. (Those 'questionable assumptions' included a Tory totting up of Labour's spending promises to produce a total of £38 billion, which Norman Lamont insisted would mean an all round average tax increase of £1,250 per head.)

But the tabloids took it all to heart and ran front page stories with headlines such as 'Road to ruin with Kinnock' (*Daily Express*),

'Kinnock's policy is economic suicide' (*Daily Mail*) and 'Labour to squeeze backbone of Britain' (*The Sun*). (Barbara Castle wrote after the election – in *The Guardian* – that her enduring memory of the campaign was of talking to residents of sheltered accommodation for old people. One elderly gentleman timidly said he had been told that Labour would take £1,000 a year from him in tax, and he couldn't afford that. Lady Castle asked, astonished, where he had got that idea. He replied: *The Sun*. 'We explained newspaper politics to him, but I don't know whether we offset the effect on him of seeing this assertion in print.') Kinnock was to say later that a lot of people who did not pay tax, or were going to pay less tax, 'nevertheless believed the propaganda that said they were going to pay more. It was the degree to which the falsehood was lodged in five or six per cent of the electorate.'

On the day that Labour's manifesto, *It's time to get Britain working again*, was published, two opinion polls gave them a 5 per cent lead. The manifesto contained strong commitments to the European Community, and promised to retain a nuclear deterrent for Britain until the world's stock of nuclear weapons had been removed. Commentators noted that the words 'class' and 'socialism' were nowhere mentioned! The only promise of renationalization was to take the national grid and the privatized water companies into 'public control'.

On Europe, Kinnock maintained that his 'conversion' predated the 1983 election, which Labour fought on a pledge to leave the Community. He had long been in favour of the EC but he saw the potentially destructive effect of saying so until the time was right. On the question of public ownership, he said that in Europe there were many versions of state ownership, and that the notion of 'wholesale takeover' was no longer appropriate for Britain.

Neither issue proved particularly contentious during the campaign, and Kinnock concentrated on presenting Labour's caring policies. In the first of his public appearances, a speech to the Scottish Labour conference, he promised investment to build a strong economy in partnership with industry and condemned the 'selfishness' and 'stagnation' of the Government's rule. Returning to a favourite theme he promised: 'We want people to be free of the fear of falling ill, free of fear of walking the dark streets at night, free of fear of being old and lonely.'

Robin Oakley, then political editor of *The Times*, wrote that the campaign lacked excitement: the long 'practice period' had ensured that most acts were well rehearsed and there were few gaffes. Kinnock himself admitted that spontaneity had gone from election campaigns, but blamed television which, he said, forced all the main parties to change their approach. He was responding to criticism that Labour 'minders' were sheltering him from reporters through a series of staged photo opportunities.

The problem was illustrated on board Labour's chartered train, the Red Rose Express. On a journey to Cardiff Kinnock set off to walk the length of the train to chat with journalists, but it took him twenty minutes to get past the television crews and photographers packing the first carriage. He regretted, too, that party rallies were now all-ticket; once again, television was to blame for providing an open door 'for people to demonstrate and disrupt'. This 'concession to disruption' had been adopted by all the parties, against his own instinct which was for 'heckling and a rumbustious style – that suits me down to the ground'.

But all-ticket rallies tended to be relatively solemn. Nicholas Timmins of *The Independent*, described one meeting, in Manchester Town Hall, where Kinnock delivered a 'carefully staged economics lecture' with an academic version of Labour's policies. Said Timmins: 'Its sub text might have been: I can be boring and responsible enough to be prime minister.' This style did not suit Kinnock at all, and the campaign did provide some moments when he could weave a magic spell with words. 'The all-important sound bites are often ad-libs,' wrote Timmins on another occasion. Such as when Kinnock followed his 'the Tories know they are losing' with the unscripted: 'You can hear their fingernails scraping down the wall of power as they hang on.'

'Neil Kinnock may be a mixed performer at Prime Minister's questions,' said Timmins. 'Not even his closest friends would describe him as the greatest television interviewee. But put him on a conference platform and there can be a magic that few have matched. It is his element.' Kinnock, said Timmins, understood the rapture that he produced. 'He drinks it in, not in any self-glorifying way, but as the fuel that keeps him going in the face of a largely hostile Press and still sceptical electorate. Unlike Mr Major, as the cheers and the standing ovations wash over him, Mr Kinnock knows why his party loves him.'

The performances were mixed, sometimes too long, sometimes verbose.

> But on his day – and particularly in election campaigns – no one matches him. Everything goes into them [the performances]: dark and light, shade and tone, humour and deep seriousness, variations of pitch and pace and volume. His body coils and strikes like a snake to deliver the harshest points while the voice avoids spitting them out. His hands illustrate, expand, explore, define.

The speeches continued to be scribbled on bits of paper. Texts provided in advance for reporters were merely the framework, not the finished article. Timmins quoted one partisan observer who said: 'Plenty of politicians can make you laugh, plenty can make you angry, some can make you cry. Neil can do all of that and include real content.'

For Barbara Castle, he did not do it often enough during the election campaign. 'The man who was packaged for the election by Labour's campaign team was not the Neil I knew,' she wrote in her memoirs, *Fighting All the Way*. 'For a long time I had been disturbed by the front bench's cult of blandness and respectability, designed to reassure a hesitant electorate ... Neil Kinnock was a captive of this approach.' When she spoke with him at election rallies, Kinnock's text was too often 'a carefully prepared speech, with verve but no spontaneity'; hers was inevitably a punchy, hard-hitting clarion call to the faithful. But Lady Castle acknowledges why he could not make a speech like that: 'I was free of the responsibilities of leadership and could make daring, mocking sallies against the government, while Neil was sanitized in case the press should pick out of context a single impulsive phrase they could distort.'

Nevertheless her frustration remained, and in despair she wrote a letter to Kinnock:

> I can't stand it any longer. What are your image makers doing to you? You have achieved so much ... but your advisers are insisting on projecting you in such a denatured form that I for one cannot recognize the man who I know would make a human, warm and caring Prime Minister. The photograph of you on the front page of the current *Labour Party News* is disastrous. It makes you look like a washed out edition of Paddy Ashdown.

In fact the letter was never posted: after watching on television a speech in which Kinnock 'radiated his old spontaneity' she hoped that this was a transformation and a changed style of electioneering, 'but it did not last. I did not send the letter because his advisers had cast him in the role of calculated respectability and it was too late to change.'

The recollection brought a wry smile from Kinnock when Barbara Castle's book was published twelve months after the election. 'Her view of me is very kindly and well motivated. But the point is, we knew Barbara was going to vote Labour. We didn't have to worry about that.' On her challenge that Kinnock had appeared to lose confidence after the 1987 election defeat, he believes that she underestimated the discipline needed for the task in making Labour electable.

> Barbara really did think I could have done it by a flourishing appeal, what I call the cavalryman's approach, and it couldn't have been done like that. My life would have been a lot easier if it could have. Barbara was solicitous, considerate, but frustrated because she thought I should have

drawn my sword and charged. Whereas I knew that if I did I might take a few with me, but I was going to go down, and the party was going to go down.

On the substance of the 1992 campaign, Robin Oakley wrote that Labour had the greater success in framing the agenda,

> while Conservatives grew edgy at their party's apparent inability to peg back Labour's small but visible lead in the opinion polls. A media pack long bored with the preliminary skirmishing of the phoney war, during which the Conservatives had been forced to expend much of their ammunition on Labour's tax plans to prevent Mr Kinnock developing momentum, criticised the Tories in particular for concentrating all their efforts on attacking Labour.

The Labour leadership team knew only too well that the three main Tory-supporting tabloid papers – *The Sun*, the *Daily Mail* and the *Daily Express* – would exploit any 'gaffe' and Kinnock was guarded closely so that reporters were denied the opportunity to trip him up. When he refused to give interviews to *The Sun* and the *Daily Mail*, the *Mail* printed a page carrying its questions with empty spaces where Kinnock's answers should have been.

As the campaign gathered momentum the tabloids directed their attacks more personally at Kinnock, culminating in the *Express* headline 'Nightmare on Kinnock Street', and the notorious polling day *Sun* front page, with its picture of Kinnock in a light bulb and the banner: 'If Kinnock wins today will the last person to leave Britain please turn out the lights'. The text ran: 'You know our views on the subject but we don't want to influence you in your final judgment on who will be prime minister! But if it's a bald bloke with wispy red hair and two K's in his surname, we'll see you at the airport. Good night and thank you for everything.'

Hugo Young wrote in *The Guardian* at the time that 'Mr Kinnock can safely be said to have endured more public insults over a longer period than any other figure in British public life.' (Some might argue that Mrs Thatcher, by the very nature of her office as prime minister, and a target for critics from overseas as well as at home, endured even more public insults than Kinnock. Certainly in the subsequent periods of assessment of their respective careers, Kinnock came to be treated far more gently. After his term of leadership, former critics were both sympathetic and generous, while Mrs Thatcher came in for insults verging on the brutal. But of course, as commentators pointed out, Kinnock was the one who resigned without his leadership being challenged! Nor was he the one to publish memoirs critical of former allies.)

The significance of such personal attacks was that the leader of the party which lost the election would almost certainly have to resign, Kinnock because he failed on successive occasions to lead his team to victory, and Major because his predecessor had led hers to victory every time. Kinnock consistently came a poor second in the opinion polls when voters were asked who would make the best Prime Minister, even when Labour had an overall lead. When questioned, many interviewees referred to Kinnock's policy reversals, particularly over nuclear defence. Fewer than a third believed that he was a good Labour leader, and most ranked his personal qualities below those of Major.

Kenneth Newton, in *Britain at the Polls 1992*, pointed out the irony that Kinnock's strongest point, his power as an orator who could move large audiences, was largely irrelevant to the 'media electioneering' techniques of 1992, 'whereas Major's nice, caring, likeable, and reasonable features shone through best on television'. (It is even more ironic that Kinnock subsequently found considerable popularity as a media entertainer, described as warm and likeable by those who watched his TV performances after the election defeat.) Newton says that it is difficult to disentangle the effects of personality and politics in assessing whether the leadership battle affected the election outcome, 'but the evidence, though circumstantial, suggests that it did. Major was always more popular than Kinnock by a wide margin, although Kinnock's policies were better liked than Major's by a smaller margin ... There seems to be a closer association between voting and approval of Major than between voting and approval of Major's policies.'

One particular incident in which Kinnock took the brunt of press criticism was the bizarre affair of 'Jennifer's ear'. A Labour television broadcast on the NHS focused on the plight of a young girl whose operation to heal a painful ear complaint was delayed by lack of funds; her story was contrasted with that of a similar young girl whose parents paid for medical treatment. The broadcast was not meant as an actual case history, more as a parable based on a number of similar sick children, but the real 'Jennifer' was named by *The Independent*, and the rest of the national press immediately accused Labour of exploiting a sick child for political purposes. They delighted in the further revelation that Jennifer's grandfather was actually a Tory councillor and no supporter of the Labour Party.

In fact, the original claim that the girl's operation was delayed by lack of funds was true and verified in letters by hospital officials; and the Tories then came under fire for admitting that they had put the consultant in the case in touch with the *Daily Express*. But the debate had moved into another arena by then: subsequent stories concentrated on Labour's lack of responsibility rather than on any shortcomings in the NHS.

Kinnock played little direct part in the entire proceedings, other than to intervene when a Labour press officer, Julie Hall, was being questioned about her part in the releasing of the girl's name. But Kinnock, of course, bore the weight of press indignation: 'If Kinnock will tell lies about a sick little girl, will he ever tell the truth about anything?' was the question posed by *The Sun*. It was the sort of issue that the campaign observers had been waiting for. (The *Express* even recalled from Moscow its reporter Peter Hitchen who had been at the forefront of attacks on Kinnock during the miners' strike and the 1987 election, and was now under his editor's instructions 'to harry Kinnock': fellow reporters believed that he was really there to taunt Kinnock into hitting him.) The stories ran and ran, but the public appeared to have been either bemused or bored very early on, and the standing of both main parties seemed to be unaffected by the issue – other than in an increase of cynicism at the entire process.

As the election campaign moved into April, several Tories were openly critical of their team's lacklustre performance, and a MORI opinion poll indicated the prospect of an overall Labour majority; Labour was leading the Conservatives by seven percentage points, its biggest lead so far. (The City took fright and billions of pounds were wiped off the value of shares. Prices plummeted, with the privatized water and electricity companies among the worst sufferers, although the index recovered slightly soon afterwards: Labour had promised to take the water industry back into public control and tightly regulate the power sector. City analysts had repeatedly warned that a firm Labour lead was bound to upset the stock market where dealers and investors were traditionally Conservative supporters.) Conservative campaign workers were said to be in a state of panic while Labour's election team was talking about the door of No. 10. On the night of 1 April, the Labour Party celebrated.

The venue was an arena in Sheffield, the crowd numbered more than 10,000, and the event was a political rally on an exuberant scale never before seen in Britain. Sceptics say that the triumphalist mood of the Sheffield rally lost Labour the election; Roy Hattersley said afterwards that, had Labour won, Sheffield would have been seen as the turning-point. It was the most glamorous and exultant staging of a political meeting in showbusiness style. It became the most analysed event of the general election post-mortem. That it gave a platform for the finest orators of the Labour movement, past and present, has generally been overlooked. And so it is worth studying the Sheffield rally in some detail, if only to see what all the fuss was about.

The event was introduced by Sheffield MP David Blunkett; both he, and the compère for the evening, the actress Charlotte Cornwell, sounded utterly certain of electoral success. The members of the Shadow Cabinet, said Blunkett, were 'committed to and sure of a resounding Labour victory'. Cornwell, in due course, proclaimed: 'It's time to meet the men and women who, within a matter of a very few days, will form the next Labour government.' The Shadow Cabinet team was hailed individually, as each entered the hall and went to their seats raised at the back of the crowd. Meanwhile pictures on a huge screen showed Neil and Glenys Kinnock arriving by helicopter and landing a few hundred yards from the arena entrance, before they too came in to rapturous applause.

It was a night for music. There were Highland pipers, a colliery band, pop singers, jazz singers, opera singers, a brass ensemble, two choirs; and throughout the repeated stirring anthem, 'Winter's Ending', written by the film score composer Michael Kamen with lyrics by the poet Adrian Henri. And it was a celebrity night, with screened messages from the famous and influential, each announcing why they would vote Labour: from athlete Steve Cram to satirist Stephen Fry; from disc jockey Paul Gambacini to scientist Stephen Hawking; with more eloquent tributes from writer John Mortimer and film director Richard Attenborough. There were flags and balloons and blown kisses, and there were speeches. Roy Hattersley and John Smith, eloquent and respectable; Barbara Castle taking up the battle cry in a more traditional vein with unforgettable clarity: 'Hang on to the simplicities, comrades'. And then, said compère Cornwell: 'Now it is time, time for the next prime minister – Neil Kinnock.'

The Prime Minister in waiting took an age to reach the platform as he – and his minders – pushed through the crowd, shaking hands and blowing kisses. At the steps he turned, waved, and bounded to the lectern. He waited for the cheering to subside a little and then yelled to the crowd, three times: 'Well all right.' Then, as the noise diminished, he wiped his brow and insisted: 'We'd better get some talking done here, some serious talking.'

He was to regret for ever bounding on to the stage. But the glitter and the razzmatazz, the songs before and the balloons after, have tended to overshadow the substance of his speech. It was not the greatest performance of Kinnock's life, but it was a very good one indeed. He was addressing friends, fans and followers and – just as he had done at every party conference – Kinnock rose to the occasion.

There was the confident opening – 'In ten days time Britain will have a Labour government.' There were a few initial jokes, just enough sarcasm, in a fundamental, back to basics call to the electorate. The Tories, he said, were a spent force. They had no vitality and were rapidly losing the last remnants of their integrity. Unable to offer any vision of the future 'they have fallen back on smears and insults and absurd fictions about us and about our programme'.

'I hear these strident and sour insults, and frankly they impress the British people even less than they affect me.' But there were personal attacks to which he objected,

> personal attacks that enrage me. They are not the ones launched by politicians on politicians; politicians are big enough to look after themselves. The personal attacks that I detest are those made by the Tories on poor people when they shrink incomes that are already too small to sustain civilised life. Those made on peoples' security when they lose their jobs because of Tory policy. Those made on sick and disabled people when they wait longer in pain as a result of Tory policies.

The British people, he said, were coming to Labour 'because our country cannot go on like this with a government that caused recession, a government that continued recession, and a government that now hasn't got a clue how to get out of the recession'.

Kinnock condemned the Conservatives' 'deliberate policies of poverty' against pensioners, the disabled, low paid families, unemployed youngsters, and single parents. 'British people want a country with a sense of community, a Britain that is whole and fair and free, free of fear.' He condemned Government policy on education, particularly on school opt-outs and the lack of nursery places.

He mocked the Tories' concept of a classless society, poured scorn on the prospect of further privatization, and attacked policies which had increased homelessness and insecurity. And silencing the critics who had read Kinnock's introduction to the election manifesto, he used the word 'socialism' time and again. In essence the speech appeared to encapsulate his entire political philosophy. As he ended with the call: 'Now is the time for Britain to pull together, now is the time for change, now is the time for Labour', the members of the Shadow Cabinet rose from their seats on steps at the back of the stage and came forward to receive the cheers of the crowd, and Glenys Kinnock stepped up onto the platform. Arm in arm she and Neil acknowledged the applause and the cheers, and joined in a rock gospel version of 'Jerusalem'.

It was, after all, a celebration rally for Labour supporters, designed to give them a boost for the final week of the campaign, and as Glenys Kinnock said later, 'We should sing and dance at political rallies.' But even within the Labour Party there were those who felt uncomfortable with the air of certain victory. Dennis Skinner said that the Sheffield rally was like a football team throwing a party to celebrate a half-time lead. And from some quarters came criticism of Kinnock's performance, described variously as that of a US evangelist, a pop star and a boxing champion.

'That was one of his mistakes,' says friend and ally Tom Sawyer. 'That "all right" was being a "boyo". It might have looked great to the people there in the audience, but watching it on TV, seeing it through the eyes of people in the south, it made you cringe.' Sheffield came to be seen as a public relations disaster by the time clips from it had been seen on news bulletins. For many this was American-style electioneering and had no place in the sober and restrained world of British politics.

Kinnock regretted at once 'bounding' on to the stage, as he explained later in an unusual televised interview for a BBC series during Holy Week in 1993, *Beyond the Shadows*. He was discussing with John Humphrys the triumphal entry of Christ into Jerusalem, and the parallels in the life of a leading politician. There were inevitably comparisons to be made, particularly for a leader accustomed to ovations at party conferences (the conversation was taking place on Brighton Pier, close to the scene of Kinnock's memorable conference performances). 'Although I don't think any politician would be foolish enough to compare himself with the sacrifice that Jesus Christ made.'

The adulation, he said, could be immensely enjoyable. 'But it is important at all times to keep your mind fixed on the objective, that you must not confuse the respect, the support, the friendship, with worship of any description.' Kinnock took the view of adulation that 'it's all right as long as you don't inhale'. Sometimes the temptation to 'inhale' was great: 'You would have to be a very cold fish not to, for moments.' And on the night of the Sheffield rally he did inhale, if only for a few seconds.

Kinnock described how he had vetoed a plan for the Shadow Cabinet to walk the length of the hall and up on to the stage. He insisted instead that they should enter from the back of the stage. And then, on the night, when he walked out of the light into the darkened arena he realized that his instructions had been ignored. 'Which made me ...', he hesitated, 'a bit fed up. I had counselled restraint, modesty, decorum throughout, because I was afraid of overdoing it, of appearing to be triumphalist.'

But by then there was nothing he could do about it.

We were under way. There was an immense tide of affection and support. There were old party stalwarts, there was a terrific number of young people. But even as I got to the stage I was holding back. It wasn't until I got onto the stage and turned round, and there were these 10,000 people really letting their enthusiasm get full vent, and for a few seconds I did inhale. I did feel lifted.

And shouted to the cheering crowd: 'Well all right!'

One journalist who had covered the Conservatives' Sheffield rally at the same venue earlier in the campaign, Eileen Brooks, was there again on 1 April in the crowd as a Labour supporter. The Tories had also put on a smooth show, she recalls, and one at which John Major seemed ill at ease. 'Kinnock was a revelation. The windbag was gone. He seemed assured, confident, at ease, among friends, and was greeted as the conquering hero. I have read since that he felt uncomfortable and did not want to do the walk from the back of the hall, but this wasn't obvious. He seemed totally in control.'

She admits that with Labour riding high in the opinion polls, 'on reflection they got carried away and treated it as a victory rally. But on the night everyone was caught up with the heady atmosphere. Kinnock may have been preaching to the converted, but on that night's showing he should also have converted the disbelievers.'

Brooks remembers going home in a 'euphoric state, thinking we were on our way and feeling proud of the emotions and feelings from the heart which had been missing at the Tory rally. We switched on the television news and expected to see the rally get a big billing and a good reaction. Instead there were a few fleeting moments and a carping, critical commentary.' Afterwards, she says, she came to realize that Sheffield might have 'helped the downfall'. 'It was too triumphal, a bit too smug, too early, and left a vague feeling of embarrassment about being caught up in the atmosphere and losing sight of the enemy.'

It would be fanciful to suggest that the Sheffield rally had any significant impact on the election result. There might have been some among Kinnock's detractors who found further evidence of his unfitness to govern; there might well have been a few admirers who squirmed; there might even have been disbelievers who were converted.

Kinnock's interviewer John Humphrys takes a sympathetic view. 'To become a leader of a political party is to become a figure of stature,' he says.

You do tend to become idolised in some cases. The amount of sheer exposure is quite extraordinary, especially during an election campaign. It is bound occasionally to go to your head, when every word you utter is examined carefully. That's why I was interested in how Kinnock saw the adulation side. He could have created the impression that he was being triumphalist, but it was quite the opposite. I found the way he dealt with it very impressive. I do think he was being entirely honest. He freely admitted that strange things do happen, like the way he went into the hall at Sheffield. He wasn't prepared for it. He realized it was a mistake as soon as he had done it. Politicians don't usually admit to mistakes – Kinnock is unusual in this respect.

As the campaign moved into its final week, the opinion polls indicated, if not a Labour majority, then the prospect of a hung parliament. Major declared such a possibility a disaster, warning that support for Paddy Ashdown and the Liberal Democrats would let Neil Kinnock into Downing Street. Kinnock meanwhile began to talk of 'consensus' government, and hinted that membership of the Plant committee, set up to look into systems of voting, might be widened to include other parties; there were also suggestions that the question of proportional representation might be considered more closely. This provoked intensely polarized reactions among Labour supporters, and there were those who maintained this issue alone was to blame for the party's subsequent defeat after leading the opinion polls until the final week before the election. Only afterwards did Kinnock speak freely of his interest in a proportional system.

Politics professor David Marquand writing in *The Guardian* saw his pre-election efforts as 'a few modest and ill-thought-out steps' in the direction, while paying the Labour leader an unqualified tribute: 'Thanks largely to Kinnock's driving will, the Labour Party of the 1990s has become the social-democratic party which Hugh Gaitskell tried and failed to create in the 1960s.' Proportional representation continues to disturb equilibrium within the party. At the time the issue faded before the final onslaughts of the campaign.

Kinnock urged the electorate to say to the Government: 'If you think unemployment and recession are a price well worth paying, then YOU pay the price. We've paid enough. Now it's your turn to lose your jobs.' The tabloid press, in the main, highlighted the Prime Minister's 'nice guy' image while leading a last attack on the opposition leader. One of the most vitriolic pieces appeared in *Today*: 'Neil Kinnock could run a Cub group but not the Scouts. He would be fine as the manager of a suburban bank but not of a big city branch. He could manage Doncaster Rovers but not Manchester United. In other words, Neil could run a whelk stall but I wouldn't put him in charge of the fishmonger's.'

Fleet Street came out overwhelmingly in favour of the Tories. Brian MacArthur, in *The Times Guide to the House of Commons, 1992*, points out that on polling day seven of the eleven national dailies exhorted readers to vote Conservative, three Labour – among them, surprisingly, the *Financial Times* – and one, *The Independent*, remaining neutral. *The Sun*, the *Daily Mail* and the *Daily Express*, he said, launched a blitz against Kinnock and his party in the last four days of the campaign.

Robin Oakley of *The Times* wondered if campaigns mattered at all, as Labour had begun the period with an average lead of 1.6 per cent in the polls and ended it with an average lead of 2.3 per cent. 'Certainly the 1992 campaign justified the Prime Minister's quiet optimism all through,' he wrote. 'It testified to his coolness under fire and it vindicated his judgment, just as it underlined once more Neil Kinnock's fine qualities as a platform orator and demonstrated a new discipline in the Labour effort. But history has since been rewritten about the campaign simply because of the result.'

13   Never Mind, Miss,
At Least You Came Second

By election day Kinnock was beset with doubts about success. Both he and Glenys admitted later that their instincts, their political antennae, sensed a shift in public sympathy during the last few days of the campaign. Until then Kinnock believed he had a 'better than even chance of being in Government. Then I felt the sentiment slipping away from us. There wasn't a lot of evidence. It was just instinct.' Glenys, it appeared, felt the same, although it was not until the Monday night that she said aloud: 'You don't think we're going to win, do you?' Glenys had noticed that on the campaign trail people were shaking hands, 'they were very kindly and friendly, but it wasn't in their eyes'. When polling closed on the night of 9 April they knew, at best, that the result would be close.

Political correspondent Julia Langdon believes that Kinnock knew even before the polls closed that he had lost. She was covering the election for Irish television, and was collecting an appropriate green dress from the cleaners at around 5 p.m. when she heard him being interviewed on the radio. 'He said "The sun is out and so are the Tories" but I could tell from the tone of his voice that he couldn't believe it.' Glenys Kinnock recalled that until the results started coming in they were 'not confident, but still hopeful'. In an interview with Hunter Davies in *The Independent* she said:

> I didn't at first have time to think a lot. I lived from minute to minute. When we got to Neil's count in Islwyn it was obvious we hadn't won the election but we were still not really thinking about that, only about the constituency people, who are all great friends of ours. They were clearly wounded that Neil would not be Prime Minister. People were crying and shouting bitter things, feeling they'd been cheated. Hundreds waited and waited for him, to cheer him up.

The Kinnocks drove back up the M4 to London in a police convoy. 'I was listening to results on the radio,' said Glenys. 'He was thinking about the speech he was going to make at Walworth Road. The most important thing was to be dignified in defeat, which he was.'

At Labour's HQ in Walworth Road the planned celebration had become a wake, but the partygoers turned up in the early hours of the morning all the same: some of the showbusiness stars who had played their part at pre-election rallies (among them actress Susan Tulley, writer Ken Follett and comedian Ben Elton), and the inside team who had worked towards a Labour victory. Nicholas Timmins in *The Independent* described how Joyce Gould, Labour's organization director, stood at the stair top, 'a single long-stemmed rose ready for her leader, its colour a bleeding red against her lime green jacket'.

Charles Clarke, 'a man who is a cross by physique and temperament between a teddy bear and a brown bear' was still, somehow, smiling. Larry Whitty, Labour's general secretary, was there, and David Hill, the party's communications director. The only Shadow Cabinet member with a London-based constituency, who could therefore arrive from his own count, Bryan Gould, hugged the Kinnocks when they arrived. It was, wrote Timmins, a moment of ashes, dignity, bitterness, courage and agonizing defeat.

The results indicated a clear Conservative victory: in the final analysis they had an overall majority of 21 seats, well down on the 102-seat majority of 1987 but far better than any opinion poll had suggested. And in a handful of key seats the Tories won by fewer than 100 votes in some cases. This was no consolation to Kinnock as he tried to control his voice and address the crowds who had gathered outside. 'I naturally feel a strong sense of disappointment. Not for myself, for I am fortunate, very fortunate, in my personal life. But I feel dismay, sorrow, for so many people in our country who do not share this personal good fortune.'

He said later that in the small hours of 10 April he had felt:

shattered – immediately and primarily because of the people around me. They had worked very hard. Glenys's consideration was for me; you always care more for those that you love than you do for yourself. That was how both of us felt in that respect. But we both felt for people around us. Dedicated supporters who had had the oxygen taken away. And then the implication for the country – when I said Britain deserves better, that was how I felt and that is how I still feel. The combination of physical tiredness and dismay, and the sense of depression for my dear comrades and the future of the country – it doesn't do much for your physical appearance. But I did have a clean shirt and clean shoes on!

The Kinnock family locked themselves away for a quiet weekend at home. Friends arrived in tears; Kinnock himself was the only one who did not give way to emotion. The letters, telephone messages and flowers began to arrive; a small boy turned up at their door with a daffodil and a note which read: 'Sorry'. Over the next few weeks and months Kinnock received around 30,000 messages of sympathy and support.

> I felt a strong sense of personal rejection. But it was like getting letters after being bereaved. Instantaneously the messages that were coming in from people round the country and around the world were expressed in such generous terms that although they didn't make me feel comforted, they did say, you shouldn't feel a personal sense of failure. I know what I felt. And I know what a personal failure I felt. But other people whose views I respect, and other people offering sympathy, that did help. And so did the kids.

There was no doubt that his leadership of the Labour Party was over, but by the time he stood before the cameras in the Shadow Cabinet office beneath a South Wales trade union banner on the Monday to make his statement, Kinnock must have felt that he was not entirely without friends.

His critics did not wait for an announcement before launching their own post-mortem on the election result and pinning the blame on Kinnock's style of leadership and his changes to party policy. Ken Livingstone was one of the first to suggest that by abandoning unilateralism and public ownership, Kinnock had moved the party 'in a more right-wing direction'. And the almost inevitable call for Kinnock to resign came from miners' leader Arthur Scargill, who said that the policy changes had been a desperate attempt to win the middle ground.

Kinnock had already made his decision to stand down. He thanked his supporters, and members of the Labour Party: 'I deeply appreciate their great kindness.' The action he was taking was, he said, an essential act of leadership. 'It is not to do with any personal sensitivity – it arises entirely from my desire to see that the Labour Party will gain further strength and be better able to serve the people of Britain and the wider world community.' There would be many opportunities to consider the causes and consequences of the election result.

He drew attention to the 'heroes' of the campaign (as they had been labelled by the former treasurer of the Conservative Party, Lord McAlpine), the editors of the *Daily Mail*, the *Daily Express* and *The Sun*, and, in the words of Lord McAlpine, 'the other editors of the grander Tory press. Never in the past nine elections have they come out so strongly in favour of the Conservatives. Never has their attack on the Labour Party been so comprehensive ... This was how the election was won, and if the politicians, elated in their hour of victory, are tempted to believe otherwise, they are in real trouble next time'. Kinnock added: 'Lord McAlpine could not be expected to acknowledge the degree of misinformation and disinformation employed in the attacks on the Labour Party but in all other respects his assessment is correct.'

Kinnock had already warned that as the process to elect a new leader got under way, the Labour movement at every level should not feed and should not believe the press and broadcasting media in their reporting of events. He said that the newly elected government did not have the policies necessary to strengthen the economy and would not try to address the injustices in society.

> My only regret is that I failed to ensure that enough people understood that and the implications which it has for the future. My sorrow is that millions, particularly those who do not have the strength to defend themselves, will suffer because of the election of another Conservative government.
>
> I make and I seek no excuses, and I express no bitterness when I say that the Conservative-supporting press has enabled the Tory Party to win yet again when the Conservative Party could not have secured victory for itself on the basis of its record, its programme or its character.

The tabloids responded to the attack the next day, with *The Sun* calling Kinnock's claim 'an insult to the 14 million people who voted Conservative', and the *Express* dismissing his remarks as 'sour grapes and the ranting of a man lost'. The *Daily Mail* editor, Sir David English, said: 'To suggest that the Daily Mail single-handedly won the election for the Conservatives and brought about a Labour defeat is very flattering. But it ascribes far more influence to us than we would give ourselves.'

It remains a matter of conjecture. Labour eventually calculated that the Tory tabloid assault in the final weeks cost them 400,000 votes, although such calculations cannot be precise. Kenneth Newton, in *Britain at the Polls 1992*, agrees that after initially criticizing the Conservative campaign, the tabloids did throw everything into the last few days in their efforts to get the Government re-elected. 'Everything included the race card and the threat of immigrant hordes; Kinnock's dismal failure as a future prime minister, as a Labour leader, and as a human being.'

He says further that the claim by *The Sun* that 'It's *The Sun* wot won it' implied that the Conservative campaign was not good enough to claim the credit.

> There is evidence to support this claim, including figures showing that *The Sun* had a high penetration in a few key Conservative held marginals. For example, it was taken by 50.5 per cent of homes in Basildon – above its national average – and Basildon registered only a small Labour swing. But such evidence is at best circumstantial and is not supported by

evidence from other Conservative marginals where high sales of *The Sun* were accompanied by large Labour swings.

But he goes on to estimate that the Conservative tabloids, with their daily circulation of around 8 million and a readership of well over 20 million, and their wave of personal attacks on Kinnock culminating in the last heave of the remaining days of electioneering, 'must have been worth the equivalent of millions of pounds in advertising for the Conservative party'.

As the election inquest got under way, there were tributes to Kinnock from the two rivals in the contest for leadership of the Labour Party, John Smith and Bryan Gould. Smith, who had been Kinnock's Shadow Chancellor, described him as

> a courageous and inspiring leader. I have been privileged to work closely with him over these years and I will always admire the utter dedication and the immense skill with which he rescued the Labour Party from near oblivion and brought us to the edge of victory. In addition to his qualities of integrity and commitment, he is a decent and warm hearted man who will always be respected and admired by a Labour Party so much in his debt.

Gould, at the time Shadow Environment Secretary, praised Kinnock's tough leadership and relentless drive to modernize the party. 'In that process he has had to endure the most savage personal attacks on him and his family, all of which he has borne with quiet dignity. He is a bigger man than any of those who have devoted so much time and effort to attacking him.'

There were tributes, too, from leading trade unionists. 'Mr Kinnock was the only man equipped to reorganise and modernise the Labour Party,' said Bill Jordan, president of the Amalgamated Engineering and Electrical Union. And the general secretary of the Transport and General Workers' Union, Bill Morris, said: 'Neil Kinnock has shown great courage, integrity and commitment towards the Labour Party during the difficult years in which he provided inspiring leadership.'

But Derek Hatton, the target of Kinnock's attack on Militant-dominated Liverpool council, was without sympathy: 'He was the one who put everything on the line – at the end of the day it didn't come off.' And a critical account of the Kinnock years by Richard Heffernan and Mike Marqusee in *Defeat from the Jaws of Victory* concludes: 'The painful fact is that the Kinnock leadership threw away an election that was there for the taking. It did so not only in the five weeks of the campaign but in the five years preceding it.'

Kinnock's own view, expressed at the first post-election meeting of

Labour's NEC, was succinct: 'It was a choice between fear and hope, and fear won out.' Awaiting a definitive account which would be presented to the party conference in the autumn, a preliminary report to the NEC pointed to a late swing against Labour, a poor showing among young male D-E social groups and older women, reaction against the tone of the Sheffield rally, and the difficulties in a recession of easing voters' fears over the impact of Labour's tax and interest rate proposals.

Senior figures, including Kinnock's office, expressed concern on the sharply differing swings in individual constituencies within the same area. For instance, Labour won Bristol East on a 6.78 per cent swing, but achieved only a 1.7 per cent swing in the nearby target seat of Swindon. Similarly, a southern seat such as Southampton Itchen fell with a 6.6 per cent swing, but another key southern marginal, Slough, saw only a 3.3 per cent swing. Had the party's better swings within regions been reproduced across each region, it was argued, then Kinnock would now be inside No. 10.

David Sanders, also writing in *Britain at the Polls*, produced indirect evidence that the 'Kinnock factor' harmed Labour's political fortunes to some extent. Major's government, he said, lost no opportunity to attack Labour at what it saw as its weakest point: Neil Kinnock.

> With the support of large sections of the popular press, the opposition leader's character, judgement, and abilities were insistently questioned; and with some success ... And although it is almost impossible to demonstrate this empirically, it seems likely that Kinnock's weak image was in part responsible for the consolidation of Conservative support that appeared to take place at the very end of the campaign.

Further to his argument, he points out that only 28 per cent of respondents to Gallup's election survey considered that Labour had 'the best leaders', compared with an equivalent figure for the Conservatives of 53 per cent. And when respondents to the same survey were asked how they would have voted if John Smith had been Labour's leader, Labour's share went up by three points. 'While it would be foolish to place too much reliance on the responses to this sort of hypothetical question, it would be equally foolish to dismiss the "Kinnock factor" as having been of no electoral consequence.' At the same time, he stresses that most political acts have multiple causes, and when some 30 million votes are cast in a general election, 'the full causal picture is necessarily one of enormous complexity.'

However, Sanders draws the conclusion that the critical factor underpinning the Tory victory was the fact that enough people, drawn from all social groups, were moved to vote according to their pocketbooks.

In the nine months or so before the election, the beneficial effects of the interest rate reductions initiated in October 1990 were starting to feed through to people's pockets. Economic optimism was rising and even began to accelerate quite sharply in the final weeks of the campaign. The Conservatives' political triumph was to make the satisfaction of these rising expectations conditional on a Conservative victory. By the end of the campaign, almost half the electorate believed they would be worse off under Labour's taxation policies; and a large proportion of them – most of them, falsely, avowing to the pollsters that taxation had not been an issue affecting their vote – duly voted Conservative.

It was in June that Kinnock began to reveal his own analysis of the defeat. In his first full account of what went wrong, he said the basic reason was 'the fact that there are still people in Britain in significant number who cannot forget the wounds that the Labour Party inflicted on itself in the early 1980s.' They remained, he said, 'Reserved in their attitudes to the Labour Party so that when they came to make a choice they manifested some alarm and reservation about giving the votes to us.' The regrets, he said, were not for himself but for those who needed Labour. He would have liked to be Prime Minister – 'and certainly I would have done a very good job' – but he felt most sorely about the impact of the election defeat on the people who needed a Labour Government. When the NEC met shortly afterwards, to plan ahead as well as analyse the past, Kinnock repeated what he said in a *Times* article in July 1983, that 'to help the have nots, we have to get the support of the haves and the haven't enoughs'.

Kinnock spoke further of the instinct which had warned him, four days before the election, that Labour would lose. 'From the Sunday I had my doubts. Of course, in the last final heat of battle you couldn't afford to show them.' He said that between 4 and 5 per cent of the electorate did not have sufficient trust in the party because of the 'months of turmoil' under the last Labour government in the 1970s and the years of conflict in the early 1980s. He told also of how he was bound to state until the last moment that 'we were absolutely confident of victory, because to do otherwise would have sabotaged any remaining chance of a last minute swing towards us. I couldn't let down the people I had been leading. I couldn't give people the impression that all their efforts had been for nought.'

So why was it that Kinnock's leadership of the Labour Party still worried voters? 'It was partly because of the changes that had had to be made,' he told David Dimbleby in an interview for BBC 2. 'Partly because of the way I had been represented over the years, partly because of the way I had represented myself. Some people say it's to do with

Welshness.' But Kinnock had never, at any stage, considered standing down as leader.

> I had the belief that my replacement with anyone else would not have made an improvement, and that no one else could do it better. And I wasn't being arrogant in that. I don't think you would have found a combination that was sufficiently determined, willing to go into fine detail, expend the time and detail on endless discussions, and someone who could get up and light the Labour Party's touch paper when the occasion demanded.

Kinnock said, categorically, that Labour would have defeated a Conservative government still led by Mrs Thatcher. During the election campaign it had been 'very difficult to hit Mr Major'. In another interview, with John Humphrys for Radio Four's *On the Ropes*, Kinnock admitted: 'Yes, I failed in getting the Labour Party elected. I think there's a variety of ways of measuring whether it had become electable. There was the general assumption, which I didn't share, right up to the day of the election, that we were going to win'. He added frivolously: 'I wouldn't have minded if we had been thought not electable but nevertheless got elected.'

He went on:

> The reason for us being defeated, above all else, was that we still hadn't secured enough trust among enough people. And that was partly because of the scale of the changes that had to be undertaken. It was right to make the changes, no question about that. But all change carries the risk of the accusation or the fear of inconsistency. Our opponents were able to exploit ideas articulated by Mrs Thatcher and repeated by John Major that if they will move away from those things that they have said to be fundamental parts of their conviction in order to get support, can't they move back again? There was a great question mark of trust in people's minds.

What image had people had of him on polling day?

> I think it was an amalgam ... some people would have thought of me as being weak, because a lot of the propaganda over the previous years was of someone who was unsure, and the impression was given that I was a weak person. Even when the newspapers were writing about strength – taking on Militant, for instance – it then became translated as the strength of a weak man.
>
> Then another element ... was that I didn't have the intelligence to do the job. There was a perpetual story about the shallowness of my intelligence and intellect. And a lot of it was the idea that I was frivolous and short-tempered. I just think they are generally false assumptions of what I am. But people had eight or nine years of the presentation of me as a mixture of these inadequacies.

When a major ITV series on the Kinnock years, *Kinnock: The Inside Story*, was previewed in the press, and the papers singled out the former leader's admission that he believed himself to be a personal and political failure, his postbag filled up again with hundreds of letters from sympathizers insisting that he had not failed. 'That was because of the way the stories were focused,' Kinnock says. 'They accurately quoted the words I used on the television programme, but when people heard them I think they understood that I was simply being candid about myself. I wasn't consigning myself to the abyss, whereas the papers gave the impression that I was almost suicidal.'

While Kinnock was still able to smile, and was seen publicly to be a good sport as he developed a part-time career as a media entertainer, it was Glenys Kinnock who admitted to feelings of bereavement. She told Anthony Clare on BBC Radio Four's *In the Psychiatrist's Chair*: 'I felt a sense of loss. I knew a period of our lives was over now and that Neil was having to make lots of decisions and changes in his life. He did it with such impressive smoothness and determination. I expected him to be like that, but he even impressed me.'

The week before the election she had been optimistic, but never taking it for granted that Neil would be in No. 10. 'But in the week leading up to 9 April I felt it slipping, I felt that people were shifting. I never ruled out the possibility of a very close result.' But she did not feel bitter, 'just very, very sorry'. Afterwards Kinnock was 'amazingly strong' she said. 'I took refuge in reading all the hundreds and hundreds of letters, I read every one. I did cry, yes.'

She allowed herself some time to grieve, but not so much that it became self-indulgence. After about three weeks, at Easter, the Kinnocks went on holiday to Devon. 'We saw lots of friends there and I think I more or less decided that that was it, and then I went back to school soon after that.' She was aware that the head of her school had asked colleagues and pupils not to mention the election, but there were seven year olds who came to her and consoled: 'Never mind, miss, at least you came second.'

In another interview, with Hunter Davies in *The Independent*, Glenys Kinnock declared:

Neil got over it more quickly than me. Ask anyone in his office. He has been stronger than me ... For a long time I was devastated. I believed he'd earned the right to be Prime Minister, and that he would have made a very good one. I wasn't sad for my own sake. It was the country's loss. I still feel that.

I'm managing now to come to terms with it, getting it in perspective. We have got so much which many people long for – a happy marriage, wonderful kids. We have friends in hospital and we visit them and friends with marriages breaking up. So what have I got to moan about?

Those nearest and dearest to him, says Neil Kinnock, expected a kind of cathartic anger.

But I took a very conscious decision that that would be self indulgent. I have a wonderful life. I can't succumb to introspection. I'm fit, I was only 50, I've got a marvellous wife, great kids, lots of friends, health, a terrific constituency, a lot of ideas. It would be destructive for me to be despondent.

He wrote at length in *The Guardian* at the end of 1992 of his concern for his supporters, those who had put so much effort into trying to secure victory 'and suddenly they found themselves facing a very unsure future.' He had said on the day after the election that Britain deserved better,

and I think that now a lot more people understand what I meant. I had guessed two days before the election that we were going to lose, so I suppose I had had some sort of preparation. My instincts told me that there was a definite movement taking place – and it wasn't in our direction. I've been a political activist for 35 years and you develop a sense of smell or sensitive bones or something like that, which warns you what's going to happen without any firm proof.

Kinnock said that it would be ridiculous to describe his mood as anything other than sad and grieving,

but for the opportunity which I thought the country had missed, rather than for myself. No good political leader, in that situation, could possibly reflect on their personal position. Only after about 24 hours and an endless stream of messages, telephone calls, flowers and other expressions of support did the defeat actually begin to sink in.

On the Saturday after the election, Rachel had received her unconditional acceptance into the University of Western England.

The joy and relief of securing a future for your children completely preoccupies you. It's not that I was looking for something to take my mind off what had happened, it was just such a strong demonstration that a fulfilling life existed for me beyond defeat. That realisation offset a lot of the loneliness I would otherwise have felt.

He said that he was aware of how many people in his situation would have felt isolated: 'And I know just how lucky I am to have the people around me whom I love, and who love me in return.'

Broadcaster John Humphrys says that he does not believe Kinnock when he maintains that he was not deeply hurt, personally, by the election defeat. 'He clearly was. But he has succeeded in persuading himself that he wasn't. I have no doubt that he was devastated. Early on in the campaign he thought he was going to win, and so did a considerable number of other people.' Humphrys believes that Kinnock was unsuccessful in the end

> much more for personality reasons than any other. There is a kind of latent anti-Welshness among the English and that is his bad luck, that and his hair colour. It is often the case that the things that don't matter at all are the ones that have the greatest influence over your destiny. But he never says, I was robbed, or there's no justice.

But Charles Clarke, who was Kinnock's chief of staff until the election, does not believe that the experience 'floored' the former leader of the Opposition. 'He's a young man, and there's a lot ahead. He was deeply disappointed and he saw that an opportunity had been missed,' says Clarke.

> That was naturally a very disappointing thing. But I don't think it was his own personal ambition. He was the longest serving leader of the Opposition since the war, and it is acknowledged as the hardest job in British politics. He had a task that had to be done, but it was very hard. It kept him away from his family, for example. The defeat was a deep disappointment but I don't think it floored him.

NEC colleague Tom Sawyer, on the other hand, says: 'I would think he was devastated. Not shocked, because nobody goes into an election prepared only to win. But he's got this thing about not letting people down. He feels very responsible for what happened.' Sawyer, who has known Kinnock for a long time, describes him as a very private man. 'Only Glenys knows what he really thinks. He's quite a shy man in some respects. I think his bravado and powerful personality, and the capacity to entertain, is something that hides quite a shy and sensitive person. It is often the case that the life and soul of the party is often glad when the party is over.'

Sawyer says Kinnock did have a 'downside' as leader of the Labour Party. 'It goes back to when he first got the job. He was very inexperienced and youthful, and he looked it. And he allowed people to see in him the Welsh boyo side. It was a very warm, happy go lucky part of him, but I don't think that the electorate took to it.' He could lack confidence on occasions, says Sawyer, and he made some mistakes: bad performances in the Commons, some 'dicey' interviews with the press, some arguments which the tabloids latched on to. 'The Labour Party still doesn't have people's trust. It has the knack of making two or three big mistakes each year, and there were a lot in his time. I have to try and see the situation as others do. Neil as leader didn't get the British people to trust him.'

The non-specialists had their own views too. Dame Barbara Cartland, the romantic novelist, had been busy writing letters to the media before the election, and afterwards she had another of her contributions published:

> During the election I wrote to every newspaper pointing out that Neil Kinnock and his wife were atheists and that his wife had announced that when she got to No. 10 she would go on teaching. I sent this to 92 newspapers, and I received very strong letters from people shocked by the Church's silence, saying they had written to the Archbishop of Canterbury protesting about Mr Kinnock, and still not a word.

An eccentric view, but is there a point here to be taken seriously? Kinnock had never hidden his lack of belief, and there are those who say that the British want an actively Christian political leader, in spite of their own general indifference to religion. These critics were surprised and impressed when Kinnock appeared on *Beyond the Shadows* on BBC TV discussing in depth the life and ministry of Christ and demonstrating a considerable knowledge of the scriptures.

John Humphrys, the interviewer for that programme, says that he is always sceptical when he sees politicians at public church services, wondering if they are there because they believe or because it is required of them for the sake of the voters. 'It is always interesting talking to politicians about their faith,' he says. 'Kinnock was absolutely straight about it – he does not have a faith. I was puzzled why he agreed to do the discussion in the first place, and intrigued at the idea that he would talk about it publicly.' (Kinnock's view, for all his unbelief, is of Christ as a messiah rather than a politician. 'And while there are politicians with messianic aspirations, I certainly wasn't one of them!' Christ had an objective and knew the sacrifices he would have to make in pursuit of that objective. A politician, said Kinnock, would have done a deal with Pontius Pilate, in order to sustain his position.)

What would have happened if the result had been different, if Kinnock's objective had been realized? In April 1993, marking the anniversary of the election defeat, *The Guardian* carried a highly detailed speculative account of how a Kinnock government would have handled the crises of the past twelve months. The writer, Will Hutton, hypothesized that Labour had in fact won the 1992 election, with a working majority of thirty seats. But the problems for Kinnock's newly formed cabinet began immediately. The foreign exchange markets did not believe the Labour commitment to hold the parity of the pound within the ERM. For the pound to survive, Chancellor John Smith would have had to raise interest rates. When Kinnock announced this intention the Cabinet was instantly divided; his opponents insisted that the pound would have to be devalued sooner or later.

Following a scenario of real and imagined events in the financial world, Hutton's apocalyptic fantasy led to rebellion in the Labour ranks, a vote of no confidence in the Commons, and a subsequent general election in November 1992 at which John Major regained power with a fifty-seat majority. It was only a fairytale but, given that economics can never be a precise science, did Hutton's fable carry any truths?

His analysis was quite wrong, insists Kinnock.

And Will knows it's wrong. We would have cut interest rates savagely within three days of the election. That would have actually taken the pound down, but we would have done it in conjunction with the other members of the ERM. So it would have been a managed realignment, with a terrific cost-weight off the backs of the British people and British industry. And once you acknowledge that, the whole scenario changes.

You must not suppose, as Will Hutton does, that we would not have made any shifts in policy, but that an incoming government would have the wit and the guts to act as I would have insisted we act. And I knew exactly what I was going to do. But of course, any hint of that before the election would have caused us to be crucified. We would have been wiped out for being what the papers and Tories would have called reckless and irresponsible.

It was on the Opposition front bench that Kinnock spent a final two months in the early summer of 1992 before the contest to choose his successor. On the opening day of the new Parliament he faced John Major once again. 'I had a job to do in responding to the Queen's Speech, so I got on with it,' he says. His name was put forward for another job, that of President of the Confederation of Socialist Parties of the European Communities. But on 15 June he withdrew his nomination, stating that the possibility of Labour opposing the Tory version of the Maastricht treaty in the Commons could clash with his duties as confederation president. 'I believe in these circumstances it is my duty in the Commons and my duty to the Parliamentary Labour Party which is my primary duty.'

He made his last appearance at the despatch box on 14 July at Prime Minister's question time to attack the Government's economic record (which is precisely what he had done during his first question time as Leader of the Opposition in October 1983). The Prime Minister, on this occasion, was able to smile warmly in reply and pay tribute to

Kinnock's scrupulous fair dealing and support in times of crisis. Kinnock replied: 'I consider it a great honour to have been able to serve my country in the way that I could.'

Four days later, on 18 July, John Smith was elected new leader of the Labour Party. On the same day, coincidentally, Kinnock was awarded an honorary degree at University College, Cardiff.

14   Whatever Next?

A few years before he became leader of the Labour Party, Neil Kinnock prophesied that he wanted to retire at fifty, 'to play cricket in the summer, geriatric football in the winter, and sing in the choir'.

It was evidently a flippant remark from the man who has as much energy now as he had as a teenager, and even more commitment to an ideal for which he will never stop working. The irony of the timing, that he had celebrated his fiftieth birthday less than two weeks before the election defeat which led to his resignation, is not lost on Kinnock. But, as he has pointed out, patiently and repeatedly, he has not retired. He is still an MP – 'a job I worked hard to get and one which I hope to do until I am 65', still a member of the Labour Party's national executive committee, still consulted for his views on matters of national and international importance.

And by late summer 1993 he was still looking forward to watching his first cricket match of the season. 'And my team, Glamorgan, are top of the county championship.' Displayed proudly on a shelf in his office is a glass crystal cricket ball presented to him as only the second ever life vice president of Glamorgan County Cricket Club.

Kinnock's office is a bright and comfortable room overlooking the Thames at the top of Parliament Street, its walls decorated with family photos and a few small paintings. Kinnock lost more than the chance to become Prime Minister when he stepped down as leader of the Labour Party. He left behind the panelled suite of rooms allotted to the leader of Her Majesty's Opposition, and his salary dropped from £59,736 to £30,854. The chauffeur-driven Rover was replaced by a second-hand Ford Scorpio. The dozen-strong staff of minders, tacticians, press officers and advisers went; Jan Royall remains as his highly valued personal assistant, and he gets help from a secretary and part-time researchers.

He was at least relieved of the responsibilities of a position which, for more than eight years, had offered little in the way of rewards but a great deal in the way of frustration. The task of saving the Labour Party from itself had demanded a concentrated, relentless, determined effort which

might have left a lesser mortal with little energy for the role of leader of
the Opposition. Kinnock's enthusiasm had been sustained only by the
prospect of reward – of leading Labour into Government, into the
position where philosophy and policy could be implemented. They had
not been enjoyable years.

As a professional politician for most of his life – apart from the three
years as a WEA lecturer – Kinnock had no career to return to, no family
firm waiting to cushion him. After the 1992 election defeat, Nicholas
Timmins wrote in *The Independent*: 'He is just 50 – the age at which most
senior politicians begin to contemplate Downing Street, not have to
accept that they will never get there.' Timmins pondered on Kinnock's
future:

> There may be memoirs – he does, after all, have quite a story to tell – and
> there are his constituents, a bunch of people as fiercely loyal to him as he
> to them: a loyalty that at times, as in the miners' strike, helped to constrain
> his actions. There is rugby and song. In time the young man of 50 will
> grow into an elder statesman. Neil Kinnock, despite moments of Celtic
> gloom, will survive the fall.

He has survived the fall, and survived it with a strength and resilience
which some observers did not expect. As one acquaintance observed,
Kinnock is a 'very balanced bloke. He's got a belief in himself.' He still
attracts a certain degree of adulation, 'like being a pop star without the
fortune' says another, adding: 'When he is pestered by people in the
street there is an enormous warmth there. Maybe he loves it, maybe it
feeds his vanity, but he treats people remarkably well. There's not a
touch of remoteness about him.'

Kinnock's sense of humour was another saving grace. 'I like laughing
a lot,' he says. He enjoys physical humour as much as the things people
say. And then there was plenty to smile about in family terms during the
twelve months following the election defeat: Rachel got into university,
Stephen graduated, and then worked for an MA, Glenys was selected as
MEP candidate for South East Wales, the family moved into a new
house, Glenys's parents were in good health. There were a few more
jobs available in Kinnock's constituency.

The Celtic gloom was kept for private moments and brief
observations, such as when discussing his favourable image since the
1992 election: 'It's like Paul Newman said, the nice guys come second.'
The bitterness and anger are directed at the Conservative
administration. 'What the Tories were going to do was evident within
days after the election and that's what upsets me. It's the outrage of
decline and decadence, the economic, industrial, cultural and moral
decadence. The effects are on other people, not on me.'

Kinnock tells of an evening when he and Glenys were on the way to a reception at the home of a 'friendly socialist millionaire'. Driving slowly through the London traffic they saw five people on the street 'who should not have been there, they shouldn't have been out of hospital. One of them I see frequently. And I think that if there was no other reason to have a Labour government, it was so that they would have a safe place to put their heads at night. Britain has gone downhill and the world has become a more dangerous place.'

There are two books in the offing, but not his memoirs at this stage, they would be too closely scrutinized for evidence of dissent within the party, he fears. One is on the state of Britain's manufacturing industry, the other is linked to a BBC programme about the future of socialism.

He did expect to have more time to relax, 'But we have been to the theatre less than at any time since I became leader. This is about to be corrected.' He does spend more time in his constituency, going down to Wales most weekends – he and Glenys still have a house in Pontllanfraith. And at least there he has the chance to eat at one of his favourite restaurants, The Countryman, at Blackwood. In fact, the food he likes best of all is Glenys's home cooking, especially fish.

There is a little more time to read. As guest of *Desert Island Discs* the one book Kinnock chose to take with him was the *Essays* of R.H. Tawney, the political theorist. But his favourite writer is Dickens and his favourite novels *Great Expectations* and *Our Mutual Friend*. He reads poetry – Shelley, Wilfred Owen, Dylan Thomas and the archetypal poet of the south Wales valleys, Idris Davies. Dickens was taken along when the Kinnocks headed for California and Arizona for a holiday in the summer of 1992 with Glenys's brother Colin Parry and his wife Barbara.

When they returned home the spotlight on their personal lives had been turned down, if not moved away entirely. (Kinnock had once remarked, during a hot summer with a hosepipe ban in force, that he was the only man in Ealing who didn't dare go out at night to water his roses.) They moved to their new home in the autumn, leaving the semi-detached in Lammas Park, Ealing, for a similar but bigger, six-bedroomed Victorian house with a conservatory and a walled garden about a mile away in the Montpelier area of Ealing.

Rachel, by then nineteen, was off to college, after taking her BTEC in media studies and writing a dissertation on Doris Day. She began a degree course in media studies at the University of Western England, formerly Bristol Polytechnic. Stephen had graduated in French and Spanish at Queens' College, Cambridge, and then won a scholarship to the College of Europe in Bruges to take an MA in European Studies. He now works as a Brussels-based research assistant to Gary Titley,

Labour Euro MP for Greater Manchester. Neil and Glenys would be on their own for the first time in more than twenty years.

As further reflection of the upheaval in their lives, Neil and Glenys decided to lose some weight. It was a sudden choice, says Kinnock, after a meal at a Mexican restaurant in Tucson, Arizona, during the holiday, when he was struck by the excesses of the American food culture. 'I decided there and then to go on a diet.' He lost two stones, Glenys lost a stone-and-a-half, and the result was that a much leaner and more gaunt-looking Kinnock returned to the public arena in the autumn.

His appearance led to much speculation: was he ill, had the stress and strain of the preceding months taken their toll? Some acquaintances believed that he was 'mortifying the flesh', punishing himself: at the same time he stopped drinking for a while, and gave up smoking with the help of a nicotine patch. *The Observer* political diarist Alan Watkins observed: 'Mr Kinnock appears to have been fasting, whereas one would have expected his release from the burdens of leadership to lead to the opposite effect. I hope there is nothing the matter with him.' Letters from worried sympathizers flooded in to Kinnock's office to the point where his personal assistant, Jan Royall, begged him: 'Please don't lose any more weight, we just can't reply to any more letters!'

Subject to even greater speculation and scrutiny was Kinnock's future career. Acquaintances said that he appeared to be at a 'loose end', wanting to spend time with plenty of people around him, swapping jokes. 'He is always mixing, an immensely sociable man.' Was this to mask the upheaval in his career? 'It is one thing for Mrs Thatcher, at her age, to move on, but it is another thing completely to be one hop away from the "big one" and have it all taken away from you,' said one colleague. 'So what is left? I don't think he's written himself off, but what does he do? There's no possibility of a political reincarnation, or of taking a senior post in the shadow cabinet. What he might do next is perhaps more intriguing than what he has achieved so far.'

In spite of Kinnock's insistence that he would continue to represent his Islwyn constituency, it was widely felt that this alone would not sufficiently tax his talents and energy. For a time it looked as though he might be given a Brussels-based appointment as a European Commissioner – a role which would have demanded his resignation as a Member of Parliament.

The powerful £108,000 a year post would have required the approval of the Prime Minister: Britain nominates two European Commissioners, one Tory – currently Sir Leon Brittan – and one Labour. The Labour leadership can put forward a preferred choice but the selection has to be ratified by John Major. But in Tory circles it was feared that Kinnock would represent a much more critical figure in Brussels and would hand

Labour a powerful propaganda weapon, and eventually the Prime Minister vetoed the move because of fears of further provoking critics of the European Community in his own party.

Contrary to reports that he felt hurt and let down, Kinnock says that he did not actively seek the post, and that he was not disappointed with the outcome. He joked with comedian Clive Anderson that: 'I didn't even get an interview. But I put in a good CV.' Although lucrative, it was not a job ideally suited to Kinnock, anyway. As Alan Watkins wrote in *The Observer*, Kinnock 'is not in his element when confronted by mounds of paper ... In any case, why should the Brussels Commission be treated as a Sunset Home for politicians who have resigned, retired, been dismissed or become merely embarrassing?'

More of a diversion than a serious career move was Kinnock's week as a BBC Radio Two disc jockey, standing in for Jimmy Young in November. He found the experience great fun. And, after a somewhat stilted and laboured start, was performing like a 'true professional' by the end of the first day, according to his producer. 'Very few people could go on the air and do such a good job on their first day. He grew into the role as the show progressed.' The BBC reported dozens of complimentary phone calls from listeners, and offered him another slot, as a stand in for the early evening show hosted by John Dunn.

On BBC television soon afterwards Kinnock gave a sparkling performance on the panel of the satirical quiz show *Have I Got News For You?* where he was to be seen completely at ease with the sparring of top comedians Angus Deayton and Paul Merton. This was Kinnock at his most relaxed, obviously enjoying every moment. His appearance on Clive Anderson's show on ITV was also robust and entertaining. Had Kinnock been annoyed, asked Anderson, by his consistent low performance in the polls compared with Mrs Thatcher. 'Annoyed,' he replied laughing, 'doesn't do justice to how I felt.'

On every occasion Kinnock insisted that such appearances were mere diversions, that he had no thoughts of a career in television: he was, first and foremost, an MP representing his constituents. 'Being a back bench MP is, in my view, a fine job – I fought hard enough for it! I'm taking some time to think about the future, obviously, but I can't envisage any real changes – and I'm certainly not searching for them.' But he does mention the hope that when – not if – Labour win the next general election he might have the opportunity to serve in government under John Smith.

He is no less politically active for being out of the limelight. The major political crisis of the autumn of 1992 found Kinnock back among his roots addressing a Welsh mining community. On the day after the announcement that thirty-one British collieries were to be shut down, by chance he was at Clydach Vale in the Rhondda to unveil a plaque commemorating the thirty-one miners killed in an explosion at Cambrian colliery in May 1985. 'Among the large crowd the tears of mourning for the dead miners mixed with tears of outrage at the wanton destruction of a national asset,' he wrote of the event in *The Observer*.

At Westminster, he attacked Michael Heseltine, the President of the Board of Trade, with a hint of his old fire; and he made some lively interventions against Heseltine during the Commons debate on the Matrix Churchill affair. But as the year drew to a close, the focus of attention was on the new leadership of the Labour Party. At the end of December, a group of Labour MPs challenged Kinnock's successor John Smith to take the initiative in key policy areas. Among them, Roy Hattersley, the former deputy party leader, said that Smith's task was to supply the reasons for voting Labour, adding that: 'Neil Kinnock removed the reasons for not voting Labour.' Kinnock himself has remained quietly loyal to Smith and has consistently refused to be drawn into comments on his style of leadership or style of oratory in the Commons.

There is more time to spend on constituency problems, and Kinnock campaigned for Glenys in her bid to become a member of the European Parliament when she was selected as the Labour candidate for South East Wales – one of the safest seats in Europe with a Labour majority of more than 108,000 in the 1989 elections. And Kinnock continued to play a prominent role in the effort to modernize the Labour Party, and in particular the move towards one member, one vote for the selection of parliamentary candidates. He believed that most of the party wanted reform, and that a revised voting system would not destroy Labour's union links.

In some respects, when the spotlight does fall on the Kinnocks nowadays it falls more regularly on Glenys. It might be thought that Glenys Kinnock has chosen to pursue her own political career once that of her husband had peaked. Neil Kinnock stresses that the timing is connected with the children growing up and leaving home.

> I'm certain that she never thought in those terms while the kids were growing up. But we were driving down to see Rachel after she had started at university and the fact that we were by ourselves, and the kids were on their way, was physically evident. I felt it very strongly at that time. We were chatting about the European elections and who would stand to replace the retiring MEP. There was a pause and then Glenys said 'I'm going to do it' and I nearly drove off the road! But I'm certain it was a product of the understanding that was just dawning on both of us, that she could act as if her first obligation was to herself, for the first time in her life.

Glenys has also had a book published, *By Faith and Daring*, a series of interviews with remarkable women, co-written with journalist Fiona Millar. She has continued teaching two days a week. She is the chair of One World Action, to which she is utterly dedicated; she is on the UNICEF British board; she is involved in campaigns concerning education, women's opportunities and carers – and she runs the home.

Neil Kinnock continued to be a popular guest on TV chat shows, and some time after the first anniversary of his resignation as Labour leader, the probing continued into his personal reaction. On the Terry Wogan show (BBC 1) he said: 'As one who aspired to lead the country it was natural that I had more concern about the welfare of the country than about my personal welfare.' A fellow guest on this occasion was the actress Sheila Hancock who interrupted: 'Well, I was gutted for you. I've never felt so sad in my life.'

Kinnock says he spends very little time reflecting on what might have been. 'That was yesterday. It's tomorrow that matters. Clearly the questions are put by others and I believe now, as I have said for a long time, that we lost at least a year on the miners' strike. It was a complete distraction from all other efforts for the whole movement.'

He is driven still by the urge to try to make the world a better place:

It sounds banal, it's so simple. It's something I never will stop doing, paid or unpaid, professional politician or not, that's what I always would have done, and I always will do.

Why have kids if you haven't got any commitment to the future? Why bother?

Postscript

Whatever the reasons for Labour's defeat at the 1992 general election and Kinnock's subsequent resignation as party leader, there can be no doubt that he saved the Labour Party from either extinction or fragmentation. And his term of office as the longest serving opposition leader in the history of British politics was far from time wasted, in spite of the ultimate outcome. But for his efforts, there would be no platform today on which the modernizers are debating with the traditionalists. The Labour Party of the 1990s would not exist as such without Kinnock's influence.

Whoever led the Labour Party during the 1980s was going to have to deal with the disintegrating party structure and the splintering ideology. And even adversaries admit that Kinnock was the only one who could do the job. That he did it, but still failed to win a mandate to govern, might in itself be testimony to the size of the challenge.

No other leading Labour figure of the period would have possessed the necessary determination, single-mindedness and energy to reunite the mainstream, dismiss the extremists, and persuade the party to modernize both its policies and its image. If he failed to command the House of Commons, he seldom failed to ignite the touch paper among his own party colleagues. And if he failed to win the majority verdict of trust and respect nationwide, it may well have been that even nine years of leadership were not enough to restore public faith in Labour as a credible alternative.

According to *Guardian* writer Hugo Young, to shift the public mood of the time would have required the talents of a Lloyd George or a John Kennedy. 'Kinnock, in common with every one of his colleagues, did not have them. He was, even so, remarkable. He is the only leader in Labour's history never to have served in government: a telling expression, perhaps, of the regression from power, rather than its gradually increasing normality, that Labour's history consists of.' On the other hand, said Young, he left a deeper mark on the party's character than any leader since Clement Attlee, and little that he did would have to be undone. Rather, it would have to be extended further.

Kinnock himself talks of the constant effort which had to be made to have Labour perceived as acceptable, respectable, digestible and trustworthy, and that effort demanded an enormous measure of discipline. Those who found the intensity of his determination at times verging on the obsessive have to remember that in the early 1980s Labour would probably have lost a great many more waverers to the SDP but for Kinnock's moderating influence. Many more still would have been driven away had the influence of Militant been allowed to develop, and Kinnock's energy and strength of purpose in expelling the extremists was fired by an obsessive force.

Essential though he saw this action, Kinnock viewed the period as time wasted in his efforts to rebuild the Labour Party. He was similarly frustrated by the 'lost year' of the miners' strike, which he saw as a serious distraction to his purpose. Indeed, there were few enjoyable moments during his nine years as leader. It was seldom a rewarding post to hold, and those who were critical of what they saw as Kinnock's overwhelming ambition for power overlook the fact that without that aim, there would have been little point to anything he undertook.

Kinnock's critics say that by the 1992 election, the Labour Party had been changed beyond recognition; had it not been so, it is highly unlikely that Labour would have even won second place. The policy review, born out of the conviction that British socialism had lost its way, created the new Labour Party. Kinnock forced through a series of reforms designed to properly democratize the party he led, and constructed an efficient fighting machine. He was also responsible for the policies which saw Labour in 1992 as a pro-European, pro-nuclear deterrence, pro-market forces party.

All of this, says Hugo Young, was mobilized into a campaign that, by any conventional test, was highly credible. 'Under Kinnock, Labour abandoned its aversion to modern techniques, its contempt for the methodology of populism. It knew every trick and its leader was the master conjuror.'

The shortcomings which were highlighted when Kinnock took office – his supposed political immaturity and his lack of ministerial experience – were other obstacles to be overcome. But during nine years in what is considered to be the toughest job in British politics, he displayed supreme managerial skills and gained wide experience of Government procedure. His political philosophy – appreciated or otherwise – was developing apace. He had grown in the estimation of his colleagues, and his personal rating among the electorate was also rising.

Hughes and Wintour in *Labour Rebuilt* consider that Kinnock's quest for power 'forced him to shut down part of his character, and some of his beliefs, probably for good'. He had to graft on the thickest of skins to withstand the constant jibes directed at his character, his ability, his verbosity. Yet he managed to survive the experience with his dignity intact, and emerged to be viewed as a man of warmth and humour.

Kinnock made the Labour Party electable, and while he did wipe eighty seats off the Conservative majority, he still failed to see Labour elected. He admits now to no other burning ambition than to see a Labour Government voted in. He is wholeheartedly supportive of John Smith's new leadership team, and has carefully avoided anything which might undermine the new leader's progress or credibility – hence, no memoirs. The new team is extending the work begun by Kinnock. Should they prove successful in leading Labour to election victory, Kinnock can take satisfaction in his role as architect of that winning party.

Bibliography

Adeney, Martin, and Lloyd, John, *The Miners' Strike – Loss without Limit* (Routledge, 1986)

Benn, Tony, *The End of an Era – Diaries 1980–90* (Hutchinson, 1992)

Castle, Barbara, *Fighting All the Way* (Macmillan, 1993)

Drower, G.M.F., *Neil Kinnock: The Path to Leadership* (Weidenfeld and Nicolson, 1984)

Foote, Geoffrey, *The Labour Party's Political Thought* (Croom Helm, 1985)

Harris, Robert, *The Making of Neil Kinnock* (Faber and Faber, 1984)

Healey, Denis, *The Time of My Life* (Michael Joseph, 1989)

Heffernan, Richard, and Marqusee, Mike, *Defeat From the Jaws of Victory – Inside Kinnock's Labour Party* (Verso, 1992)

Hughes, Colin, and Wintour, Patrick, *Labour Rebuilt* (Fourth Estate, 1990)

Kellner, Peter (ed.), *Thorns and Roses – Neil Kinnock Speeches, 1983–91* (Hutchinson, 1992)

King, Anthony (ed.), *Britain at the Polls 1992* (Chatham House, 1992)

Kinnock, Glenys, *By Faith and Daring* (Virago, 1993)

Kinnock, Neil, *Making Our Way* (Blackwell, 1986)

Leapman, Michael, *Kinnock* (Unwin, 1987)

Marquand, David, *The Progressive Dilemma* (Heinemann, 1991)

Smith, Martin J., and Spear, Joanna (eds), *The Changing Labour Party* (Routledge, 1992)

The Times Guide to the House of Commons, 1987 (Times Books)

The Times Guide to the House of Commons, 1992 (Times Books)

Newspapers and periodicals include:

The Guardian, The Independent, The Times, Daily Telegraph, Sunday Times, The Observer, Financial Times, New Statesman, Yorkshire Post, Manchester Evening News, Evening Gazette (Blackpool) and *Labour Party News.*

Index

Abse, Leo, 35
Africa, visit to, 1985, 81
    1988, 116
Alfonsin, President, 81–2
Anti-Nazi League, 33
Archer, Peter, 106
Ashdown, Paddy, 170

Beckett, Margaret, 46, 106
Bedwellty constituency (later Islwyn),
    25–7, 29–30
  election, 1970, 27–8
  election, 1983, 52
Belgrano affair, 82–3
Benn, Tony
  Kinnock's attitude towards, 43–4
  stands for deputy leader, 43–5
  loses seat, 52
  opinions of Kinnock, 59, 69, 77,
    86, 90, 150
  & miners' strike, 68, 69
  challenges leadership, 1988, 109,
    111, 117, 118–19
  opposes policy review, 1989, 131
Bennett, Andrew, 122
Bevan, Aneurin, 19, 21, 29
Biffen, John, 161
Blackpool, *see under* Labour Party
    conferences
Blakelock, PC Keith, 83–4
Blunkett, David, 74, 85, 180–1
Brighton, *see under* Labour Party
    conferences
Brittan, Leon, 82
Broadwater Farm riots, 83–4

Brooks, Eileen, 184
Brown, Gordon, 106, 154
Burns, Terry, 26
Bush, George, 148
Byrne, Colin, 162

Cartland, Dame Barbara, 198
Caerphilly by-election, 1968, 26
Callaghan, James
  as prime minister, 35, 37
  calls election, 37
  attitude to Kinnock, 38
  attacked by left, 40
  resigns, 42
  advice over S. Atlantic, 48
  & defence policy, 50–1
Campaign Group conference, 1987,
    109
Campaign for Labour Party Demo-
    cracy (CLPD), 33, 40
Campbell, Duncan, 83
Capstick, Ken, 168
Carlisle, Mark, 41
Castle, Barbara, 34, 45, 73, 75, 177,
    181
Chesterfield by-election, 1984, 68
Clarke, Charles, 94, 105, 173, 188,
    197
Concannon, Don, 29
Cook, Robin, 54, 106, 119
Corfu, 107
Cornwell, Charlotte, 180
Costa, Charilaos, 160–1
council houses, right to buy, 78
Craigie, Jill, 26

cruise missiles, 62, 89
Curry, Edwina, 94

Davies, Denzil, 54, 113–14
Defence & Security for Britain (NEC
    document, 1984), 88–9
Desert Island Discs, 56, 112–13
devolution debate, 34–6
Dobson, Frank, 94
Dunwoody, Gwynneth, 54

Eastbourne by-election, 1990, 151
Edmonds, John, 121
Enright, Derek, 168
Epping by-election, 1988, 122
European elections
    1985, 70–1
    1989, 133–6
Evans, Gwyn, 49

Falklands War, 48, 51, 82–3
Fields, Terry, 161–2, 165
Finch, Harold, 26
Fitzwater, Marlin, 92
Foot, Michael
    early friendship with Kinnocks,
        25–6
    Kinnock works under him at
        Employment, 32
    views on devolution, 34–5
    becomes party leader, 42–3
    weaknesses as leader, 48–9
    resigns, 53
    supports Labour's multilateralism,
        126
    'duffel coat scandal', 156
Fox, Sir Marcus, 93

general elections
    1970, 27–8
    1974, 32
    1979, 37–8
    1983, 49–52
    1987, 95–102
    1992, 172–99
Gorbachev, Mikhail, 125, 162–3

Gould, Bryan, 94, 106, 135,
    188, 191
Gould, Joyce, 188
Gould, Philip, 105
Govan by-election, 1988, 122
Grant, Bernie, 83
Greece
    visit to, 1984, 81
    holiday in, 1987, 107
Greenham Common, 62, 89
Greenwich by-election, 1987, 94–5
Gulf War, 150, 155–6
Gummer, John, 135

Hamilton, John, 74
Harry, Bill, 21
Hattersley, Roy
    views on structure & aims of party,
        42, 43
    in leadership contest, 54–5
    becomes deputy leader, 57–8
    views on Kinnock, 73, 154, 206
    Shadow Home Secretary, 106
    quality of partnership with Kin-
        nock, 117–19
    at Sheffield conference, 180, 181
Hatton, Derek, 74, 191
Healey, Denis
    candidate for leadership, 42
    becomes deputy leader, 43–5
    views on Kinnock, 73, 99
    visit to Moscow, 81
    support of nuclear weapons, 89
    account of Kinnock's talks with
        Reagan, 92
    leaves shadow cabinet, 106
Heffer, Eric
    contests leadership, 54, 57
    reaction to Kinnock's attack on
        Militant, 74
    attacks Kinnoc, 109
    stands as deputy leader, 111, 117,
        119
    death, 161
Hemsworth by-election, 1991, 168
Heseltine, Michael, 82, 206

Hewitt, Patricia, 94–5, 96, 105
Hill, David, 162, 188
Howarth, George, 78
Howe, Sir Geoffrey, 135, 151
Hutton, Will, 198–9

Islwyn constituency, 52

Jenkins, Clive, 53
Jenkins, Roy, 43
Jimmy Young Programme, 37, 205
Jones, Barry, 106, 110
Jordan, Bill, 191

Kaufman, Gerald, 106, 125–6, 128
Kilroy-Silk, Robert, 77
Kinnock, Glenys (née Parry – wife)
    early life, 23
    early relationship with Neil, 22–4
    marriage, 25
    strains of separation, 29
    during leadership contest, 57
    unilateralism, 62, 125
    accompanies Neil abroad, 81, 116,
        147–8
    dress style, 86–7
    political & moral causes, 87, 141
    injured in road accident, 138
    family life, 140–1
    independence, 140–1
    feminism, 167–8
    at Sheffield conference, 181, 182
    reaction to defeat, 195–6
    MEP selection, 202, 206
    life after defeat, 206–7
Kinnock, Gordon (father), 19, 29
Kinnock, Mary (mother), 19, 20, 28,
    29
Kinnock, Neil
    childhood, 19–21
    early socialism, 21–2
    student life, 22–4
    marriage, 25
    becomes MP, 26–9
    death of parents, 29
    moves to London, 29–30

on Common Market, 30,
    33–4
on devolution, 34–6
media appearances, 37
elected on to NEC, 37
becomes Education spokesman,
    38–9
supports Foot in leadership contest,
    42
& deputy leadership contest, 43–6
struggles with Militant, 46–7
1983 election campaign, 49–52
leadership contest, 1983, 53–7
road accident, 55–6
unilateralism, 50–1, 56, 62
on Common Market, 56
private life under scrutiny, 56–7
becomes leader, 57–60
reorganizes party structure, 61–2,
    77
defence policy, 62
& printworkers' dispute, 1983,
    62–3
& miners' strike, 1984, 63–70, 72
European elections, 1985, 70–1
fights & expels Militant, 71–8
popularizes image, 78
& council house sales, 78
relations with unions, 78–81
printworkers' dispute, Wapping,
    80–1
trips abroad, 1984–6, 81–2
& Westland affair, 1986, 82
& Ponting prosecution, 82–3
& Broadwater Farm riots, 83–4
review of defence policy, 88–92
fall in popularity, 90–5
doubts over unilateralism, 91
visit to US, 1987, 91–2
& overseas aid programme, 95
pre-election campaign, 1987,
    95–102
Welsh Labour Party conference,
    Llandudno, 98–9
election manifesto, 99
defence policy attacked, 99–100

assesses defeat, 103–4
policy review, 1987, 104–6
new shadow cabinet, 106
involved in boat rescue, Corfu, 107
Labour Party conference, 1987,
    107–8
opposition within party, 109–10
leadership challenge, 118–19
opposes poll tax, 111–12, 121
moves away from unilateralism,
    113–14, 124–8
lack of intellectual credentials
    criticized, 114–15
tour of Southern Africa, 1988, 116
relations with Roy Hattersley,
    117–18
image problems, 122–4
changes in defence policy, 124–8
policy review, 1989, 129–32
European policy, 133–5
European elections, 135–6
reforms to electoral college &
    membership organization,
    136–7
strength of his leadership, 137
policy on trades union legislation,
    137–8
road accident, Ireland, 138
attitude to journalists, 139
Labour party conference, 1989,
    139–40
family life, 140–1
policy review, 1990, 145–6
visit to US, 147–9
Labour Party conference, 1990,
    150
attitude to Thatcher, 151–2
attitude to Major, 153, 158–9
fall in popularity, 153–4
policy review document, 1991, 159
local elections, May 1991, 159–60
linked with Costa fraud investiga-
    tions, 160–1
Walton by-election, 162
& fall of Gorbachev, 162–3, 164
Labour Party conference, 1991,

165–7
feminism, 167–8
Tory 'dirty tricks' campaign,
    169–70
low-key image, 172–3, 176–7
tax proposals attacked, 173–5
Manifesto, 1992, 175
attacked by tabloids, 178, 180, 185
'Jennifer's Ear' broadcast, 179–80
Sheffield rally, 180–4
defeat, 187–9
stands down as leader, 189–90
defeat analysed, 192–4
reactions to defeat, 196–7
atheism, 198
last Commons appearance as
    leader, 199–200
life after leadership, 201–7
weight loss, 204
considered as possible European
    commissioner, 204–5
media appearances, 205, 207
political activities, 205–6
assessment of achievements,
    208–10
Kinnock, Rachel (daughter), 29, 40,
    141, 196, 202, 203
Kinnock, Stephen (son), 29, 41, 141,
    202, 203
Kinnock: The Inside Story (TV), 195
Knight, Ted, 71–2
Knowsley North by-election, 1986,
    77–8
Kuwait, invasion of, 150

Labour Listens regional meetings, 110,
    131
Labour Party
    electoral college, 43, 53, 71, 108,
        136, 206
    Manifesto, 1983, 50
    Manifesto, 1987, 99
    Manifesto, 1992, 175
    membership organization refor-
        med, 136
    policy review, 1987, 104–6

policy review, 1989, 129–32
policy review, 1990, 145–6
policy review, 1991, 159
structure reformed, 61–2, 77
labour party conferences
Blackpool, 1975, 34
Blackpool, 1976, 34
Brighton, 1977, 36
Brighton, 1979, 39
Blackpool, 1980, 42
Blackpool, 1984, 66
Bournemouth, 1985, 72–3
Blackpool, 1986, 85
Brighton, 1987, 107–8
Blackpool, 1988, 118–21
Brighton, 1989, 128, 139–40
Blackpool, 1990, 150
Brighton, 1991, 165–7
Labour's Better Way for the 1990s
(policy document), 159
Lambeth Council, 71–2
Lawson, Nigel, 140, 142
Liberal Democrats, 157, 160, 161,
170
Limehouse Declaration, 43
Liverpool City Council, 71–5, 76
Livingstone, Ken, 72, 109, 139, 154,
189
Looking to the Future (policy docu-
ment) 130, 145–6
Maastricht summit, 1991, 169
McNamara, Kevin, 29
Made in Britain (policy document),
169
Major, John
becomes Prime Minister, 152–3
clashes with Kinnock in parliament,
158–9
rise in popularity, 162–3
tribute to Kinnock, 199–200
Making Our Way (book), 84
Mandelson, Peter, 71, 86, 96, 105
Manifestos, *see under* Labour Party
Meacher, Michael, 54, 55, 74, 85,
106
Meet the Challenge, Make the Change

(policy document), 129–30
Mid-Staffordshire by-election, 1990,
143
Mikardo, Ian, 34
Militant Tendency, 46–7, 71–8, 93,
165
in Liverpool, 71–4, 76, 161–2
mining industry, 63–4
miners' strike, 1971–2, 30–1
miners' strike, 1984, 63–70
Durham Miners' Gala, 1984, 65
Yorkshire Miners' Gala, 1987, 104
NUM conference, 1988, 115–16
NUM conference, 1991, 162
Modern Britain in a Modern World
(policy document), 90–1
Monmouth by-election, 1991, 160
Moore, Barry, 25
Morris, Bill, 191
Mulhearn, Tony, 77
Mullin, Chris, 30

National Executive Committee
(NEC) elections
1976, 34
1978, 37
1979, 40
1980, 42
1981, 45
1982, 47
NATO HQ, visit to, 1985, 81
Nellist, Dave, 165
NHS
Kinnock's maiden speech on, 28–9
attacks Tory policy on, 1987,
109–10
attacks Tory policy on, 1992, 166
Nicaragua, visit to, 1985, 81
NUM, *see under* mining industry

Orgreave, 65
Orme, Stan, 65
Owen, David, 43, 151–2

Parry, Cyril (father-in-law), 23
party political broadcasts, *see under* TV

& radio broadcasts
Patten, Chris, 158
Pengam School, 20
policy reviews, *see under* Labour Party
poll tax, 109, 111–12, 143, 144, 153,
    158
Ponting, Clive, 82–3
Pontllanfraith, 25, 203
Prescott, John, 106, 109, 117, 119
press, images of Kinnock & Labour,
    54, 123–4, 160–1, 170
    effect on voting, 1992 election,
        174–5, 178, 180, 185, 189–91
printworkers' dispute, 1983, 62–3
    Wapping dispute, 80–1
proportional representation, 185

Radice, Giles, 106
Reagan, Ronald, 81, 92
red rose symbol, 70, 86
Red Wedge, 78
Reykjavik Summit, 1986, 125
Richardson, Jo, 106
Ridley, Nicholas, 150
Ribble Valley by-election, 1991, 157
Rogers, Gen. Bernard, 99
Rogers, Bill, 43
Rogers, Lance, 26–7
Rooker, Jeff, 78
Ruddock, Joan, 126

Saddam Hussein, 150
Sawyer, Tom
    supports anti-Militant stand, 76–7,
        85
    role in reshaping party, 105
    views on Kinnock, 106, 124, 127,
        183, 197
Scargill, Arthur
    & miners' strike, 63–8, 72
    subsequent relations with Kinnock,
        104, 109, 162, 189
SDP (Social Democratic Party), 43,
    102, 103, 122
Sharples, Adam, 105
Sheffield rally, 1992, 180–4

Shore, Peter, 54, 57, 106
Short, Clare, 122, 155, 162
Skinner, Dennis, 30, 68, 93, 131, 182
Smith, John, 106, 154, 181, 191
Straw, Jack, 78, 106
Sun newspaper, 160–1, 178, 180,
    189–91

Tatchell, Peter, 47
tax proposals, 146–7
    attacked by Tories, 169, 173–5
Thatcher, Margaret
    & Falklands, 48
    & miners' strike, 69–70
    & Westland affair, 82
    & Belgrano affair, 83
    Kinnock's view of, 84, 101, 129,
        151
    relationship with Reagan, 92, 148
    TV interview technique, 111–12
    attacked at Blackpool conference,
        1988, 120
    loss of popularity, 129, 135, 142,
        145
    & poll tax, 144
    & televised parliament, 142–3
    relationship with Bush, 148
    resignation, 151
    effect on Kinnock, 151–2
    treatment by media after loss of
        power, 178
Todd, Ron, 121
trades unions
    relations with Kinnock in early
        years, 53, 78–80
    printworkers' dispute, 1983, 62–3
    *A New Partnership, A New Britain
        (1985)*, 79–80
    Wapping dispute, 80–1
    Labour policy on union legislation,
        1990, 137–8
    TUC conference, 1990, 149
    see also mining industry
Tribune, 30, 33, 34, 44
Tribune Group, 30, 46, 47

TV & radio broadcasts
  Behind the Headlines, 152
  Beyond the Shadows, 183, 198
  Clive Anderson Show, 205
  Desert Island Discs, 56, 112–13
  Have I Got News For You, 205
  Jimmy Young Programme, 37, 205
  Kinnock: The Inside Story, 195
  On The Ropes, 174, 194
  Panorama, 1981, 45
  Panorama, 1990, 147
  Panorama, 1993, 207
  party political broadcast, May 1987
    ('*Chariots of Fire*'), 97
  party political broadcast, autumn
    1991, 165
  party political broadcast, spring
    1992 ('Jennifer's ear'), 179–80
  Wogan, 147
  World at One, 135

Ullman, Tracey, 78
Underhill, Reg, 46
Underwood, John, 162
unilateralism, 50–1, 56, 62, 88
  move away from, 91–2, 113–14,
    124–8

US, visits to
  1984, 81
  1986, 90
  1987, 91–2
  1990, 147–9
USSR
  visit to, 1984, 81
  visited by Kaufman, 1989, 125–6

Walters, Sir Alan, 140
Walton by-election, 1991, 161–2
Wapping dispute, 80–1
Warburton, David, 110
WEA, 25
Wembley conference, 1981, 43
Westland affair, 82
Whitty, Larry, 71, 105, 188
Williams, Shirley, 43
Willis, Norman, 67, 149
Wilson, Harold, 26, 35
'Winter of Discontent', 37
Wise, Audrey, 68
Wood, Deirdre, 94

Yeltsin, Boris, 163

Zircon affair, 83